LINCOLN BIBLE INSTITUTE

P9-CPY-102

THERE ARE SERMONS IN STORIES

THERE ARE SERMONS
IN STORIES

By

WILLIAM L. STIDGER

ABINGDON-COKESBURY PRESS
NEW YORK ● *NASHVILLE*

THERE ARE SERMONS *IN* STORIES

COPYRIGHT, MCMXLII
BY WHITMORE & STONE

All rights in this book are reserved. No part of the
text may be reproduced in any form without written permission of the publishers, except brief quotations used
in connection with reviews in a magazine or newspaper.

K

PRINTED IN THE UNITED STATES OF AMERICA

251
Stt

Book Store.

q Aug 48 - 1 cop - Baptist

4734

DEDICATED TO
HAZEL AND MARK HOPKINS, WHO
IN "THE WINTER OF MY DISCONTENT" MADE ME SEE THAT
"IF WINTER COMES, CAN SPRING BE FAR BEHIND?"

CONTENTS

A WORD TO LAUNCH THIS BOOK

MY DEAR FRIEND, William J. Cameron, who has been speaking over the radio for five minutes each week on the Ford Sunday Evening Hour, once wrote me a letter about Dr. George A. Gordon, the immortal Boston pastor of the Old South Congregational Church. In that letter he described the prayer part of Dr. Gordon's Sunday morning service. He said:

"I never heard Dr. Gordon preach a brilliant sermon, but he always imparted something of his granite and fire. He moved simply amongst the profoundest ideas. Everybody understood him. His power was not in what he said, but in the sense of immense reserves and background which he created. Homely of face, hard and shrewd of thought, he was a most reverent man in prayer. After he had prayed the service immediately moved up one story. And it was on that higher level that he preached."

So is it that the heroic and sacrificial actions of simple, sincere human beings lift life to higher levels. This simple book is a series of such stories which I have picked up in my reading, living, adventuring way across the continent and around the earth. They grew out of the lives of the people, and as such I return them to the people from whom they came in this permanent form. They are not *my* stories, but the stories of the people themselves; and in that mood I dare to present them in this form, hoping that just as they have thrilled and stirred my soul so will they stir and thrill the souls of the readers of this book. I am not a creator here, but a reporter passing on something I have seen and felt and heard.

In this foreword I want to thank several individuals who have been of great assistance in research and writing, friends who have searched their own personal scrapbooks and gone through their experiences to help me enrich the life-lifting quality of

9

these stories from human life. These gratitudes go out to Dean Earl Marlatt of Boston University School of Theology, Professor C. M. McConnell of the same institution, Marie Cole Powell, Lucille LeSourd, Mrs. Russell Cole, my own daughter Mrs. John Hyland, Sidney Adams, Helen Feussle, Albert Wiederhold, and Grace Noll Crowell. Also my thanks go out to that larger group of friends who have sent me some of these stories, acknowledgment of which I have tried to make in the stories themselves as they appear in this book. The authors of poems which I have used herein have given me permission to use their poems and writings in this manner, for all of which I am duly grateful, and to all of whom I hereby acknowledge my debt of gratitude.

WILLIAM L. STIDGER

AND LET THE GLORY OUT

ACCORDING to my friend Marie Powell, Margaret Prescott Montague tells a story which dates back to the setting of the World War of 1914-1919, but which has a message for any day and age. It is the story of a drab-looking little Virginian seamstress returning from Europe on one of the great ocean liners shortly after war had been declared. Her neighbor in the adjoining deck chair who had been watching her, had noted how the lines in her face appeared to have been overlaid by something big which had given her face an entirely different look. It was not long before the little seamstress was pouring out her story, for she needed nothing so much as to share with someone the soul-shaking experience that had been hers.

Her name was Sadie Virginia Smithson, and her home was in Johnson Falls, West Virginia. She had grown to young girlhood in that small town before she realized that she did not "belong" to *the* social set of the community. After her graduation from high school she had been deliberately kept out of the Laurel Literary Society, which stood as the symbol for all that was to be desired in that little community. She was being excluded because her father kept the livery stable and because she herself was obliged to take in sewing. So there grew up in her thoughts one great obsession—one day to be elected into membership in the Laurel Literary Society. Since not many people in that small town went to Europe, she determined to save enough money to travel there; and in her dreams often she could hear the soft gloved hands clapping after she had read her paper, "My Trip to Europe."

After many years she saved the money. She went to Europe with a professor and his wife, only to have war declared shortly after they had arrived. The professor's daughter was ill in Paris, and they were in Belgium. An army officer offered to drive them to Paris in his car. In some way they lost the road and suddenly found themselves crossing a battlefield shortly after the battle had occurred.

Right beside the car lay one young fellow with part of his side torn away, and he looked right up at Sadie Virginia Smithson and moaned, "Water, for God's sake!" Before she knew what she was doing, the little seamstress had jumped out of the car with her drinking cup and was making her way to a spring.

Then there followed the remarkable story of her night spent on the battlefield with those dying boys, for she utterly refused to get back into the car, which finally drove off and left her. Back and forth to the spring she went with her little cup. She tore her skirt up into bandages. She scribbled notes and messages for loved ones at home. As she tramped back and forth through that blood-stained field she kept her mind sane by singing under her breath over and over again the first thing that popped into her mind:

> I don't want none of your weevily wheat,
> And I don't want none of your barley.

This little chant soon gave way to a prayer which she repeated as she offered each cup of water: "God bless us, and keep us, and make his face to shine upon us." After a night of horror with suddenly reddening skies and distant thunder and dying and moaning boys the dawn came, and with it an ambulance car and a young doctor, who, confronted with the astounding spectacle of the little seamstress amid all that carnage, shouted, "Who are you, and what in thunder are you doing here?"

To which she replied, "I'm Sadie Virginia Smithson, and I've been holdin' hell back all night."

"Well!" said the young doctor in a quiet voice. "Well, Miss Sadie Virginia, I'm glad you held some of it back, for everybody else in the world was letting it loose last night."

As she told her story she said, "I've never been married—never known what it was to have children—but that night all those

12

men were my children, even the biggest and roughest of them, an' I believe I could have died for any one of 'em. I reckon bein' so crazy with pity had stretched me out of bein' a scary old maid into bein' a mother."

At the close of her story, her new friend, too overcome to know what to say, ventured, "Well, the Laurel Literary Society will be glad enough to have you belong to it now."

The little seamstress sat bolt upright. "But—but you don't understand. I've been face to face with war an' death an' hell an' God—I've been born again. Do you reckon any of them little old things matter now?"

"What does matter?" whispered her companion.

"Nothin'," she answered, "nothin' but God an' love an' doin' things for folks."

*   *   *

HOLY BREAD

RECENTLY one of my friends sent me a beautiful story she had read. It was written by Zelia M. Walters, and appeared in *Unity* magazine under the title "Holy Bread." It was the story of a man named Donley based on a real experience in life. This man Donley had been out of work for months and had finally got down to begging, which he despised with all his soul.

One cold winter evening he stood by a private club and saw a man entering accompanied by a woman and asked him for money to buy food.

"Sorry, fellow, but I've no change with me," the man replied crisply.

The woman, overhearing the conversation, said, "What did that poor fellow want?"

"Price of a meal. Said he was hungry," replied her husband.

"Oh, Larry! We can't go in and eat a meal we don't need and leave a hungry man out here."

13

"There's one on every corner now. Likely he wants the money for booze."

"But I have some change. Let me give him something."

Donley, with his back turned to them, heard every word that was said. An electric shock passed through him. He was about to run away when he heard a woman's kindly voice:

"Here's a dollar. Buy yourself food. And don't lose courage, even if things do look hard. There's a job for you somewhere. I hope you'll find it soon."

"Thanks, lady. You've given me a fresh start and a new heart. I'll never forget your kindness."

"You'll be eating Christ's bread. Pass it on," she said with a friendly smile, as if he were a man and not a bum.

Donley found a cheap eating place, spent fifty cents, resolved to save the rest for another day. He would be eating Christ's bread for two days. Again that feeling as of an electric shock passed over him. "Christ's bread!" But, look here! One could not save up Christ's bread just for oneself! And far in the distance he seemed to hear the echo of an old hymn humming in his memory, a hymn he had learned as a boy in Sunday school.

An old man shuffled along just ahead of him. Maybe the old fellow was hungry. Christ's bread must be shared.

"Hey, fellow, what do you say to going in and getting a good meal?"

The old man turned, blinking up at Donley. "You wouldn't fool me, would you, Buddie?"

And he couldn't believe it until he was seated at an oilcloth table with a bowl of stew before him.

During the meal Donley noticed that the old man was wrapping up part of his bread in a paper napkin.

"Saving some for tomorrow, hey?" he asked.

"No—no. There's a kid down my way. He's had tough luck and was crying when I left—hungry. I aim to give him the bread."

"Christ's bread." Donley was shaken as by a mystic presence, a third guest at that oilcloth table. It was as if he heard far-off church chimes playing an old hymn.

14

The two of them took the bread to the hungry boy, who began to eat greedily. Then he stopped and called a dog, a frightened, lost dog.

"Here, Jack, you can have half of it," said the boy.

"Christ's bread!" Ah, yes. It would go to the four-footed brother too. St. Francis of Assisi would have done that.

The kid acted like a new boy now, stood up and started to cry his newspapers. "Good-bye," said Donley to the old man. "There's a job for you somewhere. You'll find it soon; just hang on. You know"—his voice sank to a whisper—"this that we've eaten is Christ's bread. A lady told me so when she gave me that dollar. We're just naturally bound to have good luck."

Donley turned as the old man left and found the lost dog nosing at his leg. He bent over to pat it and found a collar around its neck with its owner's name on it; he took the long walk uptown to the owner's home, rang the bell. Soon the owner came to the door and when he saw his lost dog was delighted.

The keen-eyed man was about to say sharply, "Didn't you steal that dog just to get a reward?" But he didn't say it. There was something of dignity about Donley that day. Instead the man found himself saying, "I advertised in last night's paper. Ten dollars reward. Here it is!"

Donley looked at the bill half dazed.

"I don't like to take it! I just wanted to do the dog a good turn."

"Take it along. What you did is worth more than that to me. And do you want a job? Come to my office tomorrow. I need a man like you, who has ideas such as you have." Donley started off down the avenue with a hymn singing in his soul, a hymn which he had remembered from childhood: "Break Thou the Bread of Life."

✳   ✳   ✳

LOST HARMONY

Now and then I receive from my friends beautiful stories, and I am always grateful for the interest that they show. Recently I received a letter from Rufus Mallilieu of New London, Connecticut. He's one of my loyal friends, and he has sent me a splendid story which he calls "Lost Harmony."

Two famous Scandinavians, Ole Bull, the marvelous violinist, and John Ericsson, the clever inventor who revolutionized ocean travel by introducing the screw into steam navigation, were great friends in their youth. Eventually they drifted apart, and did not meet again until they had both become famous. It was during one of Ole Bull's American tours that the two friends met again.

Bull tried several times to persuade his friend to attend one of his concerts and hear him play the violin, but Ericsson declined. He was too busy; he had no time to waste on music. After several more invitations Bull finally said to him, "If you won't come I'll bring my violin down here to your shop and play."

The engineer laughed heartily. "If you do I'll smash the thing to pieces."

The famous musician, knowing the strange power that his instrument had over the human heart, was eager to see what effect it would have on the engineer. To realize his ambition, he decided to use a bit of diplomacy.

One day he arrived at Ericsson's workshop with the violin under his arm. Taking the instrument to pieces, he pointed out certain defects. He asked the engineer several questions about the scientific and acoustic principles involved. Ericsson's interest was aroused. They discussed the varying effect of the different grain of certain woods, and then the sound waves. Finally, to illustrate his meaning, Ole Bull replaced the parts, and drawing the bow across the strings, played a few bars of marvelously sweet music.

Ericsson's soul was stirred to the depths as he listened. Tears glistened in his eyes, and when Ole Bull paused he said softly:

16

"Play on! Don't stop. Play on! I never knew before what it was that was lacking in my life."

What is lacking in our lives? Is there a lost chord? Is there no harmony, no music, nothing but discord? What causes this discord, which throws us out of tune with the Infinite, disturbs the balance of our lives, and robs us of the highest enjoyment? Perhaps Milton knew when he sang long ago:

> Disproportion'd sin,
> Jarr'd against nature's chime, and with harsh din
> Broke the fair music that all creatures made
> To their great Lord.

Sometimes the Spirit of God touches a lost chord in our lives, and we confess, "I never knew before what it was that was lacking in my life." Charles Darwin, after he had spent a lifetime in research, giving to the world what is called "The Evolutionary Hypothesis," finally in his old age cried out in despair: "Oh, my friends, I have made a great mistake. I have left music out of my life; and now I have lost all capacity to enjoy great music—and that is an irrevocable tragedy!"

For, after all, there is an unbroken harmony and rhythm in life, and if we miss that we miss everything. The harmony already heard in life gives us promise of a harmony yet to come, as an unknown poet sings in "The Unbroken Rhythm":

> Perhaps we shall find at last that life and death
>   Are part of the same poem, rhyme on rhyme,
> With but a natural pausing of the breath
>   As a sentence ends; that swinging out from time
> Into eternity will make no break at all;
>   That still the perfect rhythm will be there;
> That the singing, high, sustained notes will not fall,
>   Nor the music falter on the waiting air.
> I trust that there will be no stumbling feet
>   To mar the progress of that perfect thing.
> The epic we call "Life" is strangely sweet
>   And yet, God, grant upon its upward swing
>   It may take on, beneath an abler hand,
>   A meaning that the heart can understand.

17

"SWEET MYSTERY OF LIFE"

LATE one afternoon a few months ago, Mr. Lawrence Nye, one of my students, with his bride of but a few weeks, stood in beautiful Forest Lawn Memorial Park, in Glendale, California. He says of that experience:

There we stood in this new park, looking upon acres of green sod, and catching the odors of profuse flower gardens. From somewhere near a great organ was playing the familiar strains of Victor Herbert's masterpiece, "Ah! Sweet Mystery of Life."

The music came floating to our ears, truly as sweet and as mysterious as the name itself implies. It was played over and over as though there was a message of endless value that needed to be told. Upon investigation we learned the reason. There, close to us, was a brilliant white group of statuary by Ernesto Gasseri called "The Mystery of Life."

It consisted of eighteen life-sized figures, ranging in ages from that of a tiny baby in its mother's arms to an aged patriarch leaning intently forward as though attempting to keep up with the procession. The characters seemed to come to life. The children were watching the slow movements of a turtle, and two white doves. A man in his full years gazed wonderingly out into vistas of the unknown. Sweethearts embraced. An aged man sat patiently, having long ago ceased his attempts to pierce life's mysteries.

We walked slowly away, and spoke not a word until we stood before a great temple. Inside was that renowned reproduction in stained glass of da Vinci's "The Last Supper," executed by Mosetti.

Six years it had been in the making, and was shipped from Italy. Carefully placed, the window was all that it was supposed to be. The low western sun was shining directly through it, and the colors changed many times, giving life and breath to the thirteen characters portrayed.

It was silent in that room—reverently silent. Suddenly the two characters on either end of the great window seemed to disappear. Then, one by one, as the sun sank lower and lower, the disciples in turn seemed to fade from view. The picture narrowed more and more until the full power of a fading sunset was pouring through the central figure, the face of Christ. It was as though an electric wave swept through the people watching. It was as though He who had lived so long ago were seeking an answer to the great mystery of life.

And as the halo of light upon the head of that figure became more

18

intense, an orderly opened a door. It was only for a moment, but long enough for the answer to come in. We heard again the strains: *" 'Tis the answer, 'tis the end and all of living! For it is love alone that rules for aye!"*

The light soon faded, and that central figure joined his beloved men in the shimmering shadows. Our hands were clasped tightly and understandingly, for a mystery had been made plain. And the benediction of that hour never ceases to touch us again and again, every day of our lives.

I think I understand how that gay couple felt as they had this beautiful experience on their honeymoon and found that " 'Tis love and love alone that rules the world."

> Time is itself a restless dream,
> A swallow's flight across a stream.
> Dawn dims the splendor of the moon,
> The dusk of evening nudges noon.
> A flash, a flame, a flickering,
> The flutter of a weary wing;
> A pitcher broken at the well;
> A whispered word, a muffled bell;
> And yet the gods are good to me;
> Love lives through all eternity!

*   *   *

FRANCONIA NOTCH AND ECHO LAKE

DR. GEORGE A. GORDON used to tell a story of an experience which he had in New England.

There is in the Franconia Notch a sheet of water called Echo Lake. If one is a good singer let him go there about sunset and sing clearly and slowly the first verse of "Nearer, My God, to Thee"; and listen as the great mountains return his voice magnified and the song glorified. But let another sing a ribald song, with a voice harsh and torn with discords; let him sing it into the great receptive heart of the mountains, and the ribald song will come back, and all the singer's discords with it. "This Echo Lake seems to me to be a symbol of the moral world and the universe in which we live."

I have a daughter who used to marvel at the large number of letters that I received each day. She herself wanted as many, but she did not get them. One of her first queries on coming home from school was an eager, "Did I get a letter?" She could never understand why she did not receive more letters. One day I said to her: "Betty, I receive a lot of letters because *I send out* a lot of letters. I get back just about the same amount of correspondence that I send." Then I told her the story of Echo Lake in Franconia Notch.

And now that this marvelous medium of the transference of words and thoughts, which we call the radio, has come to us, we have an unusual opportunity of testing this principle. A radio broadcaster sends out through the air a simple, universal, helpful thought; and that thought is that we get back from life just about what we send out to life—no more; no less. The broadcaster hopes to get many responses. He does not always get them. People accept what they receive on the radio as a matter of course. But it does gladden the sender's heart when those who listen in take time to send a letter confessing that the sender's little light was seen. Yet in spite of the fact that only a small percentage of those who listen in ever give any response to what they receive, even though they may be grateful in their hearts, the principle still holds true that we get back just about what we send out into life.

I remember once in Kansas City when we were entertaining Ethel Barrymore and Sinclair Lewis. We had all been to see Miss Barrymore's play that afternoon. Sinclair Lewis, in a facetious remark, said: "Ethel, I don't believe you did as well as you could this afternoon. You let down on us."

Ethel Barrymore's eyes flashed fire and she replied: "No Drew or Barrymore ever goes on the stage, no matter how he feels, or how large or small the crowd is; no matter whether it is New

20

York City or some small town; that he does not give the best that he has to an audience. For we have learned through four generations that we get back just about what we give."

I also remember a story that the famous comedian, Fred Stone, once told me. In the early days of his career he was playing with the famous Montgomery and Stone team in Keith's Theater in Boston. As they started on the stage Dave Montgomery said, "It's a small crowd this afternoon; we'll save ourselves for this evening."

Fred Stone stopped his partner dead still in the wings and replied: "Dave, we must never go on the stage that we don't give the best we have. There may be a manager out there in those shadows; a lonely fellow who needs to laugh; a poor girl who has paid her last half dollar to hear us."

It is an easy thing to figure this out for ourselves: Hate begets hate! Indifference begets indifference! Listlessness begets listlessness! Anger begets anger! Jealousy begets jealousy! Friendship begets friendship! Love begets love!

> There are loyal hearts, there are spirits brave,
>   There are souls that are pure and true;
> Then give to the world the best that you have
>   And the best will come back to you.
>
> Give love, and love to your life will flow,
>   A strength in your utmost need;
> Have faith, and a score of hearts will show
>   Their faith in your work and deed.
>
> Give truth, and your gift will be paid in kind;
>   And honor will honor meet;
> And the smile which is sweet will surely find
>   A smile that is just as sweet.
>
> Give pity and sorrow to those who mourn;
>   You will gather in flowers again
> The scattered seeds from your thought outborne,
>   Though the sowing seemed in vain.

"WATCH FOR MY RED ROSE"

TIM was the elevator boy in a dye factory and his car was used by one great wing of the place. Up and down he carried workers, officers, and visitors, and all loved him because of his friendliness and winning smile.

Tim's clothes were shabby, his knowledge of the world was very limited, and his English was very poor. Yet his cheerful "Good morning" was an event in everyone's day.

"My, my! Ain't you glad to be alive today?" he said to Mary Flynn just before seven o'clock one morning. "Look at that 'ere sunshine. Don't it make yer want ter shine too? Come in and I will put yer up higher where the air is jest great."

When Mattie Mack came to the elevator door she had in her hand a bunch of flowers for her desk. But as she left she slipped a tiny red rosebud into the hand of the boy. "Bless yer kind heart," he whispered. "I hain't got any garden, but a posy on me coat jest makes me happy all the day. This rosebud is sure a dandy."

This morning he did his work quickly and found some time to glance at the morning papers. He couldn't read them all, but he loved to read what he could and look at the pictures. As he was glancing over the papers he heard a loud sound and then another. Then came a terrific explosion, and dirt, bricks, and wood flew in all directions. The building trembled. Tim rushed out to see what had happened. In some unknown way a great tank of acid had exploded, people told him as they hurried by with white faces.

Like a flash there came the realization that all that lay between the employees in his building and death was himself and his elevator.

"May God help me," he thought as he shut the door of the car and started up the swaying shaft. On every landing were screaming, anxious women. Could he ever get them down? If they pushed and struggled all would be lost. When he reached the top floor he called cheerily: "Here I come fer ye. Ain't it great to be in a building that is all right? Now if yer won't push and only fifteen will come inter the car ter once, I kin get every one of yer down. But if yer push, then I'll never come up again after yer. Now I'll see what yer will do. Only fifteen, remember. Twelve, thirteen, fourteen, fifteen. Full up. Now, Aunt Beckey, stay right there and watch fer me. Watch fer me red rose." The shaft swayed and shook as, very slowly, he took them down. But he sang cheerily from the foot of the shaft, "I'm coming. I'm coming. Tho' me car is running slow."

The people watched him breathlessly as he tried to save them. Up and down he went. A great crash told him that more of the building had collapsed, and the heat from the burning structure was intense. But Tim wanted to save others and forgot about fear. "Do yer best, Tim. Some of them folks have little uns at home. Yer must get them all down." Having this thought in mind, and looking at the red rose, he carried on his rescue. One floor after another he emptied, but the face of the elevator boy was becoming white and drawn. Suddenly there was a scream of terror. The flames were spreading through the shaft—and one more trip must be made. Waiting women below covered their faces with their hands and wept as they heard Tim say: "I guess she'll hold for another trip, and I promised to come back fer them. There's only five more up there and one of them is Mattie Mack, the one that is so good ter me. Sure. I'm going up." The car went up very slowly; the watchers below heard the elevator door open and a fervent "Thank God" from one of the women. Then Tim's merry voice again called out, though this time it was all of a tremble. "Now, here we go down. Ain't yer glad ter be alive ter tell how yer went through fire and wasn't burned? Ain't fire pretty, though? Sure, the shaft will hold if we go slow. Jest look at my red rosebud. Ain't it one fine match for my red hair? Why, here we are so soon. Now out with yer —and Mattie—thanks agin fer my posy. It sure helped me a lot."

A moment later everyone was looking for the elevator boy. On every tongue was the story of his bravery. But he wasn't about the buildings and he wasn't in the street. Where could he be?

23

Sitting on the steps of a little house in a back alleyway was a freckle-faced, red-haired boy. He was patting the head of a big yellow cat and saying: " 'Twas great, Tom, jest great. Ain't it good I wasn't burned! I am glad I could help. But I don't want folks ter thank me so I am goin' ter sit out here with yer fer a spell." And the big cat rubbed against Tim's knee and seemed to understand.

* * *

"THROUGH THEE THE ROSE IS RED"

IN THE city of Weimar, in Germany, there is a statue which was set up in 1857. Standing before it we see the figures of two men. Both are Germans. Both are poets. Their names are Goethe and Schiller. Schiller wrote the drama of "The Robbers," the poem of "The Diver," and many other pieces. Goethe wrote the drama of "Faust," the poem of "Herman and Dorothea," among other things.

The German people like to see the plays of these two poets produced and performed at the theater. They like to raise the question, "Which one is the greater?"

Schiller and Goethe were friends; they met each other frequently and enjoyed talking to each other. If Goethe heard people say, "Sir, you are the master poet of the Germans," he was quick to rejoin, "But do not forget Schiller."

And if Schiller heard folk praise him as the finest singer in verse, he would say, "But there is my friend Goethe."

The sculptor of the statue of Weimar expressed their mutual friendship beautifully. He has put a wreath of laurel leaves in Goethe's hand. The poet is raising his hand to place the wreath on his friend Schiller's head. But Schiller does not wish for the crown, which he thinks Goethe deserves more. He is thrusting it back, as if saying, "No, it is more fit for you to wear than me." Thus the two friends nobly disagreed, each refusing to be

24

crowned. But in their hearts they loved each other, appreciating each other's qualities.

The Talmud, a work much prized by the Hebrew people, contains a story which shows us what it means to be a friend. We are told that a man had three friends. A heavy step is heard at the man's door. The gleam of a helmet is seen. The stranger is an officer of the court of the emperor of Rome, who asks him to come to the court and to defend himself against certain charges made against him. The Jew is in terror. His limbs shake and his heart sinks—he is helpless. He thinks of his three friends. He will go to them and ask them to accompany him to the palace of the king.

The first friend answers, "No, I can do no good by going, either to you or to myself."

The accused departs with sadness and seeks out his second friend. This one says: "Well, it is a very dangerous thing to stand at your side. The emperor may charge you with some offense against the law. If I am seen with you, he might think I share your guilt. However, I will go with you as far as the palace gate."

"No, that will not help me at all," he replies. "I can manage to keep up my courage as far as the gate. It is just at that point that my spirit would fail me."

So he goes to his third friend, who says, "Fear naught; I will go with you. I will go with you right to the emperor's presence. I will tell him that I know you and that I trust you, and I will speak on your behalf, and I will not leave till the affair is settled and you are delivered—as I hope you will be—from your trouble." And he kept his word. The real friend is ready to go to the very end, and to help to the utmost. Not of himself does he think, but of his comrade's need and his comrade's good name. The real friend does not want the wreath of laurel on his brow if it is taken from his comrade.

A small boy was lying on an operating table ready for a serious operation. He had asked that his father stay with him to hold his hand as they gave him the ether. Just before they slipped the ether mask over his face he looked up at his father and said with trusting confidence, "You'll go all the way with me, won't you, Dad?" And the father replied through his tears of understanding, "I sure will, Son!" That's what true friendship really means. It means going all the way. Emerson seemed to catch the meaning of friendship when he wrote:

O friend, my bosom said,
Through thee alone the sky is arched,
Through thee the rose is red,
All things through thee take nobler form
And look beyond the earth,
The mill-round of our fate appears
A sun-path in thy worth.
Me too thy nobleness has taught
To master my despair;
The fountains of my hidden life
Are through thy friendship fair.

✳   ✳   ✳

WHO SENT THE RED ROSE?

THE other day I received a letter from a friend who had listened to the broadcast of mine about an elevator boy who wore a red rose while at work—the story which I have just told in the preceding pages. I am passing on the letter and the story it tells:

MY DEAR DR. STIDGER:

A friend and I were making an automobile trip through the Midwest not long ago. Along about noon we turned on the radio in the car and picked up your broadcast. You told the story of an elevator boy who wore a red rose at work. It brought to mind a story of a red rose which I am passing on to you.

Early in the depression a thoroughly good businessman got heavily in debt and the collapse of his business seemed inevitable. But he had

26

faith in his business and in himself and believed that he could weather the crisis.

Some of his larger creditors continued to have faith in him and were lenient with him. Word came to him in roundabout ways of friends who wished him well in his fight to save his business. He never could forget the coming into his office of an old friend who had sung with him in the choir in former years—a big, whole-souled bass singer, who took his hand in a hand like the paw of a bear, and in his deep voice said, "Just a word. Keep going—fight it through," and was gone within fifteen seconds of his arrival.

Each incident that brought cheer photographed itself on his memory, and later he could recall every detail of it.

One day, when the load was very heavy, and he was almost ready to give up the struggle, this man found on his desk a single red rose. With it was a card which said simply, "From one who prays daily for you."

The rose soon faded and no other appeared on his desk, but the simple message stuck in his mind. It started a chain of inquiry in his mind which amounted almost to a mystery. "Who sent the red rose?"

Possibly, he thought, it was his wife. Perhaps it was one of the office force. He remembered how loyal the whole force had been, and how fine an organization it was that could hold its spirit and discipline through such a crisis.

There were others who might have sent the rose. There were people whom he had helped. Possible the red rose was a sign of gratitude.

There were men with whom he had worked in civic and religious organizations. But on second thought it did not seem likely that any among this group of co-workers would send him a rose—and yet again maybe one of them did.

This process of calling the roll of friends who might have sent the red rose and the message it bore, continued. The rose seemed to remind him of them. He had a list he went over in a mental roll call and every day he added names to the growing list.

Finally he ceased to want to know who sent it. On the whole, he was glad he did not know.

The strain and stress of his business crisis finally passed and the long fight was eventually won. This man still thinks of the red rose and wonders who sent it to him at an hour when his courage was at its lowest ebb.

And aside from the mystery of the red rose there is that deeper mystery of the message of the unknown sender, "From one who prays daily for you." Maybe this had something to do with the man's successful effort to pay his creditors and save a useful business.

Theodore Parker said, at the end of his long ministry, with a perfect understanding of the problems, tragedies, and disappointments of humanity, "If I had my ministry to live over again, I would preach more to broken hearts." That man had an understanding heart or he could never have said that perfect thing. Therefore we are not at all surprised to hear him also saying this: "Every rose is an autograph from the hand of the Almighty God on this world about us. He has inscribed his thoughts in these marvelous hieroglyphics which sense and science have been, these many thousand years, seeking to understand."

And he might have added that every kindly thought and deed done in this weary old world is an autograph from God's hand —a rose from his Garden of Love.

* * *

"THE LOVELIEST ROSE IN THE WORLD"

And since we are thinking of roses just now, let me tell this story of "The Loveliest Rose in the World."

Once upon a time in a country far away there reigned a queen in whose garden were found the most glorious flowers at all seasons and from all the lands of the world. But more than all others she loved roses. She had every imaginable kind of roses. They grew against the garden walls, wound themselves around the pillars and window frames, and crept through the windows into the rooms, and all along the ceilings in the halls. And the roses were of many colors and of every fragrance and form.

But there was great sorrow in the house because the queen lay upon a sick bed, and the doctors said that she would die, "There is still one thing that can save her," said the wise men. "Bring the loveliest rose in the world, the rose that is the symbol of the purest and brightest love. If that is brought to her before her eyes close, she will not die."

The old and young came from every side with roses, the loveliest that bloomed in each garden; but none of them was of the right kind. The flower was to be plucked from the *garden of love*. But what rose in all that garden expressed the highest and purest love?

The poets sang of the loveliest rose in the world, of the love of youth and great heroes. "But they have not named the right flower," said the wise men. "They have not pointed out the place where it blooms in its splendor. It is not the rose that springs from the hearts of youthful lovers, though this rose will ever be fragrant in song. It is also not the rose of heroism and that magic rose of science to which man devotes many a night and much of his fresh life."

"But I know where it blooms," said one mother, who brought her pretty baby to the bedside of the dying queen. "I know where the loveliest rose of love may be found. It springs in the blooming cheeks of my sweet child, when, waking from sleep, it opens its eyes and smiles tenderly at me."

"Lovely is this rose," replied the wise men, "but there is a lovelier still."

Another woman exclaimed, full of joy: "I have seen the loveliest, purest rose that blooms. I saw it on the cheeks of the queen. She had taken off her golden crown. And in the long, dreary night she carried her sick child in her arms. She wept, kissed it, and prayed for her child."

"Holy and wonderful is this white rose of a mother's grief," replied the wise men, "but it is not the one we seek."

Also the Bishop came to call upon the ill queen. "The loveliest rose in the world I saw at the altar of the Lord," he said— "the young maidens that went to the Lord's Table. Roses were blushing and pale roses were shining on their fresh cheeks. A young girl stood there. With all the love and purity of her spirit she looked up to heaven. That was the expression of the highest and purest love."

"May she be blessed," said the wise men, "but not one of you has yet named the loveliest rose in the world."

Then a child came running into the room. It was the queen's little son. "Mother," cried the boy, "only hear what I have read." The child sat by the bedside and read from the Book of Him who suffered death upon the cross to save men: "Greater love there is not. . . . ."

A rosy glow spread over the cheeks of the queen, and her eyes gleamed for joy and happiness. Now she understood that from the leaves of the Bible there bloomed the loveliest rose, that sprang from the blood of Christ shed on the cross.

"Now I see," the queen exclaimed; "he who beholds this, the loveliest rose on earth, shall never die, but have eternal life."

That child was right. And Edgar Saltus, one of the world's truly great writers, saw that and described it in his drama entitled *Mary Magdalene* when she stood that morning of the Resurrection:

"Then suddenly the sky began to open in dawn; open like a great red rose. What the sunset had sown the dawn would reap.

"At that moment the tomb opened and Jesus stood beside her. His eyes were golden parables; and in his face shone Truth revealed. She started, dumb and blinded by the light of his face, and Jesus passed quietly into the budding day, where a great Rose was unfolding."

✶　　✶　　✶

"THERE'S ONE FOR THE 'GIPPER'!"

GEORGE GIPP, the son of a Congregational minister, was one of the greatest football players the game ever knew. He was on one of Knute Rockne's famous Notre Dame teams. He will go down as one of the great heroes of football, and if ever there was a hard-hitting, hard-fighting player it was the "Gipper," as his team-mates always called him.

Knute Rockne himself tells of how that boy, after a brilliant football and scholastic career, lay dying at twenty-three. Coach Rockne had been called in to see him at the hospital. The coach bent over George Gipp in that hospital bed, as he had bent over him many a time before that in the huddles of practice on the football field.

"It's pretty tough to go," said Rockne, not knowing just what to say at such an hour. Since that day Knute Rockne himself has gone, falling from the sky while on his way to help create a football picture at Hollywood, starring the story of this same team on which the "Gipper" played.

"What's tough about it?" Gipp smiled back. "I've no complaint." Then he turned to Knute Rockne and said: "I've got to go, Rock. It's all right. I'm not afraid. I'll plunge into this game of going as I did into West Point or Southern California games. But sometimes, Rock, when the team is up against it, when things are going all wrong, and the breaks are beating the boys, tell them to go in there with all they've got and win one game; just one—for the 'Gipper.' I don't know where I'll be, Rock, but I'll know about it and I'll be looking on from somewhere; you can count on that, old man!"

Two years later the famous Notre Dame team had a hard season. The boys were crippled. They were all but demoralized. Then came the hardest game of the season, the Army game—Gipp's old love and hate. At the end of the first half the score was a tie—nothing to nothing.

Then Knute Rockne, who knew his men—and, what is better, knew human psychology—felt that the hour had come to tell the boys that story. It was just the hour which Gipp had anticipated. It was the West Point game, the very game which had stirred Gipp most of all each season he had played on the team before his death.

Between halves Rockne walked into the dressing room. The

31

boys were lying down on benches resting, a bit demoralized, but determined. They needed something. Rockne started to talk in a quiet voice—hushed, in fact. He felt that way. It was a reverent moment for him. There was something beautifully sacred even to this big, burly coach. He told that half-defeated team Gipp's last words. Most of the boys on that particular team had never met Gipp, but he had become a legend at Notre Dame. The story hushed their hearts but it sent an electric thrill through them, as it had been intended to do by the coach. Following that story they ran out to the field. The West Point band was playing. The tail end of the usual cadet parade was just leaving the field. The stands were full. There was an expectant attitude in that great crowd. It might have been anybody's game if it had not been for that story and for the unseen presence of the spirit of the old "Gipper" on that field. The Notre Dame team, as newspaper reporters said, "seemed inspired, exalted, overpowering. There was something about them that is seldom seen on a football field. They were invincible. You could see it as they ran onto the field. They looked like a caravan of crusaders." That's the way the hard-boiled sports writers wrote of that Notre Dame–Army game.

The second half had hardly started when, with several sweeping end runs and forward passes, Notre Dame got within striking distance of the Army goal line. It had been done so swiftly—as often happens when a team is inspired with confidence—that in almost seconds Chevigny was given the ball and smashed through the line for the winning touchdown. As he lay on his back, with two or three of his own teammates on top of him, who had been forming his interference, he looked up with a smile and said, "That's one for the old 'Gipper,' boys!"

That is one of the classic stories of football and will remain one for a good many years to come, because it comes up out of life, and out of reality. We smile at talk about the invisible, at talk about the presence of our loved ones about us everywhere and all the time. We smile at talk about the invisible world in all of its manifestations, but when a tall tale like that comes along, of the power of the presence of the invisible, we sit up and listen, especially when it works out in practical life, and when it inspires hard-boiled, disciplined men to turn defeat into victory; when it takes a depressed group of crippled boys and turns them into young furies, unbeatable.

You ask me what "presences" are with us, and I reply: the presence of our parents—our mothers and fathers, the memory of them and their expectations, their sacrifices for us in the past; the presence of our friends who have faith in us and look forward to seeing us do great and heroic things; the presences of our pals, our sweethearts, our ancestry, our better selves, our idealism, our dreams, our goals, our hopes. These are always hovering about us like so many invisible spirits; hovering about watching and waiting for us to achieve; waiting and expecting us to be our best selves.

✳　✳　✳

"THAT KID IS HOPELESS"

ONE of my good friends, Clarence Westphall, who is especially interested in boys' work, sent me this story.

I should like to take you with me to a crowded courtroom in a New England city. A boy about sixteen years of age, who has been accused of stealing an automobile, stands before the judge awaiting sentence. In a chair nearby a mother sobs hysterically. An attorney has just testified that the young offender has been a constant nuisance to the community. Previous to that the chief of police had told how the boy had been arrested on numerous occasions for stealing fruit, breaking windows, and committing numerous acts of vandalism.

Now the stern, cold-eyed judge, glaring over the rims of his spectacles, launches into a bitter tirade against the youth, reminding him of the dire consequences which will result from his lawless acts. Every word from the thin-lipped judge is like the crack of a whip, as he mercilessly berates the defendant for his irresponsible conduct. He seems to be searching his vocabulary for the cruelest words he can find with which to humiliate the lad who stands before him.

But the boy does not *cower* before this bitter tongue-lashing. His attitude is one of reckless *defiance*. Not once does he lower his eyes from the face of the judge. With lips compressed and eyes flashing he glares at his persecutor with a look on his face of utter disdain; and when the judge pauses for a moment to let his words take effect the boy looks him straight in the eye, and from between clenched teeth come the sneering words, "I'm not afraid of *you*."

An angry flush spreads over the face of the judge as he leans over his desk and snaps out, "I think about the only language you can understand is a six months' sentence in the reform school."

"Go ahead and send me to the reform school," the boy snarls. "See if I care."

The feeling in the courtroom is tense. Spectators look at one another and shake their heads.

"That kid is hopeless!" an officer has just remarked.

"A good horsewhipping is what he deserves," whispers another.

Up to this time not a sympathetic word has been spoken for the lad. The chief of police, the attorney, the judge—all have branded him as a nuisance to the community, a criminal at heart, and all of the invectives which were hurled at him have served only to stir up in his heart a deeper feeling of hatred and resentment. The scene is much like that of a lion trainer jabbing at a caged beast with a pointed stick, with every thrust goading the victim to renewed fury.

At this point the judge spies among the spectators a young man from a nearby town, the superintendent of The Golden Rule Farm for problem boys.

"Mr. Weston," he says, in a tone of weary resignation, "what do you think of this boy?"

The gentleman in question steps forward. He has an air of assurance that immediately commands respect, and a kindly look in his eyes which makes you feel that here is a man who really understands boys.

"Judge," he says quietly, "that boy isn't really tough. Underneath that bluff of his he is completely and thoroughly frightened—and deeply hurt. My belief is that he has never had a chance. Life has been bewildering to him. He has never known a father's love. He has never had the hand of a friend to guide him. I'd like to see him given a chance to show what he's really worth."

For a moment the courtroom is quiet. Then the silence is suddenly broken by a stifled sob—not from the mother, but from the boy! The kind, sympathetic words of Mr. Weston have broken him completely. There he stands with shoulders drooped and head bowed, as tears slowly trickle down his cheeks. One kind word has reached the boy's heart, whereas a half hour of denunciation had served only to make him the more resentful.

The judge coughs to hide his embarrassment and nervously adjusts his spectacles. Then the chief of police, who had testified against the lad, slips from the room, followed by the attorney.

After a moment of deliberation the judge turns to Mr. Weston and says, "If you think you can do anything with the boy, I'll suspend sentence and turn him over to you."

The conclusion of the story is that the lad was given into Mr. Weston's charge, and from that time forth he caused no more trouble. The friendly gesture of the man who had come to his defense that day in the courtroom had put his feet on a new path, and had helped to bring out those finer qualities of character which no one previously thought even existed.

✳   ✳   ✳

"HIS SOUL GOES MARCHING ON"

Two years ago while lecturing for a month in California, I was visiting one evening in the home of an elderly minister in Pasadena who got to telling me stories of that vicinity. One of his stories deserves a wider hearing.

It seems that two quaint old men were spending the last days of their lives in Pasadena, keeping a little garden. Everybody respected them because they were always mentally alert and interested in social and political questions.

During those years the Chinese Exclusion Act was being debated and the racial feeling against Orientals was running high.

But one day there appeared in the Chinese section of Los Angeles two dignified-looking, white-whiskered old men driving a buckboard. They hired two Chinese to go out to Pasadena to work in their garden, put them in the back of their buggy, and started to drive down the main street of Los Angeles. The rumor soon spread throughout the then small city that two old white men had hired two Chinese laborers, contrary to public sentiment. A crowd gathered and followed that old buggy. One of the old men was driving; the other sat in the front seat with a shotgun lying across his knees. There was a determined look in their faces, set like steel. Finally the jeers and taunts turned to mob anger as the crowd grew larger, and there were cries of "Lynch them! Kill the whole lot of them! Let's string all four of them up to a tree!"

But the two old men never flinched. There was a twitching of the shotgun in the hands of the old man on the right, but no menacing movement. The crowd grew so large that finally it blocked the street and the horse stopped.

"Give us those Chinese! Hand those Orientals over to us! Cut off their pigtails and hang 'em up to a tree!" What at first seemed to be only a threat finally turned into madness, and in a last burst of mob violence that crowd started to climb into the wagon to lynch both the white men and the Chinese. Someone had found four ropes and men were whirling them in the air. It looked bad until a preacher who happened to be in that crowd climbed up on the wagon, held his hands up for silence, and said to that mad mob: "Just a minute, please! I don't think that you would molest these two old men if you knew who they were. These two old men are the sons of old John Brown of Harper's Ferry, my friends, and they think they are making a stand for social and racial justice, liberty and fair play. They

36

may be wrong in your eyes, but at least we Americans will have to respect them!"

A sudden silence fell on that mob. Then somebody started to sing what was then a familiar melody: "John Brown's body lies a mold'ring in the grave, but his soul goes marching on."

That crowd then formed a procession in front of those two old men, with their Chinese laborers who were huddling on the bottom of the buggy under the seat, and actually escorted them out of the city singing that great old anthem of freedom and liberty in memory of their patriot father.

Oh, these fathers! There's no Father's Day universally recognized, but every day is father's day. I have noted this reverence, gratitude, and the long-continuing influence of the father's spirit in the great American personalities I have interviewed. Ralph Adams Cram said to me: "My father was the greatest man I ever knew. He was the last of the squires." Vachel Lindsay said to me: "My old doctor father used to take me with him on his errands of mercy at Springfield, and even today his memory is sweet in a thousand homes. They never think of me as a poet, but always refer to me as 'The Doctor's Son.'" And one of the richest memories I have of the tribute of a son to his father comes from San Francisco, where I met a young doctor named Wilson, son of a big six-foot Methodist preacher who in his younger days had been a sailor. They called him Jab Wilson, for he was a battling giant. That boy once said to me: "Father was a giant in body, intellect, and spirit. We boys—and there were six of us—worshiped him. He died during the earthquake; and now after ten years his personality is so real to me that often as I am walking downtown on Market Street, an old trail of my father's where we used to meet when he was alive, and I suddenly turn the corner of Powell and Market, I swear to you that I still run into him face to face and find myself saying, 'Why, hello, Father. I want to tell you what happened this morning.' And then I suddenly realize that he is no longer of this world although his virile personality still lives in my soul." Yes, thank God, the souls of most of our fathers are still marching on through our lives.

YUDISTHERA and his four brothers were great heroes. They had fought many a good battle as they reigned as kings in India.

For a good many years they had ruled gloriously, and now the time had come when they considered giving up their reign to their descendants, and starting for heaven.

They started their journey up to the Himalaya Mountains, for they thought the dim peaks of heaven lay just beyond. Dressed in clothes of abject poverty the brothers set out on their great journey. The Himalayas were easily reached, but the mountains of God lay a long way beyond.

One by one Yudisthera's brothers fell by the way and died because each had been guilty of some kind of sin. Even Yudisthera felt a pang shoot through him whenever his foot touched the earth, as he thought of some untruth of which he had been guilty.

At last, from the mountains of God he heard a thunder, and out of it came a golden chariot and upon it sat the Angel of God.

Then he heard a wondrous voice saying: "It is ordained, thou blameless one, that thou shouldst enter heaven without tasting death. Therefore, enter this chariot."

"Nay," said the good king, "all of my brothers are left behind; I must wait for them!"

"Thy brothers are not behind thee," replied the angel. "They have died, and so reached heaven before thee. To come with me is to go to them."

With this good news he stepped aside to let his dog enter the chariot before him, but the angel Indra objected: "Send away thy dog. He cannot enter heaven with you."

"But how," cried Yudisthera, "could I enjoy eternal blessing without my faithful dog?"

"For men with dogs there is no place in heaven," said the angel, "so you must leave him behind."

"Nay, nay, Eternal Being," said the good king with firmness. "To abandon one who has loved us is sinful. Never while I live shall I forsake one who has given me devotion or sought my protection or mercy."

But as he finished and turned away, the stern face of Indra smiled and he said: "I was only testing thee. Thou hast refused the divine chariot in behalf of thy dog. Verily, in heaven there is none like thee. Enter in with thy faithful animal."

So Yudisthera and his faithful dog entered heaven and he began immediately to look around for his brothers, for the celestial regions were nothing to him without his brothers.

The angel therefore took him down into a dark and terrible road, gloomy as a night without a star, till at last the messenger would go no farther.

Yudisthera could not quite trust his eyes and ears when he saw his brothers way down there in pain and sorrow. "Come away," shouted the angel, "this is no place for thee." But Yudisthera replied: "You return, but I shall go where my brothers are and remain with them forever. Heaven without them would be a dreary desert."

Then again the illusion vanished, and he found himself and his brothers in a land of love and light, and a celestial voice spoke to him: "These things have seemed to happen to thee, to test thee, but now arise and dwell in the highest heaven with thy brethren. Thy faith is full, thy self-mastery complete. Lo! All life is mine, and I am all that is. It was as a dog I followed thee. In loving thy brothers thou didst love me. Therefore enter into the joy of eternal life."

I think I have understood for years that feeling, which I have tried to express in this verse called "Dear Lord, if you please!"

I want no heaven
Without the vast event
   Of spring when birds nest and sing,
Without white dawn, magnificent,
   And wide winds that swing.

I want no heaven
Without autumn, when leaves
   Turn crimson and gold,
And I can hear eaves
   Creak and feel time grow old.

39

I want no heaven
Without love of friends
    And work to do, with rest
At dusk when the day ends
    In the wide west.

I want no heaven
Without children, home and wife
    About me, over there.
Without these, to me no life
    Eternal would be fair.

I think I'd almost rather be
Dead through all eternity
Than not have these,
Dear Lord, if you please!

✳   ✳   ✳

"THE LOOK OF EAGLES IN HIS EYE"

SEVERAL years ago I saw a motion picture entitled "Kentucky."
It had something which gave me a thrill I seldom get in a motion
picture, and that was a great phrase. It was Uncle Peter Goodwin in this picture, the lovable old Southern horse-lover, who
was given a chance to select, from a herd of what looked to be
ordinary two-year-old colts, the one that would be the most
promising to win the Kentucky Derby. He chose one which
everybody else in the scene thought was a second-rater and not
likely to develop into a thoroughbred. That colt turned out to
be Blue Grass, who won the Kentucky Derby—a matter about
which I know little and care less. But what I do care about is
the reason old Uncle Peter Goodwin gave for selecting this particular colt. He said he took the one that had "the look of
eagles in his eye."

That phrase is full of meaning for humans as well as horses.

40

History has had some great men who had the look of eagles in their eyes. There is a great painting in Massachusetts. You see three men marching forward with courage, audacity, determination in their vibrant stride, without fear and asking no favors. One has a flute lifted to his lips and is playing it lustily; another has a snare drum which he beats with vigor; the third carries a flag, and that flag trails behind flying in the wind of their rapid stride. It is a militant, moving miracle of patriotism, courage, and daring. The old man carrying the flag has a bandage over his forehead, for he has evidently been wounded in battle; but that does not stop him, or them! Nothing does or seemingly could stop them. They call that painting "The Spirit of Seventy-Six." And each man in that painting has "the look of eagles in his eye!"

Lincoln had it when his face was animated. I used to talk with an old man named Henry Rankin who had been Lincoln's office boy, and one thing he told me about Lincoln I shall never forget: that usually Lincoln's face was sad, listless, unanimated; but when he was on the platform in debate, or when he was trying to comfort some mother, his face would begin to glow as though there were a great light behind his kindly eyes. "Then," said Mr. Rankin to me many times, "he looked like an eagle on a craig!" That was his expression—not mine: "He looked like an eagle on a craig!"

I know a quartet of the contemporary great who have that eagle look in their eyes—eyes which none who have seen them can ever forget; those strange blue-gray, wistful, playboy, fun-loving, happy, steel-cold, yet daring eyes of William Allen White; the haunting, dreaming, far-away, dark eyes of soft-voiced Roland Hayes—eyes which have the look in them at times of some African chieftain from whom he must have descended; the regal eyes of Fritz Kreisler as he brings his violin to his shoulder, then lifts his bow, raises his head, and plays an aria through with the gesture of a master who seems to say, "That's the way that ought to be played!" and those strange brown eyes of Edwin Markham, which are always looking out beyond the horizons. Once when Mr. Ford and Mr. Cameron were photographing him we all

41

noticed that he was looking out into the horizon. I asked him what he was looking for and he said, "I am always looking for Virgilia." "And who is Virgilia?" I asked. He replied: "Virgilia is my ideal of womanhood. I have always been looking for her coming down the horizons." But whatever he was looking for, there was an eagle look in his eyes.

I often wondered what this eagle look in the eyes of certain personalities meant, and I think that the answer can be expressed in a verse I once wrote called "Almost Omnipotent."

> I am an eagle born to fly
> Up stellar highways of the sky
> Along the Milky Way, where blaze
> New dawn, new planets, and new ways.
> I am man-born, God-led, sky-bent,
> Almost Omnipotent!
>
> I am a planet, blazing white
> Down the long world's chaotic night;
> A planet on its orbit flung,
> A new Mars in the heavens hung;
> Sky-born, sun-bred, God-sent;
> Almost Omnipotent!
>
> I am a personality;
> A spark of God's Divinity;
> A sacred thing in God's own eyes,
> An earth-born pilgrim from the skies;
> Of dust and spirit strangely blent;
> Almost Omnipotent!
>
> I am a pilgrim who has strayed
> To earth and in God's image made
> To dominate sky, land, and sea;
> The lord of my own destiny;
> Till all the veils of earth are rent;
> Almost Omnipotent!

✳   ✳   ✳

"THE HAND OF GOD"

THERE is no adventure in the world more thrilling than that of coming unexpectedly upon some vision of splendor or beauty when one least expects it. In the days before I knew Rodin's sculpture very well I came suddenly upon one of his masterpieces standing at the end of a corridor in the Metropolitan Art Museum. As one approached it there seemed to be merely a great block of white unhewn marble, but as one came nearer there emerged from the rough marble a great, beautiful, shapely hand. The hand seemed to grow right out of the marble, a device which Rodin was fond of employing. Drawing closer, one saw that this hand held certain shapes—the half-formed bodies of a nude man and woman, curled up in the great hand; and finally one was near enough to read the inscription carved beneath: "The Hand of God." There they were—men and women carved from the same piece of marble as the Hand of God itself! And suddenly there flashed upon my mind a sentence from the Old Testament: "Look to the rock whence ye are hewn."

Dallas Lore Sharp used to tell a story of being out in his garden one spring day planting seed, with his ten-year-old boy at his side. Suddenly overhead a flock of wild geese flew by on their northward journey. Dr. Sharp paused in his work and began to quote these lines of Bryant's:

> He who, from zone to zone,
> Guides through the boundless sky thy certain flight,
> In the long way that I must tread alone,
> Will guide my steps aright.

After repeating the first line of the poem he paused, and the boy took up the quotation and finished it. Then he, too, paused, and in a few moments said, "Father, I'm glad that I know that poem."

"Why, my boy?" asked his father.

"Because I seem to see God when the wild geese go flying by!" Some men lose this divine gift while others cherish it and never let it go. One astronomer can record: "I have swept the heavens with my telescope and nowhere have I found God." But Kepler can say with utmost conviction, "Almighty God, these are thy thoughts I am thinking after thee." As Elizabeth Browning said,

> Earth's crammed with heaven,
> And every common bush afire with God;
> And only he who sees takes off his shoes;
> The rest sit round it and pluck blackberries.

Yet this ability to see "God and the wild geese," "God and our daily work," is not confined alone to children. Strong men have confessed to its power to transform experience. There is that thrilling record of Sir Ernest Shackleton's in which he tells how he and two other men, Worsley and Crean, battled against terrible odds in a temperature many degrees below zero, as they made their way over the almost impassable mountains and the treacherous glaciers of South Georgia in their efforts to save the rest of the South Polar party. Of this march Sir Ernest Shackleton writes:

When I look back on those days I have no doubt that Providence guided us. . . . I know that during that long and racking march of thirty-six hours over the unnamed mountains and glaciers of South Georgia, it seemed to me often that we were four, and not three. I said nothing to my companions on the point, but afterward Worsley said to me, "Boss, I had a curious feeling on that march that there was another person with us." Crean confessed to the same idea. One feels "the dearth of human words, the roughness of human speech" in trying to describe things intangible, but a record of our journeys would not be complete without a reference to a subject so very near to our hearts.

Edward Rowland Sill knew what I am writing about today and what Shackleton experienced, and sings it in these glowing words:

> ·But as heaven deepens, and the Cross and Lyre
> Lift up their stars beneath the Northern Crown,
> Unto the yearning of the world's desire,

I shall be 'ware of answer coming down;
And something, when my heart the darkness stills,
    Shall tell me, without sound or any sight,
That other footsteps are upon the hills;
    Till the dim earth is luminous with the light
        Of the white dawn, from some far-hidden shore,
        That shines upon my forehead evermore.

*   *   *

THE MAGIC MASK

A GREAT and powerful lord once ruled over thousands of soldiers, and with them he conquered vast domains for his own. He was wise and brave, respected and feared by all, but no one loved him. Each year as he grew more severe he grew more lonely, and his face reflected the bitterness in his greedy soul, for there were deep, ugly lines about his cruel mouth which never showed a smile, and a deep frown permanently furrowed his forehead.

It happened that in one of the cities over which he ruled there lived a beautiful girl whom he had watched for many months as she went about among the people, and he loved her and wanted to make her his wife. He decided to go and speak to her of this love. Dressing in his finest robes and placing a golden coronet on his head, he looked into his mirror to see what kind of picture he would make for the beautiful girl. But he could see nothing but what would cause fear and dislike for himself— a cruel, hard face which looked even worse when he tried to smile.

Then a happy notion came to him, and he sent for a magician. "Make for me a mask of the thinnest wax so that it will follow every line of my features, but paint it with your magic paints so that it will look kind and pleasant. Fasten it upon my face so that I shall never have to take it off. Make it handsome—attractive. Use your greatest skill and I will pay any price you ask."

"This I can do," said the magician, "on one condition. You

45

must keep your own face in the same lines which I paint or the mask will be ruined. One angry frown, and the mask will be ruined forever, nor can I replace it."

"I will do anything you say," said the lord eagerly, "anything to win the admiration and love of my lady. Tell me how to keep the mask from cracking."

"You must think kindly thoughts," replied the magician, "and to do this you must do kindly deeds. You must make your kingdom happy rather than powerful. You must replace anger with understanding and love. Build schools for your subjects instead of forts, and hospitals instead of battleships. Be gracious and courteous to all men."

So the wonderful mask was made, and no one would have guessed that it was not the true face of the lord. So handsome was it that the beautiful lady became his bride. Months passed, and though the mask was often in danger of ruin, the man fought hard with himself to keep it. His subjects wondered at the miraculous change in him and attributed it to his lovely wife, who, they said, had made him like herself.

Since gentleness and thoughtfulness had entered the life of this man, honesty and all goodness were his also, and soon he regretted having deceived this beautiful wife with the magic mask. At last he could bear it no longer and he summoned the magician.

"Remove this false face of mine!" he cried. "Take it away! . . . this deceiving mask that is not my true self!"

"If I do," said the magician, "I can never make another, and you must wear your own face as long as you live."

"Better so!" said the lord, "than to deceive one whose love and trust I have won dishonorably. Better that I should be despised by her than to go on doing what is unworthy for her sake. Take it off, I say, take it off!"

And the magician took off the mask and the lord in fear and anguish sought his reflection in the glass. His eyes brightened and his lips curved into a radiant smile, for the ugly lines were gone, the frown had disappeared—and lo, his face was the exact likeness of the mask he had worn so long! And when he re-

46

turned to his beloved wife she saw only the familiar features of the man she loved.

Yes, it's an old story this legend tells: that a man's face soon betrays what he is inside of his soul; what he thinks and feels; the thoughts of his heart. "Whatsoever a man thinketh that he is" was a wise and true saying. Somebody else has said, "A man *is* what he thinks!"

A year or so ago I was able to do a favor for a Boston portrait-painter, and in return for that favor he insisted upon painting my portrait. I had never had that experience before. I felt a little silly at having it done, especially when I had to sit many hours in his studio. But there were compensations. I learned a lot from that painter. I learned that a true painter scorns a photographic likeness and seeks to put into his painting the soul of his subject. Early in our experience, at my first sitting, he said casually, "You seem to have a little of the angel in you but more of the devil." At that, I almost decided to give up the experience. I felt as if I had been caught with all of my soul-clothes off in a public place. Another day he said to me: "A man is what he is inside of his soul and he can't get away from it. You don't fool people—especially painters—about what you really *are!*" That man made me nervous—but we finished the portrait and it didn't turn out half as bad as I feared it would. But from that experience I certainly learned the everlasting truth that a man's face is the signature of his soul!

*   *   *

"THERE IS NO TIME FOR HATE"

MAELDUNE, according to Tennyson's version of an old Irish legend, and his men set sail with deep hatred in their hearts to avenge the murder of Maeldune's father by the king of a neigh-boring island many years before. Just as they approached the island of his father's enemy, a great storm came and carried them far out to sea, and they were left there to wander aimlessly.

Their wanderings brought them to many strange islands—islands of mystery, of fantastic experiences. The first was the Island of Silence, an island where no sound was heard. The weird absence of sound awed them and they left the place in haste, only to find themselves approaching the Island of Shouting, where wild birds and even the cliffs screamed constantly, as in terror, until the very earth shook and cattle dropped dead. In the midst of this horrible din, Maeldune's men began to fight one another, and Maeldune hurriedly set about getting them away from such a dreadful place.

Once more out at sea, the men became conscious of an almost overpowering fragrance, as of many gardens, and they were irresistibly drawn to the Island of the Flowers, which was a veritable paradise of beauty. The earth was red with passion flowers and the mountains were crowned as with drifts of snow-white lilies. The fields were colorful beds of roses, tulips, and poppies. One could not walk anywhere without stepping upon a delicate blossom. The men were so attracted by this great and gorgeous array that they ran among the flowers and stooped down and gathered them to their breasts and pressed their faces into the fragrant flower-hearts. At last they lay down to sleep among them and drifted into a stupor-like slumber, only to awaken and discover that there was no food—nothing but flowers, flowers, and their deadening fragrance. They soon tired of this place, for they were sick with hunger and they hated the pollen which covered them from head to foot and left them yellow and ugly. They tore at the flowers and ground them under their feet and went in haste to the blessed safety of their ship, to sail away.

The next island they reached was the Island of Fruits, where trees and vines bent low with luscious ripe fruits of all kinds. "At last!" cried the men, "here is food—all that we need!" And they rushed forth to gorge themselves first at a tree and then at the vines, until they fell upon the ground, too full to move. The next day they went again from one tree to another, eating the delicious fruits of the island, for there was more than an entire army would need. But there was nothing else on the island—no flowers, no people, nothing but fruit. And soon they tired of this life and in their discomfort they quarreled and fought with each other, forgetting their mission of revenge upon the man who had killed Maeldune's father. But Maeldune kept the hatred smoldering in his heart and took the men from the Island of Fruits before they should kill each other.

They went from one island to another, each an individual experience, each one seeming to offer them something which they desired deeply, but of which they soon tired and went on in search of something more.

Even the largest island of all, the Island Bounteous, which seemed at first to offer them all they could ever desire, did not appeal for long. In the morning the skies would open up and from them would fall all the food they would need for the day, and all their desires were supplied. The island was peaceful and beautiful, and they had naught to do but bask in the sun and sing of their homeland. But there was no work to do—and men must work—so again they became dissatisfied and fell to fighting, until Maeldune put them back on the ship to sail away, more discouraged than ever. Weary of the many experiences and the resulting dissatisfactions, they sailed in angry silence for many days, fearing they would never again sight land.

But at last they came to an island where a saint lived in a little hut near the shore. Dragging themselves wearily up the path, they flung themselves at the feet of the old man and told him their pitiful story. The old saint's face was kind and his voice was low and sweet.

"Oh, ye men," he said feelingly, "give up this purpose of thine. Remember Christ said, 'Forgive your enemies.' 'Vengeance is mine, saith the Lord.'

"For countless ages his fathers have killed your fathers and your fathers have killed in return. The earth is weary of the never-ending murders of human vengeance. God commands you to live in peace and forget the past."

And the aged man taught them to pray: "Father, forgive us our trespasses, as we forgive those who trespass against us."

And the men sailed away again, grateful for this message from one who had lived so long and who knew whereof he spoke. Deep within the heart of each man was the prayer that they should be allowed to return safely to their homes and to forget the mission of vengeance upon which they started. But the winds carried them to the island of the king who had murdered Maeldune's father, and the men watched anxiously to see what Maeldune would do. But this chieftain, in whose heart the hatred had been deepest, said, "Turn away, men; we shall not land, for we have learned that *the spirit of love is greater than vengeance,* and that spirit of love shall guide us henceforth even as it guided the Son of Man."

And Edwin Markham said it for us and for all time in "The Hidden Glacier," from *The Shoes of Happiness.*

> There is no time for hate, O wasteful friend:
> Put hate away until the ages end.
> Have you an ancient wound? Forget the wrong. . . .
> Out in my West a forest loud with song
> Towers high and green over a field of snow,
> Over a glacier buried far below.

⁂   ✳   ✳

"YOU IN YOUR SMALL CORNER"

BROWNING wrote a poem entitled "The Boy and the Angel" which has as its theme the great thought that "all service ranks the same with God." The story which I am going to tell is based upon this poem. It tells the story of Theocrite, the little boy in Browning's poem.

Theocrite was a little boy, but nevertheless he had to support himself and work at a poor trade, earning a few cents to pay for his living. All day long he worked, but this did not discourage him. He sang at his work and thus brought joy into his own heart and into the hearts of others; but more than that, it

50

brought joy to God's heart, who heard him from on high.

One day, as he was singing, a monk passed by the place where he worked. Upon hearing the cheerful song of the boy, he stepped in and said: "Well done, my son. I do not doubt your praise is heard by God as well as if thou wert Pope of Rome and in St. Peter's Church, singing the glad songs of praises at Easter time."

Theocrite was very happy at his work, but at the suggestion of singing in the cathedral of St. Peter, he said, "Would to God that I might praise him in the great St. Peter's Cathedral before I die!"

We are told by Browning that the angel Gabriel heard this pious wish, and the next day Theocrite was gone, for the angel had started him on the way to become none less than the Pope of Rome.

Immediately after Theocrite's disappearance from the workshop God missed him and said to the angel, "How is it that I do not hear the sweet voice of Theocrite singing at his work?"

Then the angel Gabriel left the heavenly sphere, and became a boy like Theocrite, taking his place as well as he could. The boy's work he could do very easily, but could not sing as well as Theocrite had done.

God said: "I hear a voice of praise, but in it there is no doubt and no fear, like that of the song of Theocrite. I miss my little human praise."

Then the angel Gabriel cast off his disguise. No man can fill another's place, and even the angel found that he could not entirely fill the place of the little boy.

And so he went to Rome at Eastertide, where the new Pope Theocrite was about to praise God in the great way, and said:

"I took thee from thy trade and made thee Pope of Rome, but it was all a mistake. I did not do well. Thou couldst be a great Pope, but no one can take thy place in thine old home. I have tried to take thy place. I have left my angel sphere to take thy place, but I cannot do it.

"At first thy voice seemed to be very weak, but, alas! when it stopped I could not take up thy song. God was not satisfied.

51

"All the songs of praise rise as a wondrous chorus to the ear of God, but without you the great chorus was incomplete, and God missed your little voice of praise.

"Therefore, come back with me to your old home and workshop; come back to your boyhood, and sing again your song, 'Praise God.' "

And so Theocrite grew old at home. He never had the chance to sing the praises of God "the great way" in the St. Peter's Cathedral in Rome; but when he returned home his song brought joy to the hearts of all who heard him. And many a soul found happiness through him. The beauty of his songs helped them to understand the glory of God. And when Theocrite and the Pope of Rome came to die, God saw to it that they came to heaven side by side.

It is a simple story Browning has told in this great poem. A Billy Sunday hymn used to put it, "Brighten the corner where you are." And a childhood hymn sang it, "You in your small corner and I in mine, for Jesus bids us shine like a clear pure light, burning through the day and burning through the night." And that gives a place for all of us to do our work: the mother darning little stockings, washing little hands and feet; the father toiling day by day to keep the home together; the child doing his chores with laughter in his heart—all of us doing our humble best and bit in the great God's scheme of things.

I often go to the Boston Symphony and sit as close as I can to the orchestra. I like to watch each musician—the drummer, the violinist, the man who plays even the great clanging cymbals. I like to watch him most of all. There he stands waiting, sometimes through an entire number, without much to do until the vast crescendo climax of the composition, and then I see him lift his two cymbals—waiting, eagerly, on his toes—and bang they go together—maybe just once—but that once makes that orchestration perfect. Not much to do, but the omission of that one bang would spoil the piece—and the proper timing of it perfects the piece.

✳   ✳   ✳

PUT OUT THE FIRE, FRIENDS!

COUNT TOLSTOY, the great Russian author and Christian reformer, gives us the following parable.

Ivan was a hardworking and prosperous Russian peasant. Gavrilo, his neighbor, was a cripple. Both of them had very large families, but they liked each other. Then one day something happened which made them bitter enemies.

A bantam hen belonging to Ivan's daughter flew over into Gavrilo's yard. He and his family were eyewitnesses of this fact. A little bit later they heard her cackle as though she had laid an egg. But when they came to look for the egg they found none.

The quarrel began when Ivan's family accused Gavrilo of stealing the egg. In typical Russian anger they began to tear one another's clothes and to fight. Ivan pulled out part of Gavrilo's beard, which to the Russian was the symbol of dignity and manhood. Upon this Gavrilo swore by heaven to have Ivan sent to jail for revenge.

Ivan's father tried to straighten out the quarrel, accusing them of behaving like foolish children; for, after all, they were fighting over nothing. An egg was worth little. But neither one of them listened. They went to court about it; and while the case was being heard a bolt was missing from Gavrilo's wagon, and immediately he accused Ivan's boy of stealing it. So there was another case in court. During all this time the two families quarreled with each other. First Ivan would have Gavrilo arrested for some supposed bad deed, and then the cripple would have Ivan fined for something he did, or was supposed to have done At last a deep hatred filled the hearts of all concerned. Since they would not reason together they resorted to violence.

At a wedding attended by both families Gavrilo struck Ivan's wife when she accused him of horse-stealing; and she was confined to her bed for several weeks. Ivan thought that the cripple should be sent to Siberia, but he only succeeded in having him punished with twenty lashes. When Gavrilo heard this sentence imposed he turned pale and swore revenge. "All right," he muttered; "he may lash my back. It will burn; but I will set his house on fire."

Ivan heard what Gavrilo said and reported it to the judge. The judge called Gavrilo back and asked him what he had said, to which he replied, "Nothing!" Even the judges were frightened. The oldest of them spoke to Gavrilo in a friendly manner. "See here, you had better make up, and be friends again. You might have killed Ivan's wife, and we would have put a rope around your neck and hanged you. Confess, now; ask his pardon, and he will forgive you. Then we will change the sentence." But this did not make any impression upon Gavrilo; the sentence was carried out, and both neighbors went home hating each other.

That night it occurred to Ivan to look around the yard before going to bed, to see whether any harm had been done. There by the fence he noticed something moving. He listened, and heard a rustling of leaves and hay. Then he saw a man kindling a bundle of straw in his shed. "Now," muttered Ivan, "I have caught him in the act."

The dry straw blazed up and set the whole shed on fire. Ivan, instead of putting the small fire out, tried to catch Gavrilo; but, lame as he was, he jumped away and ran behind the shed. Ivan grasped his coat, but it tore away. He rushed after him, only to be struck by a blow that knocked him senseless.

While he lay unconscious on the ground Ivan's shed and house burned down, for there was none to put it out. Then the sparks flew over and caught Gavrilo's own house and shed, until at last the whole village was burned, and all were homeless. The old father was rescued with difficulty; and when Ivan went to him he said, "I told you so. Now tell me, who really did all this damage?"

"He, Gavrilo. I caught him at it. Right before my eyes he touched off the straw," cried Ivan.

"Ivan," said the father, "whose foolishness was it? In God's name, whose fault was it? You could have put out the fire and yet you preferred to chase Gavrilo." Only then did he realize

54

what he had done, and he fell on his knees before his father and asked his and God's forgiveness.

Then his father told him not to tell of Gavrilo's crime, to spare him, and then God would forgive them both. So he followed his father's advice. No one ever knew who set the fire.

Ivan forgave Gavrilo. Gavrilo was much surprised that Ivan did not tell the judges who had set the village on fire. At first he was afraid of Ivan, but he got over it. While they were rebuilding their houses both families lived in one shed, and there was never any more quarreling. Ivan had learned his lesson. He knew now that a fire ought to be put out in the beginning, and that getting even through revenge results only in creating another wrong. An evil act can be corrected only by a good deed. Love and forgiveness are the pillars of friendship, in both a personal and national sense. Europe and Asia had better read Tolstoy's parable.

$$* \quad * \quad *$$

"THE PASSIVE MASTER LENT HIS HAND"

ONCE, in a hotel in Switzerland, a mother was staying for a few weeks with her little girl. Evidently the mother did not want that little girl to get out of practice for her piano lessons; so every day following lunch that little girl would go into the lounge room at that hotel and do her half hour of practicing on the piano there. That practicing was so full of discords and so monotonous that the hotel guests got very weary of listening to it day after day. But they were too polite to complain about it.

When she started practicing, however, the lounge room, lobby, and hallways would suddenly become mysteriously deserted. The other guests would go to their rooms rather than have to listen to that awkward half-hour of pounding the piano keys.

But one day there came from that lounge room the most beautiful harmonies they had ever heard. They could not believe their ears. Had they not actually seen the same little girl go into the room and sit down at the same piano? Had they not heard her start once again on that monotonous thumping? Yes, they had, but suddenly the most beautiful music was pouring forth from that room.

Then the guests started back to see what strange miracle had transformed that awkward child into a musical prodigy. From every room, from every nook and corner where they had sought refuge from that ardent child, they trooped back into the lounge. When they came back a strange sight met their eyes. Josef Hofmann, the great pianist, had been taking a rest cure at that hotel incognito. For weeks he had watched this little girl practicing, had seen the disgust of the other guests, and in a sudden impulse had gone into that room where the child was practicing. When the startled guests hurried back into that room they saw the great pianist seated on the piano stool by this child's side, and as she strummed with her two fingers, the great musician, with delicate touch and infinitely beautiful expression, lifted her childish theme into his own magnificent improvisation.

The child's face was beaming with pride as the strong, vibrant hands of the great musician played over her small delicate fingers, transforming her awkward touch into music that lifted that crowd up until they stood looking into the room with hushed hearts.

The child seemed delighted to lend her hands and her heart to the great master, who hovered above her until that crowd was entranced with what they heard. And when the impromptu concert ceased the uninvited audience began to express their thanks.

With the humility of true dignity the pianist replied to their congratulations: "It is this little lady whom you must thank for any pleasure you may have derived from the music."

So is it with those who understand. The great tenor Roland Hayes understands the power of this idea, and once in his home he told me that his life motto comes from Ralph Waldo Emerson.

The passive Master lent his hand
To the vast soul that o'er him planned.

And when I asked him what he meant by that phrase he said: "I mean that I give my vocal chords, my body, my soul over to God who gave me my voice, and I say to him, 'Sing through me. Help me to forget myself and to remember that I am only an instrument for you to sing through.'" Then he added: "It is the same thing that the immortal Lincoln had in his heart when Stanton asked him why it was that he did not worry more during the Civil War days. Lincoln replied to Stanton: 'When a man feels that he is only a pipe for Omnipotence to sound through he doesn't worry much.'"

It was so with Edwin Markham when he was asked by the Republican Club in New York City at the beginning of this century to write a Lincoln poem. He said, "I will give it to you if it is given to me." He also wrote his great "Man with the Hoe" in this same way. It sprang out of his subconscious mind after he had seen the great Millet painting of "The Man with the Hoe" in San Francisco. He brooded over it for weeks, and then it came. As he says: "It was handed down to me from above. I merely lent my soul and my hand to some spiritual power above and beyond me. I felt as if some vast hand were reaching over my shoulder and guiding my fingers as I wrote. I gave myself over to that hand, that inspiration, or whatever you wish to call it, and the poem came."

So it is with life itself. That is what the Higher Powers will do for all of us, even the most feeble, the most inarticulate, the most humble. If we try to do our part earnestly and lovingly, although it be but little, we shall not be without God's help and skill. Without him we stumble and fail to strike the true note of rapture and beauty; although we do our childish best, too often there will be unhappy discords in the music of life. But if we, through a complete surrender to his will and power, yield ourselves wholly and lovingly to his service, he will come and sit by our sides like an understanding father, and with his larger skill

57

touch the keys of our lives and our very frailties will be lifted into sublime harmonies.

> The passive Master lent his hand
> To the vast soul that o'er him planned.

*   *   *

THE KEY TO THE GOLDEN PALACE

THERE is a striking legend about the Golden Palace which comes to us from Russia.

The Golden Palace was said to have contained everything that would please the heart of any child, and all children everywhere tried every day to do good things that would earn them the key to the palace.

"What shall I do to earn the key to the Golden Palace?" asked one child. "I have brushed my hair until it shines like gold in the sun, and I have woven many yards of linen—all for the key to the Golden Palace; and no one has given it to me."

"These do not count," said the old doorkeeper, patting the child's golden head with his wrinkled old hand. "Do something each morning for somebody else, and thou shalt earn the precious key."

So the child laughed happily and ran off to find someone to do something for, that she might earn the key. The streets of the city were full of people, and the child searched among them until she found an old beggar. Running to him she poured out to him all the precious coins she had been saving for many weeks.

"Now," she said gayly to herself, "I have earned the golden key," and she ran off to tell the old doorkeeper.

But the old man shook his head sadly. "Try again, child," he said.

And the child went back to the city, disappointed. As she came to a steep hill she saw ahead of her a poor lame woman who was climbing the hill painfully and dragging a heavy bundle upon her back.

"I'll help her," thought the child. "That will surely be enough to earn the key."

Taking the bundle in her strong young arms, she trudged up the hill beside the grateful woman, and then turning she ran so fast to see the old doorkeeper that she did not notice the happy light in the eyes of the woman she had helped.

"Oh, doorkeeper," the child cried eagerly, "the key, the key!"

Tearfully the weary old man said, "You must try again, child, try again."

But by now the child was discouraged, and walking home slowly she decided to give up the work for the key. It was impossible to earn it. She didn't want the key anyway.

Passing through a wooded section she heard a faint cry among the bushes, and was frightened. When the cry came again she realized it must be a dog, so she parted the bushes and saw a little shaggy dog caught in the trap of a hunter.

"Oh, you poor little dog!" she cried as she knelt and tried to unfasten the trap. "Don't cry, I will try to help you."

The child pulled at the heavy spring until her fingers were torn and bleeding. Finally the little dog was free, and he licked her hand and whimpered. She tore some bandages from the hem of her skirt and wound them round the bruised paw. Then lifting the animal in her arms, she trudged homeward.

Suddenly there appeared before her the old doorkeeper, holding out to her the key to the Golden Palace.

"Oh!" she said in astonishment. "The key is not for me. I did not help the little dog for the key. I forgot all about the key."

In the eyes of the old man there were tears of joy. "You forgot yourself, dear child," he said; "the key is for those who forget themselves."

One day in France, during the World War, I did a favor for a soldier and he actually presented me with his Croix de Guerre which the French Government had bestowed upon him for courage. He could afford to give me that one, for that boy actu-

59

ally had so many medals for bravery that he had them to spare. It was over that gift that we got to discussing why armies and governments give medals, and I learned for the first time that they give medals to a man when he does something "outside the line of duty." He is never rewarded for doing something which comes within the line of duty. It is only when he steps outside the path of duty and does the unusual, the extra thing, that he wins a medal. In a sense that is the story of the key to the Golden Palace. We do not win the richest rewards of life for doing the things we ought to do anyway; or for doing things with the hope and expectation of reward. It is by doing things in the spirit of not letting thy right hand know what thy left hand doeth that we win the Golden Keys of life; when we do something through sheer pity, sympathy, love, and friendship.

* * *

SOWING SEEDS OF SUGGESTION

Somewhere I have read the story of how a certain wise teacher talked one day to a class of children, telling them that they had been invited to march in a parade the next day. They were all delighted and clapped and yelled to show it.

Then that teacher began to talk of what a long, hard march it would be; of how hot the weather was; of how they would get thirsty and tired, and perhaps ill, and have to drop out of the parade. Then she asked them how many of them wanted to march in the parade, and only two hands out of twenty went up.

Then she spoke again of the patriotic purposes of the parade; of how everybody along the line would be looking at them; of how the bands would be playing, flags waving; of how proud she, their teacher, and their parents and friends would be to see them in that parade; and then she asked them again how many of them would like to march in the parade and every little hand went up with enthusiasm.

Personally, I never tried to influence my own daughter by precept, teaching, or scolding. When I wanted to get a thought over to her I laid a book on her table, a book which contained the idea that I wanted to get over to her, a book about a child, a young woman, or a heroine who had the characteristics I wanted her to have. It always worked. Not long ago I gave on a radio broadcast the story of a young artist in Rome who said to a friend that he was keeping himself clean for his girl; and that was the reason he did not carouse, drink, and take part in the weekly parties the group of American artists in Rome indulged in. Shortly after that I got a letter from a mother in my audience, who said:

I was so grateful for that broadcast. I never like to preach to my sons; to admonish them to keep themselves clean and pure for their future wives and homes. I know that preaching doesn't work, but that suggestion does. So you can imagine my delight that morning when one of my young sons was listening in, and after your broadcast was over he said to me, "Gee, Mother, that was swell stuff this morning!" and he went away with a thoughtful look in his eyes. I will never need to preach on that subject again, for your seeds of suggestion were planted in fertile soil.

Sometimes these seeds of suggestion come from outside and sometimes they come from within.

Some time ago *The Psychological Review* told of an interesting experiment made by the late Dr. Slosson, with a view to demonstrating how easy this faculty can be called into play. In the course of a popular lecture he presented to his audience a bottle containing pure distilled water, which he uncorked with elaborate precautions; and then, watch in hand, he asked those present to indicate the exact moment at which the peculiar odor was perceived by them. Within fifteen seconds those immediately in front of him held up their hands, and within forty seconds those at the other end of the room declared that they distinctly perceived the odor, and several persons in the front row found it so powerful that they hastily left the lecture room.

But often we make psychological suggestions to our own

minds, and they are just as devastating as the seeds which are dropped from outside, as this story illustrates:

A distinguished clergyman who had the reputation of being remarkably cool-headed thought that on one occasion he noticed in himself some traces of palpitation of the heart. A day or two after this he went to a distant town to attend a convention which was to last several days. He was entertained in a private family, and had scarcely lain down on the bed in his room the first evening when he was astonished that the palpitation of his heart seemed to be worse than he had ever noticed it before. He felt sure that the bed moved every time his heart beat. He said to himself that he must be getting in a very bad condition when the throbbing of his heart shook the bed like that. Being a man of very determined will, he turned over on his side, forced himself to think about something else, and went to sleep. He awoke about two o'clock in the morning, and to his dismay found the bed shaking again at every beat of his heart. This both surprised and alarmed him, for up to this time he had always found his heart regular and composed when awakening from a sound sleep. He was so disturbed by it that he finally arose, dressed, and busied himself by writing until morning. On going down to breakfast his hostess inquired as to how he had rested. He replied that he had slept only fairly well, as was usually the case with him on spending the first night in a strange place. She remarked that she was fearful that he would be disturbed by an electric-light plant situated in the next block, which caused the beds to shake in every house in the neighborhood. It is needless to say that the minister saw no more traces of palpitation of the heart during the remainder of the convention.

* * *

IF YOU WOULD BE SOMETHING

A FEW years ago I spent several months in Japan, where I read a good many of the Japanese legends and parables; and no land is richer in this literature than is Japan. One of the most universal and impressive parables I read was this one about a Japanese stonecutter.

Hashmu was a very poor stonecutter. All day long he hacked and hacked at the stone. Sometimes he grew tired of his work and he would say to himself: "Why must I go on hack-hack-hacking at this stone? Why cannot I have riches as other people have?"

One day, while he was working away at the stone, he heard footsteps coming. He looked up immediately, and there stood before him the king on a great horse, with his soldiers to the right and to the left. They looked at some of his work and then passed on.

But Hashmu thought: "How fine to be a king! If only I could be a king on a great horse, with my soldiers to the left and to the right." Then he began to sing:

The king, the king,
The king I would be!

A voice said, "Hashmu, be the king!"

Then Hashmu became the king, and sat on a great horse, with soldiers to the right and to the left. And Hashmu said, "I am the king, and no one in the world is stronger than I."

But soon Hashmu felt the hot sun on his head and on his back. The soldiers grew tired, and the horses could not run. Then Hashmu became angry and cried, "Is there something in the world stronger than a king?" And he began to sing:

The sun, the sun,
The sun I would be!

The voice said, "Hashmu, be the sun."

Thus Hashmu became the great sun in the sky, and shone down on the fields. But soon there came little clouds between Hashmu and the earth, so that he could no longer shine down. Then he said, "Is there something in the world stronger than the sun?" And he began to sing:

The cloud, the cloud,
The cloud I would be!

A voice said, "Hashmu, be the cloud!"
So Hashmu became the cloud and sent rain upon the earth, and the rain became a brook, and the brook became a river, and the river carried away hills and trees and houses. Only one great rock the river could not carry away. Then Hashmu said, "Is there something in the world stronger than the cloud?" and he began to sing:

The rock, the rock,
The rock I would be!

The voice said, "Hashmu, be the rock!"
Thus Hashmu became the great rock. Then he saw coming to meet him a man. The man had in his hand a hammer, and he began to hack at the rock. The chips flew this way and that. Hashmu cried, "Is there something stronger than the rock?" and he sang:

The man, the man,
The man I would be!

The voice said, *"Hashmu, be yourself!"*
Then Hashmu took the old hammer and said: "The sun is stronger than the king, the cloud is stronger than the sun, the rock is stronger than the cloud, *but a man with a living soul is stronger than all.*"

That challenge to "be yourself" has always been one of my fundamental philosophies of life. I say that no man or woman has anything about him more valuable or precious than his own individuality. God made us all different in his wise providence. Just as each leaf and twig and tree and flower—even each petal of a flower—is different, so are we. Most of us strive for originality and greatly desire to be different from other people. But we do not do the one thing that makes us different—be ourselves. We are so apt to be imitators of other people—of their acts and ways and even their thinking. I note this so much in the ministry, and I have dinned into the ears of my young students for the ministry that if they want to be original, attract attention, they must be themselves. They must not allow themselves to be standardized or put into a mold. There is only one person on earth entirely different from all other persons, and that is *you* yourself! Surely that Japanese parable of the stonecutter and its advice, *Be yourself!* is a wise word!

✳ ✳ ✳

"NOTHING CAN TOUCH ME NOW"

GOVERNOR MOORE of New Jersey likes to tell the following story:

One day a colored chauffeur driving a car came out of Trenton at about seventy miles an hour. A trooper saw him, chased him, and caught up with him. After ordering the colored fellow to pull up to the side of the road he said to him, "What's the big idea? Don't you know you were doing seventy miles an hour?"

"Was I?" said the colored chauffeur, "that's perfectly all right with me."

The trooper looked at him for a moment and said, "You're sort of fresh, aren't you?"

"No," replied the colored man. "Give me two or three tickets if you like."

That was too much for the trooper, so he took him to jail.

When the chauffeur appeared before the judge, the judge heard the case and said, "I am going to fine you $25."

"Oh, that's all right, Judge," said the chauffeur. "Make it $100 if you like."

The judge was nonplused at that but he said, "I'm going to make it $25 and a year in jail besides."

"Oh, I'd like that fine," said the colored man. "Make it two or three years if you like."

Finally the judge said, "What's wrong with you? Who are you, anyway?"

"Well," said the colored fellow, "I'm the chauffeur for the warden of the penitentiary and I'm in for life."

Yes, there does come a time when nothing can touch you further; and it is at such a time that you become all-powerful and all other events and experiences look like child's play to you. You have reached what might well be called the ultimate!

They tell the story that one day a lot of loafers were gathered around a favorite spot in Hades discussing floods. One man there was describing the first and famous Johnstown Flood. He was doing a good job of it, giving it dramatic flourish and pleasant exaggeration. All of his audience except one little runt of a fellow seemed to be enjoying his story. That little fellow would grunt now and then with disdain—even with contempt. The story-teller from Johnstown finally got tired of the sneers of his listless listener and said, "Who are you, anyhow, to sneer at my story of the Johnstown Flood?"

The little man replied with great disdain: "Why, my name happens to be Noah, and I went through a little flood myself once which makes your flood look silly."

So it is with life. There are certain experiences that come to us which give us a lofty attitude down from which we can look on all other experiences and know that life can no longer touch us deeply; can no longer hurt us; can no longer coerce us.

Sometimes those experiences are tragic experiences. I talked with a man one morning. I said to him: "My, how happy you always are. No matter how hot it may be or how trying your work you never seem to let it bother you. Nothing seems to upset you."

He replied by saying, "Not after I got this hand." I looked at his hand and saw that it had been cruelly hurt. I waited for the rest of the story.

"A few years ago I was down in the dumps; had lost my job; didn't know where my next meal was to come from; had a family dependent on me; had been sick for six months; was just feeling better; had a call for a new position; got into my automobile to get that job; ran into a tree, wrecked my car and myself, and lost a part of my hand. Trouble and tragedy came in a heap.

Then I got better, got a job and here I am. Nothing can bother me after that experience; so I can laugh at anything."

I used to feel that General Pershing had caught the meaning of this philosophy when I saw him several times in France; looked upon his calm, poised, yet tragically sad face. When I was a young pastor in San Francisco we awoke one morning to read that a frame house in the military reservation, the Presidio, had burned down and the wife and two daughters of a certain Captain John Pershing had been killed. Only his son, Warren, was saved. Since that tragic experience I have watched General Pershing with a good deal of interest. He has never married again. He does his work and does it well—in peace or war. There is a calm dignity about him. He seems to be one of the untouchables of life; a rare person; one who seems to say: "I have suffered enough so that after that experience nothing matters any more. Nothing can touch me again!"

We come to this state not only through suffering but through experience, resolution, and fortitude. I remember that Bishop Fred Fisher once said to me: "My resolution this New Year is that never again will I allow any human being to hurt me and never again will I allow myself to hurt anybody. Never again can life touch me if I do these two things. I am immune to all harm from now on." When a man like that has made his peace with himself, his fellow-men and with God, life can no longer harm him. He has reached an ultimate of peace, poise, and power.

$\ast \quad \ast \quad \ast$

"THE ROAD OF THE LOVING HEART"

MRS. MARIE POWELL, one of the America's finest teachers of worship, tells me this story.

In the year 1801 there came riding over the mountain passes of Pennsylvania down into the valleys of Ohio a queer little man, wearing a tin pan for a hat and carrying on his horse great bulging bags which contained gifts for the future generations of his countrymen. For Jonathan Chapman on his Massachusetts hillsides had heard the tales of the pioneers who were constantly pushing westward across the mountains and prairies, but who found no fruit trees in these new lands.

Who can tell how that dream of planting a wilderness with blossoming fruit trees took shape in the mind of "Johnny Appleseed," as he was soon nicknamed? Certain it is that his dream guided him first to New York State and Pennsylvania, where there were apple orchards and cider mills. There he begged of the mill owners the waste pulp with the apple seeds left from the cider-making. Then he was gone, following the rivers and trails through the woods, making friends of the Indians, stopping at some pioneer home and sitting on the doorstep to eat his evening meal of bread and milk, looking off across the wilderness with his dream still in his eyes; and at every home where he stopped, reading the Bible and conducting family prayers.

At first he planted in the wake of the pioneers, but, as expressed in the poem by Shaemas O'Sheel,

He whom a dream hath possessed treads the impalpable marches,
From the dust of the day's long road he leaps to a laughing star.

And Johnny Appleseed was soon making his way into the wilderness *ahead* of the pioneers. For his dream encompassed the children of the future, walking under his apple trees and eating of the fruit thereof. Summer and winter he traveled on, always barefoot, always carrying his precious burden of seeds.

Yet, in spite of pioneer hardships, he had tasted a kind of joy which comes only to those who do not travel but who make the road. And even in this generation a great poet, Vachel Lindsay, immortalized his service to the future in a long poem entitled "Johnny Appleseed."

And even though it has often been quoted, I am moved to remind you again of a beautiful verse by Will Allen Dromgoole, entitled "Building the Bridge."

An old man going a lone highway,
Came, at the evening, cold and gray,
To a chasm, vast, and deep, and wide,
Through which was flowing a sullen tide.
The old man crossed in the twilight dim;
The sullen stream had no fears for him;
But he turned when safe on the other side,
And built a bridge to span the tide.
"Old man," said a fellow pilgrim, near,
"You are wasting strength with building here;
Your journey will end with the ending day;
You never again must pass this way;
You have crossed the chasm, deep and wide,—
Why build you the bridge at the eventide?"

The builder lifted his old gray head:
"Good friend, in the path I have come," he said,
"There followeth after me today
A youth, whose feet must pass this way.
This chasm, that has been naught to me,
To that fair-haired youth may a pitfall be.
He, too, must cross in the twilight dim;
Good friend, I am building the bridge for *him*."

But even a more beautiful expression of this spirit I find in a story about Robert Louis Stevenson.

Robert Louis Stevenson spent the last days of his life in Samoa of the South Sea Islands. One of his good friends among the natives was Mataafa, who claimed the throne. The authorities of the island had imprisoned Mataafa and several tribal chiefs with him. However, in their dark hour Stevenson did not forget them, but cheered their captivity by frequent visits and presents. Later, when these political prisoners were freed, they wanted to show their gratitude in some way so they determined to build a road through the brush to his house. Such a project involved terrific labor and considerable sacrifice, because labor is little loved by Samoans, and is despised as unworthy by a chief. But they set to work and completed a fine wide road which they presented to Stevenson. The name they gave the road would have

69

been a great tribute to any man. They called it "The Road of the Loving Heart."

*   *   *

"CASTLES IN SPAIN"

Dr. Harris Elliott Kirk, minister of the Franklin Street Presbyterian Church in Baltimore, once told me the story of a laundress who came to see him one day, thirty-five years ago when he first began to serve the church. She walked a long distance to tell him that she was glad he had come.

Many times after that he went to her little house and saw her bending over the tubs where the clothes were being made as white as winter snow or popcorn balls.

Her own hands were worn smooth and hard by the "suds" he recalls. "They showed the years of service that she had performed. Her work was hard and strenuous."

Every Sunday he knew that he would find her face smiling happily in the audience. One morning he came with a sermon on "Castles in Spain." He meant to lead the audience to that lovely land of visions and dreams where all our wishes find fulfillment, where the rainbow never vanishes behind the hill, and the towers stand forever. Just before time for the sermon he thought of the old laundress.

"She won't know what I'm talking about," he said. "I mustn't fail her! She comes every Sunday morning for spiritual comfort, and I can't fail her."

It was too late to prepare a new sermon. He took the one he had and told it in the simplest, yet most dignified phraseology that he knew. He made the castles rise on the glorious hills, and as he talked the room grew very still, and in the pews he could see a shining face—the face of the laundress who had come so long a distance.

When the sermon and service ended she sought him: "I want

70

to thank you for that sermon," she said. "Those Castles in Spain helped me to forget those tubs."

That great minister was a wise man, for he had learned that all of us have to have our Castles in Spain; some dream, some hope, some looked-forward-to event which helps us to forget the market place, the counting room, the hard tasks of every day.

A waiter in the hotel in New York City where I was staying was limping around one day and I asked him what was the matter. Then he told me of how he had fallen on the ice and sprained both ankles, which had kept him from work for a month. I said, "That is too bad." He replied: "It is worse than that, for I sent my wife down to Georgia the day before it happened. Our oldest daughter is expecting a baby. She always has to have mother there when that happens. I was to take my vacation and spend a month down there. I haven't seen my daughter for three years. Now I shall have to give that up, for I have already been away from work for a month and I can't afford to stay away another month to make that trip. I have been looking forward to that trip for three years."

He wiped his eyes with the back of his hand as he hobbled away, and so did I. When he came back again he said a strange thing to me: "But at least I have had the pleasure of looking forward to that trip for three years and nobody can take that away from me. And, what is more, I shall begin immediately to plan another trip to see my daughter and the new baby in a year or two. Looking forward to something, no matter how far away it may be, always helps me bear the burdens of the day."

As that waiter walked away from me, inwardly I said after him, "Good-by, Socrates, Plato; you're a wise philosopher." For that man had learned to keep his Castles in Spain always before him, no matter what his hard, greasy daily tasks were; and no matter what disappointments came to him temporarily. I respected that waiter and I respect all brave souls who, in the midst of lowly, grinding, terrifying daily tasks, still keep shining before their vagrant footsteps the kindly light of hope—their Castles in Spain.

WHEN DARKNESS DEEPENS

In a debunking mood the other day, I asked my friend Earl Marlatt, a hymn writer, if he had honestly ever known a hymn to have any practical value.

"Well," he said, wanting to be strictly statistical, "I know one that saved four lives."

"Oh, yeah?" I said. "How come?"

I shall let him answer for you, as he did for me.

It was the summer of 1916, he said. I was in Rushville, Indiana, where the Royal Welsh Male Chorus was giving a concert for the local Chautauqua Association. They concluded their program with a hymn, "Abide with Me," sung by a quartet to a low, intermittently surging accompaniment by the chorus. Such a finale seemed strange at a Wednesday evening musicale, which featured rollicking choruses rather than sacred music. I was puzzled and interested. Looking up the director, I asked him why he had closed the program with a hymn.

"We always end it that way," he said. "It's almost a rite with us."

With a newspaperman's persistence, I carried on until I got the story.

"We were on the 'Lusitania'," he said, "when it was torpedoed in the Irish Sea. We saw a crosswise ripple on the waves and heard a muffled explosion below. A few minutes later the boat began to list. We understood and decided to act at once. Having been reared on the Welsh coast, we were excellent swimmers. So we put on our life belts and planned to dive from the deck rail before the liner sank. We mapped out our course in detail. We would swim under water as far as possible and meet out of range of the suction we knew would follow the sinking of the ship.

"We were just in time. As we came up within a few yards of each other and looked back, we saw the 'Lusitania' stand upright for a second and then drop terribly, shriekingly, into the sea. We swam furiously on and on together. A damaged life raft floated out to us. It was useless except as something to cling to

72

when we were tired of floating or treading water. All the rescue boats missed us. The sun set over the spot where the 'Lusitania' had been. It was suddenly dark and very cold.

"Our fingers, and eventually our bodies, grew numb. We clung to the life raft with increasing difficulty. Without a light or a sound on the sea we gave up hope of rescue and grudgingly admitted as much to each other. Being Christians, we wanted a sacrament at a time like that. None of us felt good enough to pray. But we had always sung—sometimes sacred songs. We agreed to sing one stanza of a hymn and then slip quietly, together, into the sea. We chose

> "'Abide with me: fast falls the eventide;
> The darkness deepens; Lord, with me abide!
> When other helpers fail and comforts flee,
> Help of the helpless, O abide with me.'

"As we finished the stanza a claxon sounded. Our voices, carrying out over the sea, had reached a torpedo-boat destroyer cruising over the spot where the 'Lusitania' had sunk. We took heart and sang the remaining stanzas. Guided by the music of the hymn, the crew of the destroyer steered directly to us, picked us up, and carried us safely to shore.

"After that we feel that the least we can do is to use that hymn as a benediction for our concerts. I must be going now. Cheerio!"

And he had gone, leaving me the memory of a hymn which saved four lives with its deathless benediction.

$$* \quad * \quad *$$

A SPARK IN THE DARK

SOMEWHERE I read that striking phrase years ago. It was spoken of a lighthouse keeper who every night kept sending out his

73

spark in the dark, and never knew whether it was seen or not; never heard from the ships which were guided safely past treacherous rocks, shoals, and ledges. They simply accepted this ever-faithful flashing lighthouse, set their courses correctly and went on safely to their destined harbors. And that is the way with life, for few of us ever sit down to write a letter to those spiritual lighthouse tenders whose sparks in the dark have been our guiding beams. We just accept them as a part of the privileges of life.

To illustrate what I mean, not long ago Dr. Miller, a district superintendent in New Hampshire, handed me a beautiful poem called "Twilight" and said to me: "That poem has done me more good than any poem I have ever found and I want to pass it on to you." And in turn I want to pass it on to my friends in this book. Here it is:

> When I was young the twilight seemed too long.
> How often on the western window seat
> I leaned my book against the misty pane
> And spelled the last enchanting lines again,
> The while my mother hummed an ancient song
> Or sighed a little and said, "The hour is sweet."
> When I, rebellious, clamored for the light.
>
> But now I love the soft approach of night,
> And now with folded hands I sit and dream
> While all too fleet the hours of twilight seem;
> And thus I know that I am growing old.
>
> O granaries of Age! O manifold
> And royal harvest of the common years!
> There are in all thy treasure house no ways
> But lead by soft descent and gradual slope
> To memories more exquisite than hope.
> Thine is the Iris born of olden tears,
> And thrice more happy are the golden days
> That live divinely in the lingering rays.
> So autumn roses bear a lovelier flower,
> So, in the emerald after-sunset hour,

The orchard wall and trembling aspen trees
Appear an infinite Hesperides.
Aye, as at dark we sit with folded hands,
Who knows, who cares in what enchanted lands
We wander while the undying memories throng?

When Dr. Miller told me how much good that poem had done him I said to him: "Well, did you ever write a letter to the author and tell her that you had caught her spark in the dark and that it had done you so much good?"

He had an apologetic look on his face as he replied: "Why, I never thought of that. In fact, I don't know who wrote it!"

Several months ago I sent out a broadcast on the responsibilities that children have to their parents. I spoke of how parents sacrifice for children for twenty years: bringing them into the world; the mother travails and suffers; through their infancy both parents sit up at nights with them in their illnesses; through young manhood and womanhood they give up everything that their children may have good clothes, food, and education. When college comes these same parents go without new clothes —even food—that their children may be well equipped for life. Then comes that period of old age when parents are frequently dependent upon their children; and often children are thoughtless of them at this period, forgetting all that their parents have done for them through the years. I sent out that thought and forgot all about it. Then one day this letter came to me:

DEAR DR. STIDGER:

I am a grateful mother today. Two weeks ago I scolded my sixteen-year-old daughter for something she had done and she was angry. She went upstairs, packed her bag, climbed out a window, down the porch, and ran away. She was gone nearly two weeks and we were frantic. I telephoned the police and they kept up a secret search for her all of this time while I nearly went crazy with grief. Then one day Mary walked in, weeping, threw down her bag, literally jumped into my arms, and, between sobs, said: "Mother, you were right and I was all wrong. I ran away and went to a girl friend's home. Yesterday we were listening to the radio, to a program called 'Getting the Most Out of Life.' The man who was talking—Dr. Stidger was his name, I think—talked

75

about the responsibility that we young people have to our parents. I started to cry, looked at Jane, and she said: 'Mary, that man is right. You'd better go home to your mother.' And I packed up, and here I am, Mother; and I'm sorry, and from now on I want to do my part if you'll forgive me!" And, Dr. Stidger, you can imagine what a happy mother I am today, for your talk brought my daughter back to me. I can never tell you how grateful I am to you for that.

Yes, now and then people do catch our spark in the dark; and we hear about it and we all go about all day long with great hymns singing in our hearts.

✳   ✳   ✳

LUCK OR LOVE?

ALL MARGRET's friends called her lucky. It was just plain luck, they contended, that she managed to get such a fine husband, that she had raised two such splendid boys as Roger and Ted, that everything she had anything to do with always turned out successfully. Yes, plain, unadulterated luck it must be, as Margret never seemed to make much effort herself—she was always so calm, poised, self-possessed, and constantly cheerful all the time. Things just came to Margret without the slightest struggle on her part whatsoever—that's what they said, but Margret knew better.

Yes, her husband was successful, but she knew well enough—and he did, too—that it was her faith and belief in him that had fortified him in many a dark hour. Her sons knew well enough, too, that the devoted years of her care—her gentle, firm, and intelligent guidance—had molded them into desirable citizens. And what one of her friends would have gone to the trouble of visiting a lonely old lady who lived in a shabby house near the summer cottage Margret's family occupied? Margret made it a point to develop a friendship with the woman. She brought her many hours of happy companionship. But when the old lady died and in her will left Margret trunks full of priceless antiques that no one knew she possessed, everybody called that sheer *luck*.

Without showy effort she managed to accomplish the impossible. Such was the case with the old family farmhouse which belonged to her husband's family. It had been abandoned for years, and what protest followed when she mentioned to her family and friends that she was going to rehabilitate it! Her husband chuckled and said that the old place was good only for kindling wood. The banker in the little New Hampshire town warned that the old house stood in one of the worst neighborhoods in the community and that the rowdies would immediately destroy it. But Margret just grinned and went straight ahead with her plans. A rattling, discreditable tenement stood next to the house, but behind it were sweeping meadows and rolling hills.

The very first move Margret made was to round up all the children in the immediate neighborhood—the rougher the better —and give them each a bonus for all the rubbish and stones they would help her clear from the yard of the house. She made it a game and they willingly entered into it for the money, and finally for the sheer sport of it, as they saw the gradual improvement. She worked along with them and they soon began to consider her one of their own.

As her work progressed inside the house, she discovered valuable assets of the old place. The walls had been papered over priceless paneling that when brought to life again with oiled treatment restored a beautiful dignity to the interior. For this same paneling she was offered later an intriguing sum by a museum, but she refused that offer. The community watched with keen interest and not a little awe. If anyone had attempted so much as to throw a stone into her yard he would have been mobbed by the children, who had grown to adore her. The dilapidated old house began to assume the aspect of a mansion. In three years it was opened to the public as an historic relic. Margret convinced the town that the shabby tenement should be torn down and small, respectable, modest-priced homes put up in its place. Representatives from historical and antique societies visited the old house, approved, and lauded.

All this Margret had managed to accomplish with a modest expenditure and what seemed an easy effort. When her work was finally accomplished she gracefully stepped out of the picture. The society for the preservation of antiques in the state offered to buy the place, but one of Margret's sons said an emphatic "No." At the cost of $80,000 he and his wealthy wife moved the house and all its furnishings down to a site in Massachusetts where they now are using it as their home. Still Margret's friends say, "Aren't you just the luckiest person in the world to be able to hand down such a gorgeous place to your grandchildren." But Margret must think behind that smile that "the twilight of the wise is brighter than the noonday of the blind."

$$* \quad * \quad *$$

SIGNALING GOD

SOME years ago Alexander Irvine, the famous English writer, was a marine in the British navy. He describes his commander as a seaman of the old school, who loved to order a sail drill in rough weather. Imagine the scene: rough water, off the north coast of Cyprus.

"Clear the deck for action!" comes the command. Then follow the orders.

"Stand by! Bear out on the yardarm!"

Something happened to the captain of the foretop, out on the yardarm. He lost his nerve or his grip, and fell to the deck with a sickening thud—dead. In spite of this the same drill was ordered the next day. The new captain bungled and fell from the yardarm to a similar fate. Both were buried in old Famagusta that afternoon. The following day the drill was ordered again. The new captain, Billy Hicks, was a jovial chap who was one of the best seamen in the navy; but often when he went ashore he forgot the name of his ship and the number of his mess. Drink was his master. He had been sober for a long time and was once more eligible for promotion. He was made captain of the foretop, but the superstition of the sea gripped the marines—two men out, the third had to go! But the new captain didn't go. He performed his stuff and came down with laughter. He was the most popular man on the ship. "All the marines wanted to hug him as he descended the rigging with the agility of a cat."

There is a remarkable sequel to this story. Some days later an officer from another ship came on board and asked if there was a man named Hicks in the crew—Billy Hicks. Being answered in the affirmative he said to the commander: "We were thirty miles out at sea the other night, when I saw a light flashing on the dark clouds. I told our signal man to take down the code. This is what he gave me. "God, this is Billy Hicks. I ain't afraid of no bloomin' man nor devil. I ain't afraid of no Davy Jones's bleedin' locker, neither. I don't ask for no favors, but just one. This is it. When I strike the foretops tomorrow let me do it with the guts of a man what is clean; and, God, dear God, from this 'ere day give me the feelin' I used to have long ago when I knelt at my mother's knee and said, "Our Father." Good night, dear God.' "

Billy Hicks's idea of God may have been primitive, or anthropomorphic, or what you will, but by flashing a light on the dark clouds he was talking to God. This prayer steadied him. It was the cause of his courage.

Prayer is a very real thing, and to Billy Hicks it was real—real enough to give him the faith and courage that he could come down from that mast alive; and he did. I was greatly interested recently in noting that *Liberty*, a weekly secular magazine, was running a series of short stories on "Answered Prayer"; and they have been thrilling to me. When a secular magazine of its wide circulation goes into this field isn't it about time that we Christians and churchmen begin to get back our old faith in prayer? I also notice that another secular magazine, *True Story*, is running a series of articles entitled "God-Guided Lives"—a recog-

nition on the part of two widely circulated magazines that this
business of religion has something to it.

Yes, prayer is a very real force from childhood to the grave:

> Through Him the first fond prayers are said
> Our lips of childhood frame;
> The last low whispers of our dead
> Are burdened with his name.

✳   ✳   ✳

HIGH ENOUGH ABOVE THINGS
TO SEE THEM

In a recent book called "Toward Romance," written by Rollo
Brown, there was a young man. That young man's name was
Giles. He wanted to get out of his limited environment, for he
was a coal miner's son.

One day he was talking the matter over with an old doctor
and said, "Maybe I haven't the stuff in me to make it even if I
did start to college."

That old family doctor told Giles about the boy's own grandfather, who had also been a coal miner. "Your grandfather had
something unusual in him, and so have you, Giles. He always
got high enough above things to see them. Set him down in the
capitol at Columbus as governor and he would have hold of
things in a week as if he had been born to it. As I say, boy, he
got high enough above things to see them—and so can you if
you try."

It's a good thing to climb hills and mountain peaks even if
for no other reason than to get high enough above all physical
things to see them in the right perspective. Now and then I
take an airplane when I am in a hurry to get some place. I
always get a new perspective out of such a trip. I remember
once going up with a friend during the World War to patrol
the Bay of Biscay for submarines. For the first time that day

I really saw the beauty and contour of that glorious Bay of Biscay. I saw the little French farms laid out like a checkerboard; the green fields, streams, and hills. We flew over the little town in which I had been stationed for months—St. Nazaire. For the first time I saw our own American camps for soldiers; our machine shops, the bay, and the harbor. It was impressive and beautiful. I had never, up to that time, known what a tremendous scope our American troops had in their work. I have that experience every time I take an airplane in the United States. One never gets a true perspective of our American continent until he flies over it. Then he comes to know its wide reaches, its glorious mountains, its beautiful streams—its majesty and its wonder.

I had the same experience the first time I went to the top of the Empire State Building in New York City. I had been visiting New York City for many years but I never knew what it really looked like. I had been traveling up and down Fifth Avenue and Broadway, bewildered and uncertain as to which direction they ran, and why they crossed each other. East River and Manhattan were just names to me. But one day when I stood on top of that gigantic building, I saw New York City for the first time and the lay of its streets, the position of its rivers, and its contours. It was an exhilarating and satisfying experience. I had gotten high enough above things to see them.

A great book, a great thought, a great friend, a great experience, a great picture, a great drama, a sunset, a sunrise, a starlit night, a storm coming up over the sea, a sea voyage, a great poem —these all help me to rise above life so that I see it more clearly than I did before.

And talking about how a book may take you to the heights of some Sinai so that you may get high enough above things to see them, Rollo Brown has just published a strange new book entitled *I Travel by Train,* which really ought to be called "I Travel by Plane," for it is a bird's-eye—not a worm's eye—view of this nation; not only geographically, but its people—what they are thinking, feeling, saying; its social and political trends; its hopes and aspirations; its eccentricities; its high resolves.

81

Rollo Brown has become a sort of modern Moses for this nation in this glorious book, for he has climbed several modern Sinais to see what he could see.

Once when we lived in San Jose, California, a certain young child I knew intimately had been dressed up in a clean white dress for Sunday school. This accomplished, her pious mother went about other duties. The young child disappeared, and in a few minutes her mother heard her yelling frantically in front of the house. She ran out and found that the child had climbed the telephone pole in front of the house, a pole which had the old-fashioned spikes on it. She had got up so high that she couldn't get down. Her mother called a man, who climbed up and helped her down. The white dress was black, her face covered with dirt and tear streaks. Her mother scolded her and said, "Why on earth did you climb that pole on Sunday morning after I had dressed you for Sunday school?"

Betty blubbered and replied, "I just climbed up to see what I could see, Mother—that's all." And thank goodness her mother had enough imagination and sense of humor to smile, and inwardly to approve that adventuring spirit of a five-year-old offspring. For that young lady had the same inherent urge that Rollo Brown and his fiction character had; the same spirit that Moses had when he climbed Mt. Sinai of old, an experience I have tried to put into this verse:

> Each soul must seek some Sinai,
>   As Moses sought of old,
> And find immortal music writ
>   On slabs of stone in gold.
>
> Each soul must seek some Sinai,
>   Some far flung mountain peak,
> Where he may hear the thunders roll
>   And timeless voices speak.
>
> Each soul must seek some Sinai,
>   Some secret place, apart,
> Where he may be alone with God
>   And new-born Kingdoms chart.

Each soul must seek some Sinai,
   Some sanctity within
Where everlasting whispers
   Penetrate the deadening din.

Each soul must seek some Sinai,
   Where God's own voice is heard,
That he may see the mystic sign
   And hear the secret word.

✶   ✶   ✶

SINGING IN THE STORM

THE Norwegian freighter "Smaragd" was wrecked in the Atlantic Ocean some five hundred miles southeast of New York on the night of December 23, 1938. Two women and eighteen men, the entire ship's crew, were rescued during a raging Atlantic gale roaring sixty-five miles an hour, piling up waves forty feet high.

The rescue was made by the crew of the American freighter "Schodack." Details of the daring rescue were told by J. A. Quinlan, the "Schodack's" radio officer.

We were only five miles distance from the doomed ship when we sighted distress flares early in the evening. I began flashing my Morse light when we saw the flares, but I could not make out the "Smaragd's" distress signals. Finally someone on the distressed ship began using a flashlight and by studying it I made out what he was saying: "We are leaking badly. Our engines are broken down. We need help." We asked if they could hold out till morning, for a rescue in such a sea in the darkness was too hazardous to attempt except as a last desperate measure. They answered: "We will try. Please stand by close." We closed in on the doomed ship and circled about her all through the night. At daybreak the eighteen men and two women each made dangerous jumps from the doomed vessel into lifeboats tossing and wallowing in the treacherous sea. It was a precarious job getting each person aboard the rescue ship, for each had to be caught singly and lifted over the rail.

This heroic rescue is a deed to warm the blood. From the whole crew of thirty-six men on the "Schodack," the skipper had only to pick the ablest seamen, for they all volunteered to man the lifeboats. It is such a story as the sea has brewed these last three thousand years since certain Phoenicians grew venturesome in boats. Man still has great moments, and when it comes to manning a lifeboat there are still plenty of volunteers. And the sea, like Walt Whitman, goes on saying: "I too am not a bit tamed. I sound my barbaric yawp over the roofs of the world."

But it was not a sailor in either ship's crew, but the eighteen-year-old daughter of Captain Bernard Larsen of the "Smaragd" who was the top-ranking hero of this rescue. From the doomed ship's rescued crew it was learned that, as the water rose during the night, they were driven from one deck to another until they huddled finally in the captain's cabin on the ship's bridge. All through the night of terror Svanhile Larsen, the captain's daughter, sang Norwegian songs to keep up the crew's courage. She kept singing through the storm as the ship slowly settled deeper and deeper in the sea. While the crew of the rescue ship pumped three hundred and fifty barrels of fuel oil into the sea to film over the wave crests and quiet the restless sea this girl, still in her teens, was singing to quiet the restless, fear-ridden men.

A visitor on a Wyoming ranch asked a cowboy on night watch over the cattle why he sang so much. "Well," the cowboy told him, "my songs ain't grand opera exactly but they quiet the steers when they get restless. They tell them I'm still on the range with them and keep them from stampedin' maybe when it thunders, or a gunshot bangs somewhere." Then he hesitated before he added: "You know, stranger, you'll think it's funny, but sometimes the stars are like those songs to me—you know what I mean, as if a Greater Cowboy somewhere, herdin' people instead of cattle, was singin' through the dark so that people won't be so restless and afraid."

* * *

84

A STONE IN THE ROAD

"'Passing the buck' is an American expression which we all understand and frequently use," says Dr. C. M. McConnell of Boston University. When a hard job has to be done we like to leave it for someone else to do. This is best described by the other well-known American phrase, "Let George do it." George in this case means anyone besides oneself.

But this is not a new custom even though the two expressions may be distinctly modern and American. There is an old legend about a king and his method of breaking his subjects of the habit of letting someone else do the things which should be done. Everything was left by the people for someone else to do, and at last the king decided to teach them a lesson.

One of the roads leading to a town passed along a hillside. To a narrow spot in this road the king went late one night and scooped a hollow in the middle of the cart tracks. Then, from the folds of his cloak, he took a small bundle and placed it in the hole in the road. From the roadside he loosened a large stone and rolled it so that it completely covered the hole he had dug.

Next morning a farmer driving his cart along the road came to the stone. "Ah," he murmured, "the laziness of these people is terrible. Here is a big stone right in the middle of the road. Certainly someone has noticed it before this and everyone coming along has been too lazy to remove the stone." So saying, he pulled his horses to one side of the stone till his cart crowded the side of the hill and almost upset his load. But he passed on and left the stone where it was.

A company of soldiers marched down the road and their leader, seeing the stone, halted them. He ordered them to break ranks and form in marching order on the other side of the stone. Then he made a little speech to his soldiers about people's carelessness. But they left the stone where they found it and marched on.

Later some peddlers, with pack horses heavily laden, passed that way. "This is a fine country," said one. Another, grumbling at the delay, said, "I wonder how long that big stone has been lying there?" But no one in the company suggested that they remove the stone, so they divided and passed to the right and left of it.

This went on day after day and no one moved the stone, though everyone blamed his neighbor for letting it lie on the road. The king sent word to people near by who used this road to meet him at the stone. "I put this stone here; and for three weeks everyone who has passed by has blamed his neighbor for not moving it."

Then he lifted the stone and showed them the hollow place beneath, in which lay a small bag labeled, "For him who lifts the stone." He untied the string and a stream of golden coins poured out.

We who "pass the buck" lose the benefits which always come to the person who finally takes the responsibility. Maybe if George does it he gets the reward. "For him who lifts the stone" there is surely something worth while to be gained.

I have been told on the best of authority that a certain king of these modern times a few years ago made a test of his own in the spirit of that ancient king. When Henry Ford took over the Lincoln automobile plant in Detroit he felt that it was being run inefficiently by those in charge. There were several hundred girls in one department on the top floor. So Mr. Ford had a large tree cut down and carried to the hallway of the top floor, to see how long it would remain there before somebody with responsibility would see that tree and do something about it. That huge three remained in that hallway for several weeks. Hundreds of people, including several foremen and stenographers, had to walk around it to get to their offices, but nobody attempted to remove it. They all assumed that it was somebody else's business. What was everybody's business was apparently nobody's business, and the big clumsy tree remained where it was in the road of every person who passed through that hallway. And yet not a single one of them took the responsibility of reporting it. They all, in our good old American slang, "passed the buck" and said to themselves, "Oh, well, it looks

86

crazy, but who am I to report it? It isn't *my* business. Let George do it!"

After a few weeks of this Mr. Ford walked in one day, discharged the lot of them, and put his son Edsel in charge of the whole Lincoln plant. It was just an eccentric manufacturer's way of testing them out, to find out if anybody in that plant was actually on the job. And it worked, so they tell me.

*   *   *

"ALL GLORIOUS WITHIN"

It is surprising to hear that the largest industry in the world is the business of beautifying women! As far as I am concerned I'm all for that business, because there is something sacred in the everlasting passion women have for making themselves more beautiful. I have no sympathy with these reformers who find nothing more important to do than harangue women for using rouge, powder, clothes, and what have you, to make themselves more beautiful.

I was greatly amused when Mrs. Howard LeSourd, a friend of mine, recently told me of an experience she had had in visiting a Woman's World Fair. She said of that experience:

I visited a great hall in which there were one thousand booths displaying articles for the beautification of women. There were hats for all occasions; dresses for $1.98 to $3,000; lingerie, shoes, jewelry, and accessories.

They demonstrated many types of perfect coiffure for varying personalities; permanent-wave machines of all kinds; marcelling irons with a half-dozen different gadgets for as many different curls; the latest methods in bobbing hair; clever designs for dressing long hair, and exquisite transformations for those who have no hair. Last, but not least, they showed how to dye one's hair to match one's gown.

In the field of cosmetics they demonstrated facials, mud packs, devices for lifting wrinkles and taking freckles off. I presume they had devices for putting them on.

Further on there were books, phonograph records, and all kinds of mechanical and electrical devices for reducing, and other means for making thin people fat.

All this has been done by the business for the outward beautification of women; but an ancient beauty specialist, who was also called a psalmist, says: "The king's daughter is all glorious within."

Then this friend goes on to say:

When I was a little girl we lived next door to a child just a little younger than I. Her name was Marion. Her mother was decidedly clothes conscious and passed on this same attitude to the young ten-year-old. When Marion came to Sunday School she made life quite miserable for us, for she would lift up the hems of our dresses to see whether our little petticoats were plain, made of embroidery or fine lace. No mother was clever enough to disguise her Mary or Janet's last year's hat with a new feather because Marion would immediately discern that it was made over.

Years passed, and Marion came to visit me. I could not help admiring this perfectly groomed figure, the last word in style, her hair exquisitely marcelled and her nails manicured. But her face was a shock to me. Even the clever use of cosmetics could not cover up the selfish lines around her mouth and the rather hard look about her eyes.

Thomas Bailey Aldrich is revealing some such experience in his day when he tells of a woman he met at the opera covered with diamonds, rouge, and finery. She was a woman in whom he recognized a girl he had known long before. Something had happened to her soul, though, in the intervening years, and as he gazed on her face he says he

Read the history of her life
As it were an open book;
And saw her soul as a slimy thing
In the bottom of a brook.

88

The famous Marie Stopes adds to our theme today: "At sixteen I was vain because someone praised me. My father said: 'You can take no credit for beauty at sixteen. If you are beautiful at sixty, it will be your own soul's doing. Then you may be proud of it and be loved for it.'"

Buttressing that story is one my friend Frank Kirkpatrick tells of a tribute which Edmund Burke paid to his wife when he said: "She is handsome, but it is beauty *not* rising chiefly from features, complexion, or shape. It is not by these she touches the heart. It is all that sweetness of temper, benevolence, innocence, and sensibility which a face can express, that forms real beauty. Surface beauty is little more than the equivalent of cosmetics. Real beauty is spiritual. It is the only kind which is lasting. It is attainable through soul-culture."

Then he gives a final illustration of this principle:

A Japanese woman asked if the mission teacher took only pretty girls to be educated.

"No," replied the missionary, "we take all the girls who come to us."

"But," said the mother, "all your girls seem to be pretty."

"We teach them soul-culture," replied the teacher.

"I do not wish my daughter to become a Christian," said the woman, "but I shall send her to your school to get that look on her face."

That's the important thing to remember: "The king's daughter is all glorious *within*."

* * *

"TRAVELER, HAST THOU EVER SEEN?"

ONE dark midnight in France on the Toul line, when I was driving a truckload of supplies to the front lines, we got lost. I climbed down from my truck at a French crossroad, and walked over to a little French shrine. I knew that there would be directions carved on a little stone.

When I got to the shrine I turned my flashlight on the markings and got my directions. Then I flashed that light above the stone marker to have a look at the shrine itself. It was a beautifully carved figure of Christ on a cross, and above that figure was carved these significant words: "Traveler, hast thou ever seen so great a grief as mine?"

Those words stunned me. Then I looked away across the fields. I could hear the great shells rumbling in a continuous roar of hate and suffering. I could also see the dim flare of Very lights over No Man's Land. Within a few hundred yards of that crossroads was the first little American cemetery, in which we had buried from time to time our American dead, including the first American soldier killed in the World War.

As I stood there in the darkness I suddenly felt for the first time the terrible meaning of war. I realized all its foolish waste of human life, its useless suffering, sacrifice, and sorrow. I stood there and all the faces of all the mothers in the world flashed by me.

I saw again all the wounded boys I had seen in hospitals with their faces shot away, trembling with shell shock, husky with burned out throats.

Then I turned again and flashed my light above that wayside shrine and read again that cryptic sentence: "Traveler, hast thou ever seen so great a grief as mine?"

That night I knew for the first time all that war meant then and means now. Up to then for me it had been a glorious adventure of flag-waving, band-playing, bugle-blowing, high-sounding public addresses. But never again! From that sacred moment I knew what war meant. It meant hate, hurt, mud, rain, midnight darkness, wounded and dying boys in their teens, broken homes and hearts.

Tied up with that memory today is another. A few years ago I was called to Albany, New York, to address a crowd of young church people on Good Friday night. It rained, sleeted, and snowed all day. The time for the meeting drew near and there was only a handful of young people in the large church. As we sat there I could see that the chairman was a bit embarrassed at the small crowd. Then he turned to me apologetically and said: "I am sorry for bringing you clear from Boston to speak to so few of our young people. If it hadn't been such a bad night we would have had a big crowd out."

I turned to that chairman and in righteous anger said, "Do you realize what you are saying?"

He looked startled. Then I went on: "You are saying that if it hadn't sleeted and snowed a little this evening your valiant young soldiers of the church would have turned out in large numbers to celebrate the night that Jesus died on a cross!"

His face turned white as he said, "I never thought of that!"

Dr. George A. Gordon, the great Boston preacher, used to tell a humorous story illustrating this unwillingness to face the real test of friendship, of love, or of being a disciple. It was the story of a young man who had spent the evening with his fiancée, and on returning home thought he would write her a letter. The letter ran like this:

My dearest, I would climb the most rugged and precipitous mountain to see the light of your eyes. I would swim any body of water far wilder and wider than the Hellespont to sit at your side. I would go through tempests and torrential rains to kneel at your feet. Yours forever.

P.S. I will call on you again tomorrow, if it doesn't rain.

Of course, that boy didn't realize the terrible incongruity of that last sentence, nor did that young chairman of the meeting in Albany. But the incongruity is there just the same and it is an incongruity and a disloyalty which is shocking to a sensitive soul these days.

The unwillingness to make *any* sacrifice for a cause or a person injures us. There must be something soft and flabby in the soul of today, especially when we remember a Man who died on a cross with nails through his hands, spikes through his feet, a spear thrust through his side, bitter gall on his lips, and a crown of thorns on his brow.

91

Yes, we worship today, and we pay lip tribute, but that is as nothing unless we too are willing if need be to suffer, sacrifice, and die as He died.

$$* \quad * \quad *$$

"TUNE ME WITH MOUNTAINS AND STARS"

DR. EARL MARLATT, Dean of Boston University School of Theology, tells me this beautiful story of the writing of one of his many great hymns, the last stanza of which reads like this:

> Deepen my music, O Lord!
> Strike my heart like a lyre!
> Quicken its strings
> Till they throb in a chord
> With all things that aspire!
> Tune me with mountains and stars,
> Pulsing farther and higher.
> Deepen my music, O Lord!
> Deepen my music, O Lord!

When I asked my friend, Earl Marlatt, how he happened to write that stanza he said: "Honestly, Bill, I shouldn't have credit for that. My twin brother virtually wrote that when we were in the army together twenty years ago."

I said to him, "You mean, something like that came out of army service?"

"Well," he told me, "in a way, yes. You see, my twin brother and I went to war together. He was a practical, hard-headed newspaper man who turned into a good soldier immediately. He had every chance of becoming an officer and he did. I was a preacher and I wanted to be a poet. I couldn't keep my mind on such mundane things as bayonet drill and marching. I couldn't even keep in step or in line when we were marching to music.

"Finally I went to my twin brother and said: 'Ernie, it's no use. I just can't learn to be a soldier, much less an officer. Why, I can't even march straight.'

"Ernie was worried. He thought I was going to flunk out on the stiffest assignment we'd ever had. He did some tall thinking before he answered: 'Sure, you can learn to march. All you have to do is to pick out something high and far against the sky —a tree, or a steeple, or a star—then march right toward it. You'll go straight if you just look high enough.'

"And I did," Earl Marlatt added, "principally because Ernie had given me a rule for living as well as marching: 'You'll go straight if you just look high enough.' "

How right Ernie was. He was just a soldier and a newspaper man trying to get his twin brother out of a wartime jam, but he discovered a secret of living which doctors now are using in psychiatry and medicine.

Only the other day my friend, Lucille LeSourd, told me of a seamstress she knew who was having skull-splitting headaches without knowing why. At last she went to a doctor, who asked her, "How many hours a day do you sew?"

"All day," she told him. "I have to. My living depends on it."

"And what can you see out of your window?"

The question seemed irrelevant but the seamstress answered: "Oh, not much. Only some grass, and the trees and the road and the people that pass by."

"Nothing else?"

"No. Only the horizon and the line of hills."

"Good!" the doctor exclaimed. "At last we have it. Go back to your work, but one hour each day drop your sewing and look beyond the grass and trees and people to the hills—the hills. One hour each day—that is all."

He was a wise doctor. The headaches disappeared. There was healing in the far look. One does go straight if he just looks high enough, as another hymn writer and doctor of souls realized centuries ago when he said: "I will lift up mine eyes unto the hills, from whence cometh my help."

My friend, Grace Noll Crowell, knew what it all meant. She

93

knows what we are talking about today when we speak of tuning our souls to hills, mountains, stars, and far horizons, of keeping our eyes and dreams, as Christopher Morley once said in the title of one of his whimsical little books about a dog, *Where the Blue Begins*. Yes, Mrs. Crowell knew and sang it all in a poem called "Blue Distance":

> Blue distance always calls me like a song—
> Day and night
> Above the swirling veils of mist there lift
> Wings in flight,
> And out beyond where no seas lie are sails
> Gleaming white.
>
> The far horizons do strange things to me.
> Winds that blow
> Carry me, a spirit tipped with flame,
> To and fro,
> And though I stay at home I go the way
> Others go.

*   *   *

"SEEKING GOD, ALL UNAWARE"

RABINDRANATH TAGORE, the great Hindu poet, once visited the Henry Street Settlement in New York City.

Tagore was a tall, prophetic-looking old man with long white hair, a long white beard, brown skin, kindly, loving eyes. In addition, he always dressed in the long, flowing white robes of India. He stood out in any crowd, and children crowded around him.

One little girl edged up to Miss Lillian Wald and whispered, "Miss Wald, is that God?"

"No," whispered Miss Wald, trying to quiet her.

But the child was insistent. She had heard a lot about God,

94

and she didn't want to miss a chance of seeing him if that were he. So she whispered again, a little louder, "Miss Wald, is that God?"

Miss Wald, seeing that there was no turning her aside, bent over and whispered, "No, darling, he is just one of God's friends!"

That story reminded me of something that happened once in Boston in a public meeting when Phillips Brooks was present. He too was tall, kindly, and impressive, and a little boy suddenly ran a pin into his calf, as Brooks tells it, "to see if I was stuffed. When I looked down he said to me, 'Mister, be you Jack-the-Giant-Killer?' "

Ah, these inquiring and seeking children whom we so often push aside in their everlasting quest for something!

Once a Sunday-school teacher was telling her class about God. She tried to describe him as "kind, good, strong, thoughtful, loving; a being who could conquer the world and meet all obstacles with courage; who could take care of them in their distress; who was not afraid of the dark; who could gather them into his arms when they were afraid; who supplied them with all things they needed." Then she said to these children, "Does that description of God make you think of anybody you know?"

And one little lad put up his hand and replied, "That's my pop!"

Even so wise and sophisticated a writer as the late Don Marquis was always on the quest for God, and he once said to a group of friends as they sat around a table together: "I've been trying to catch up with God all my life, but I've never quite made it. Often I've come into a room and had the strong feeling that God was there until just one second before I arrived. But I'm going to keep trying. I'll catch up with him yet."

Don Marquis was no doubt trying to catch up with God when he wrote that beautiful play, a drama of Christ and the crucifixion which he called, *The Dark Hours*.

Now that he has passed on to that better world he has probably found God. Don Marquis was always looking beyond the things that are. Now he is where he looked. Don Marquis was always walking across the landscape of eternity in his dreams and writings. Now he is where he walked.

For those who seek earnestly sooner or later catch up with the heavenly Father, but those who rationalize over him get further and further away from him, like the young student who had been caught in the web of rationalization and said: "Some say there is a God and some say there isn't. The truth is probably half way between these two opinions."

Yes, the sincere seeker feels the universal quest, as did Gamaliel Bradford, our New England poet, who expressed it in this way:

> But my one unchanged obsession, whereso'er my feet have trod,
> Is a keen, enormous, haunting, never-sated thirst for God.

And Mary Carolyn Davies sings it in a poem, "Feet":

> Where the sun shines in the street
> There are very many feet
> Seeking God, all unaware
> That their hastening is a prayer.
> Perhaps these feet would deem it odd,
> (Who think they are on business bent)
> If someone went,
> And told them, "You are seeking God!"

And now just how *do* we find God? That is the universal question and quest. Curiously enough, I have a partial answer from Rabindranath Tagore himself, given to a friend of mine, Bishop Bromley Oxnam, who wrote me a few years ago in a letter:

While I was in India I had the honor to talk with that great poet and religious philosopher, Sir Rabindranath Tagore. I asked him what his idea of God was, and I shall never forget his answer. He said:

"When I was but a small boy, my father took me into the darkness of the jungle, just before the dawn was about to break, and he said to me: 'My son, the sweet smell of this earth is God. He is of it and in it, and it is his.'

"Then the first light of the dawn struck through the darkness of the

96

jungle and my father said to me: 'My son, God is the light of our lives and the light of the world.'

"The birds started their singing, and my father said to me: 'My son, God is music, the music of pure souls. May you so live that you strike no note of dissonance in the harmony and beauty that is God!'"

$$* \quad * \quad *$$

ARTISANS OF SERVICE

DR. BASIL MATHEWS, an Englishman and friend of mine, recently told me a story which curiously enough was typically American.

It seems that a certain boy lived thirty years ago on a little farm with his mother, father, and brother out in the Middle West. The older brother fell dangerously ill. The younger brother watched his father jump on his horse and gallop away across the prairie to the nearest doctor, twenty miles away.

At last the father came back with the doctor. These two walked into the little log house together, and the younger boy, desperately worried about his older brother, whom he almost worshiped, crept in and hid himself behind a big chair. Scarcely breathing, he looked at the lined faces of his father and mother as they gazed desperately down at their sick son.

The younger boy watched the doctor take out his stethoscope and noted every gesture and move as he took the brother's temperature and felt his pulse. The hiding boy saw the doctor open his black medicine case, take out some bottles, make up some medicine, and pour it down the sick boy's lips. Then there passed what seemed an eternity of waiting as he still huddled behind the big chair. In an hour the doctor straightened his his back, looked into the faces of the anxious parents and said, "He is a very sick boy, but in two weeks I hope we shall have him all right again."

From behind the big chair the small brother saw the lines on his parents' faces relax into smiles of hope and relief. They

97

looked happy again. Then that small boy said to himself—and the feeling that came over him was as if a great light had suddenly flashed into his young life—"When I grow up I am going to be able to do that. I am going to make boys and girls better when they are sick, and make their fathers and mothers happy."

That isn't all of that story. That younger brother stuck to his resolution against terrific odds. He was very poor. The way was long and hard, but in the end he won a distinguished degree in his university.

If you went to the city of Rochester, Minnesota, today and asked for Doctor Rosenow at the Mayo Clinic, you would find that small boy, now grown into a doctor recognized all over the world as an unrivaled authority on infantile paralysis.

In Cuba, not long ago, there was a terrifying epidemic of infantile paralysis. They wirelessed to Doctor Rosenow for help. He jumped into an airplane, flew from Rochester across the continent to Florida, thence to Cuba. As a result of that flight and his skill, thousands of Cuban boys and girls are happy—romping and laughing today. They might not even have been alive—or if they were alive, they might be crippled and twisted, hobbling around like old men on crutches. Indeed, on the decision and will power of a boy with no money or position in the world hung a considerable share in the conquest of one of youth's most deadly enemies today.

That remarkable story brings back to memory the days when Mrs. Stidger and I had the honor of entertaining Sinclair Lewis, the novelist, in our home in Kansas City. In those days we used to sit in front of the fireplace and talk of his books, particularly of *Arrowsmith,* and old Dr. Gottlieb, the research character in that masterpiece who, as Lewis used to tell us, "ached a little for research and had a divine curiosity."

Dr. Gottlieb was the idol of all the boys in the medical school, and young Arrowsmith wanted his sweetheart, Leora, to admire that old scientist as much as he did. One day on the campus old Dr. Gottlieb walked past them, bent and stooped as if moving with pain. Young Arrowsmith longed to run after him.

98

Leora said, "Is that the Professor Gottlieb you're always talking about?"

"Yes! And say!" young Dr. Arrowsmith eagerly replied to his sweetheart, "how does he strike you?"

"I don't—Sandy, he's the greatest man I've ever seen! I don't know how I know, but he is! He's a great man! I wish—I wish we were going to see him again. He's so—oh, he's like a sword— no, he's like a brain walking. Oh, Sandy, he looked so wretched. I wanted to cry!"

And as we sat before the open fireplace going over that immortal scene in that great masterpiece I said to Mr. Lewis, "That's the greatest character you ever painted, and that is the finest scene in any of your books."

"Maybe you're right. I fell pretty hard for Dr. Gottlieb, for he was a truly consecrated scientist."

"Yes, he was what I like to call an artisan of service," I replied.

And in presenting this story of these artisans of service I want to dedicate it to that noble band of country and small-town doctors, the Scotch McClures of our nation, who live so nobly, serving so faithfully, to help all their people get the most out of life.

＊   ＊   ＊

THE FINE ART OF ELIMINATION

A YOUNG wife I used to know in Detroit had baked her first pie. With eager anticipation she was waiting for her new husband to come home to have his first taste of her baking. She was not only eager but nervous, for her experience in baking pies was somewhat limited.

The evening meal progressed very smoothly, and then came the great dramatic moment with the serving of the pie. The young wife herself cut it and handed a generous piece to her husband. She could hardly wait for his comments. She also took a piece herself, and they both started to eat it.

99

Immediately she detected a strange taste to it. So did he. But neither of them said a word to each other, through sheer courtesy. That was a serious situation and demanded much diplomacy on the part of the husband. But all he could think of at that particular moment was to say nothing. He didn't want to hurt her feelings so he kept chewing away at his single piece of pie, trying to look nonchalant. But she felt that something ought to be said. The situation cried out for something besides silence. She felt that it was up to her to say something, so she casually remarked, "My dear, I don't know what I left out of that pie."

Then he replied, "My darling, it was nothing you *left out* that makes it taste like that."

Then they both had a good laugh, and ever since that eventful evening it has been a standing joke in that home.

Part of my time is occupied teaching young theological students how to write and preach sermons. Students are verbose, lengthy, and inclined to amplify and stuff a sermon rather than eliminate material and cut it down. They have not as yet learned that this is a flash age; that the short short story is now coming into its own; that the motion picture, newspapers, and advertising—everything has learned the fine art of elimination. People will no longer listen to long-winded discourses. They simply turn off the dials of their minds and their radios. So I tell the young preachers, "It isn't what you leave out of a sermon that spoils it, but what you put in."

Horace Greeley used to say, "I would write shorter editorials, but I haven't time." And that's very true. It takes more work and time to eliminate, but it pays rich rewards.

Life is so full of a number of things these days, as I recently heard Dr. Richard Cameron say, that we, in America, must learn the art of elimination. We are constantly besieged with so much material that we have more use than ever for our wastebaskets.

Indeed, he told a story of a missionary who had been in a foreign field for a quarter of a century before returning to America. Somebody asked that missionary what one thing he noticed which indicated the greatest change in American life since he

100

had left. That missionary replied, "You have and need so much larger wastebaskets."

Then Dr. Cameron told us of a day when he was a student in Boston, walking down Mt. Vernon Street one Sunday morning in spring. It was a glorious morning, sunny and bright. An old church at the foot of the hill was silhouetted against a clear blue sky and a patch of the Charles River shimmered in the Sunday morning sunlight. The green buds were tipping the trees.

When he came to Louisburg Square an artist was painting that street scene. It being Sunday morning the streets were clear of automobiles with the exception of one old battered car of a far-off vintage, probably owned by some student.

When Dr. Cameron came up to the artist he noticed an omission in the painting. Then he said to the artist, "I notice that you left out the old automobile, sir."

The artist turned with a smile and replied: "In that remark you have stumbled onto one of the greatest secrets, not only of art, but of life itself. You have to learn to leave out nonessentials, especially things which make life ugly, when you are painting. You have to learn the fine art of elimination."

So do all of us have to learn this art if we want to get the most out of life. We have to learn to discard the nonessentials of life and to cling to that which is kindly, good, helpful, and beautiful.

*   *   *

LEANING AGAINST THE WIND

BACK in 1912, when I was a student in Brown University at Providence, as I went up the hill to classes I used to stop and watch the workmen walking along the steel girders of a skyscraper. I always expected to see one of them fall, for they were seemingly careless and nonchalant. Every morning I would stop for a few minutes to watch these human ants busy about their labors high in the air above the city streets. Then one terrible morning I

101

LINCOLN BIBLE INSTITUTE

saw what I had feared would happen. A workman fell from one of those steel girders to his death in the street below.

A crowd quickly gathered around that battered and broken body. I stood on the outskirts and listened to talk about the accident. Finally a man who seemed to be in authority came down from the top of the building on a crude lift, hurried over to the body, looked down upon it, and said: "The fool was leaning against the wind! I told him to quit leaning against the wind. He was new at this game or he wouldn't have done it."

Later I got that foreman to one side and asked him what he meant by leaning against the wind. Then, seeing that I was an earnest young seeker after truth, he patiently went into some details about one of the occupational dangers of steel workers and said: "Well, you see, along the coast here in the morning hours there is often a strong wind blowing from the ocean, at fifty or sixty miles an hour, and a steel worker high on a building of this type gets to leaning against the wind. It is easier to work that way. You don't have to resist so much. But an experienced worker soon learns that he dare not depend upon that wind, for it may drop at any minute and then he topples to the ground. You can never depend upon the stability of the wind."

There was a parable for you. How many of us get to leaning against the wind in life—or against something which is just as fickle, unstable, and uncertain as the winds that blow.

Modern psychologists have discovered many new things about some of our human weaknesses. One of the things they have discovered is what they call a mother complex. That means that a child gets to depending too much on a mother. He carries that habit over into adult life, and is never happy away from that mother. A mother or a father fixation is one of the most damaging complexes that a child can carry through life, for it makes that child depend too much on that parent. He never stands on his own feet.

Just so it is with people who have come to lean on material things. Certain people who have grown up in wealth grow to depend upon money to get them everything they want or think they need. They get the feeling that if they have money that is

102

all that is necessary. In other words, they get to leaning on money. Then there comes a period like our early thirties, which we called "The Depression," and material possessions drop out from under us and we are done for. We here in America have learned well our lesson that we cannot depend entirely upon material possessions for happiness or even security.

Just as tragic are those who depend entirely upon physical energy and health. They too get to leaning against the wind. I remember that Mr. Ford once told me of a certain man who had worked in his organization—one of the big executives in that organization. Then suddenly he found himself without a job. Mr. Ford told me what the man's trouble was. He said: "Jim had taken to leaning on his youthful enthusiasm, energy, and vitality. He was able in the early days of the business, through sheer youthful enthusiasm, to talk his men into selling cars. But he forgot to inform himself on new plans, new techniques, and new methods in salesmanship. A new day had arrived, and he was still depending upon his enthusiasm, his physical energy, and his smile to sell cars. He failed to develop mentally, and the business left him behind. He was leaning on youthful vigor, and when that dropped out from under him he had nothing to fall back on and he was through! That often happens in industry."

We must learn in life to get something substantial to lean against if we want to do any leaning—the mental and spiritual things; things of character, integrity, and honor. These are the rocks of life.

✳   ✳   ✳

THE ADVANTAGE OF A HANDICAP

IT WAS proposed some years ago in the faculty of Harvard University that all applicants for scholarships should undergo a physical examination, in order that the trust fund at its disposal for indigent students should be given only to such applicants as might be expected to pay in fruitful work an adequate return upon the investment.

At first sight there seemed to be much in favor of this proposition, for it was reasonable to suppose that the possession of health and strength was essential to the maintenance of that measure of activity required in the work of the world.

In the course of the debate on this proposal it occurred to someone of the Harvard faculty to apply this test of bodily strength to the men debating the proposal. It was found that the majority of the disputants furnished in their own history evidence that a vigorous mind was not inconsistent with a frail body. The debate was closed by someone's calling attention to the fact that John Harvard, founder of the university, was himself a man of feeble constitution.

Anyone can make a long list of people who have labored continually under the handicap of ill health and have overcome the handicap.

Men unable to do enormous physical tasks turn to mental activity; hence philosophy, literature, and science are adorned by names of men whose physical powers have been scant. Immanuel Kant stands in the front rank of philosophers. During a long life of enormous labor he was never entirely free from pain. By sheer force of will he could withdraw his mind from his ailments; and when suffering from pain in his head he could concentrate his mind so perfectly on a chosen subject that the pain was treated as though it did not exist. He died in his eightieth year.

Alexander Pope has more quotations in Bartlett's *Familiar Quotations* than anyone except William Shakespeare. All the testimony goes to show that he was deformed and a helpless invalid. His body he once called "a bundle of distempers." Pope described his life as a long disease and added that he had the headache four days in the week and was sick the other three. And yet he so exerted his will and applied himself to his tasks that his writings delighted his age and remain as models of a finished style.

Deafness is one of the most common handicaps which humanity bears. Harriet Martineau was totally deaf. Besides all this,

"Never," she says, "was a poor mortal cursed with a more beggarly nervous system." She turned to story writing and wrote one a month for thirty-four months. The scene of each story, laid in different parts of the world, required a special knowledge of all the conditions of that region. In her autobiography she wrote, "Here am I, at the end of a busy life, confident that deafness is about the best thing that ever happened to me; best as the grandest impulse to self-mastery."

The wonderful cases of Laura Bridgman and Helen Keller are by far the most instructive instances of the mastery of fate of which we have any record. Cut off from the rich harvest of the seeing eye these women came to such mastery of their powers that it seems incredible to us who have witnessed their achievements. A few years ago the words of Helen Keller flashed through the air and a radio audience was thrilled by them. I never pass the Perkins Institute for the Blind along the Charles River in Watertown, Massachusetts, but I think of Miss Sullivan and her pupil Helen Keller. In her own words Miss Keller describes the great event in her life, the coming of her teacher, Miss Sullivan.

Have you ever been at sea in a dense fog, when it seemed as if a tangible white darkness shut you in, and the great ship, tense and anxious, groped her way toward the shore with plummet and sounding line, and you waited with beating heart for something to happen? I was like that ship before my education began, only I was without compass or sounding line, and had no way of knowing how near the harbor was. "Light: give me light," was the wordless cry of my soul, and the light of love shone on me in that very hour.

This was the beginning of that education which has made Helen Keller one of earth's great women and her name a household word.

John Milton, himself blind, wrote:

What though the field be lost?
All is not lost—the unconquerable will. . . .
A mind not to be changed by place or time.
The mind is its own place, and in itself
Can make a Heaven of Hell, a Hell of Heaven.

THE IMPRISONED SPLENDOR

I want to tell you one of the most stirring stories I ever heard. It came to me directly from Angela Morgan, the well-known American poet whom I interviewed not long ago, and whose philosophy of life is that every human being has what she calls an imprisoned splendor inside of her own soul. Telling of one of her own earliest experiences, she says:

I was working as a girl on a New York newspaper and my editor assigned me to interview the Rev. Dr. G. Campbell Morgan, who was coming to speak at the Fifth Avenue Presbyterian Church. I was afraid that he wouldn't trust me, so I sent him a note enclosing a poem I had written called "Kinship," which I had not been able to sell. In the note I said: "You could not be expected to know who I am, but my newspaper has assigned me to get an interview with you. I am sending you a copy of this poem so that you may know that I am a serious-minded person and can handle an interview with a clergyman in a sympathetic manner."

I went to church half an hour early but found it crowded with people; not a seat left, so I stood against the wall. After a brief preliminary Dr. Morgan was introduced, arose to speak, and said something like this: "Last week I had a sermon prepared for this morning. But I am not going to preach it, for yesterday a young lady of whom I never heard sent me a poem called 'Kinship.'" Then he raised a piece of white paper in his hand and my heart started to pound against my ribs. I thought I would faint as I stood there leaning against the wall almost close enough for him to touch me. Then he went on: "This poem has so impressed me that I cannot get away from it and I am going to read it to you and comment on it instead of preaching this morning."

I turned white and was trembling all over. A man in a nearby seat must have seen how white I was, for he gave me his seat and I slumped into it.

However, Dr. Morgan's reading and preaching on my poem didn't solve my problem of getting a hearing for it. In spite of the publicity I was not able to find a magazine market for the actual poem itself.

Months passed and one day another inspiration came to me. I would go to Mark Twain and see if he wouldn't help me. So one hot summer day I started for Stormfield, in Connecticut. I got off at a little way station three miles from Stormfield and walked down a dusty road. My shoes were full of dust, I was wet with sweat and my hair disheveled. But when I got in sight of Stormfield I stopped dead still in the middle of that dusty road, looked up into the blazing sun and prayed a little prayer: "Now you Power of the universe that is back of that sun. You can do anything, and I want you to help me get Mr. Clemens to read my poem."

I went up to that house full of confidence. I walked up the steps and rang the bell. Mark Twain came to the door, looked at me, smiled, and invited me to come in. I was never able to determine whether that smile was one of amusement at my looks after that three mile tramp in the heat and dust or what it was. He himself was immaculately dressed in a white summer suit. We went in and he read the poem over and then said, "We'll have lunch first, and then you can read it to me yourself."

My heart jumped a beat. But pretty soon I found myself sitting on the porch with Mark Twain and Charles Bigelow Paine, his biographer, eating lunch. The only thing I can remember about that lunch was that Mr. Clemens spent most of the time swatting flies. Now and then he would kill one on Mr. Paine's head. After lunch he said, "Now we are to hear the poem."

It was like a command performance and I arose to it as best I could, summoning to my help that something inside of me I had been taught was there for all emergencies.

When I had finished reading that poem Mark Twain turned to Mr. Paine and said: "I'm very glad! I'm very glad the Lord made her. I don't always approve of his handiwork but this time I do. And this poem must be published, Paine. You send it to the editor of *Collier's Weekly* and tell him that if he has any sense he will publish this poem."

And Mark Twain in that kind act of encouragement also released something inside of me and gave me my chance, a good deed for which I have always been grateful to his memory.

All of us have this imprisoned splendor inside of us. We are like the power in an atom of which they are always talking in scientific circles these days. They talk to me in learned terms of a split electron and I do not know what they mean from a technical point of view; but I know what they mean when they talk of a hidden power, an imprisoned splendor in human beings.

For, as Angela Morgan says in "Kinship,"

107

I am aware,
As I go commonly sweeping the stair,
Doing my part of the everyday care—
Human and simple my lot and my share—
   I am aware of a marvelous thing:
   Voices that murmur and ethers that ring
   In the far stellar spaces where cherubim sing.
I am aware of a passion that pours
Down channels of fire through Infinity's doors;
   Forces terrific, with melody shod,
   Music that mates with the pulses of God.
I am aware of the glory that runs
From the core of myself to the core of the suns. . . . .
I am aware of the splendor that ties
All the things of the earth with the things of the skies.

*   *   *

WHAT ARE YOUR GREEN PASTURES?

A YOUNG matron, Mrs. John Hyland, of Cleveland, Ohio, wrote me a letter recently with what I look upon as a helpful idea for us. She said that a group of women had written to the *Woman's Home Companion* telling how they had overcome troubles and disappointments. One woman wrote that when she felt blue and discouraged she went down to the pasture and watched the things that happened there. She saw how the ants whose sand hills had been trampled down by the cattle started out and laboriously built up their homes again. She watched how the little stalks of grass which had been trampled down and almost killed sent new shoots up to take the place of those which had been broken. She watched how the twigs which had been broken off of the lower limbs of the trees where the horses grazed sent out little new shoots also. Everything there seemed to know how to rebuild. Those visits to the pasture made that woman feel that people should all have some quiet place, some Green Pasture, to visit: some quiet place, as Angela Morgan sings.

> When days are full of discord
>   And every moment brings
> Its share of strife and worry,
>   I think of quiet things—
> Quiet things and calm things—
>   Lovely things like these:
> Dim woods at nightfall,
>   Snow on hemlock trees,
> A cherry tree in blossom,
>   Cobwebs hung with dew,
> Yellow leaves drifting down
>   With sunlight slanting through.
> Behind closed lids I see them—
>   Again and yet again—
> Curling wisps of wood smoke,
>   Violets in the rain.

Another woman said that she just went into the kitchen, whipped up a cake, and by the time the cake came out of the oven, all golden brown and fluffy, she had forgotten her problems. Another used to take a long walk; another tried to make a rhyme for every word that came into her mind. They were all just different Green Pastures to go to in time of stress and trouble.

When I received that letter about the Green Pastures I began inquiring among my woman friends as to what their Green Pastures were. One young mother of three children said: "I go to the piano when I am discouraged and play the old hymns, for that is what my mother did before me. When all of us girls went away from home my mother was so lonely at times that she could hardly stand it, so she used to go in to the piano and play the old hymns we used to sing together. It helped Mother, and it has always helped me."

Another friend said, "I work in my garden in summer and I tend my indoor flowers in winter for my Green Pastures." Another said, "I read a book." Another, "I write a letter to one of my children each day when I get discouraged and blue." An-

109

other said: "I turn on the radio to some good, uplifting program —and there are many of them. I find a Green Pasture in a program entitled 'Getting the Most Out of Life'—and I dare you to mention that on *your* broadcast." Another woman said, "I go to an orchard full of trees, an orchard that will make me forget all the turbulent troubles that life often brings into my day, just as Elizabeth Cheney sings in 'Overheard in an Orchard.' "

> Said the Robin to the Sparrow:
> "I should really like to know
> Why these anxious human beings
> Rush about and worry so."
> Said the Sparrow to the Robin,
> "Friend, I think that it must be
> That they have no Heavenly Father
> Such as cares for you and me." [1]

And might I add to that verse: No, it is not that they have no heavenly Father to care for them. It is just that they forget that they have a heavenly Father to care for them. And when they go away from the hurly-burly of life, the things that wear and tear and harass; go out to their own particular Green Pastures or Orchards or Still Waters, they will be reminded that, after all, they too have a heavenly Father to care for them.

And often they do not even have to leave the house to go to their Green Pastures, for this young mother who wrote to me said in her final words: "If I get to feeling blue and discouraged I try to look into something that is grand and fine. I get blue quite often and then I go into the nursery and look at my eight-months'-old son; and watch him play. I notice that if he can't manage to do something the first time he just plugs along, tries it over and over; tumbles and bumps his head, but he keeps at it until he gets it done. To me that baby boy is the answer to everything. He is *my* Green Pasture."

How true that is of us who have children, either small or grown up; they are nearly always our Green Pastures, our answer to everything.

[1] Reprinted by permission of The Gift Loft, Minneapolis.

THE WISDOM OF THE OLD

THERE was once a famine all over the world, and neither rain nor dew wet the earth for three years. All who had stores of corn ate little portions day by day, so as to make it last longer. Bakers charged high prices, and heaped up money.

When autumn came men sowed seed in hope of crops next year. But no rain fell, no dew dropped, no crops grew. Unhappy was the new year, gloomy the spring, and dark the summer. Seed sown in the spring bore as little fruit as that sown in autumn.

A young king who ruled the land in this time of famine had an idea that only young folk had a value. He had no respect for old persons. He did not thank them for the work they had done when they were young and strong. He did not even think of the service they had given to the world. He looked upon them as things useless; nay, worse than that—he looked upon them as things in the way. Old people ate food which had better be saved for the young.

So far did he carry his idea that he would allow only young courtiers in his palace, and only young officers and governors to take charge of the affairs of the country.

In the third year of the great hunger the king made a proposal to his council.

"Let us," he said, "drown all my old subjects. They are no good to anybody."

"Suppose," a young councilor put in, "the friends of an old man hide him away?"

"Then," replied the king, "he who hides shall be put to death with the one who is hidden. So I ordain."

The drownings began, and cries of woe were heard in the north, south, east, and west. Three brothers heard the royal command proclaimed, and to their aged father they told the dreadful news.

"So be it, my boys," said he. "My life is even now nearly at an end. If I go away there will be more food for you."

"No, Father," they cried. "We will not obey the king's decree. We will take care of you." They led him to a barn, and pulled up part of the floor, and made a cosy nook for him underneath. There he sat or lay on mats and blankets, and lived on bits of black bread which they handed down to him. Now and then, when no officers were near, he could creep out into the light of the day.

So passed the winter. In the spring days rain fell and the sun shone; and again rain fell and the sun shone, making rainbow colors dance in the drops of pure water, and great was the business of the folk who went out to sow seed, and they hoped for a rich harvest. But in the land of the young king there was no such hope, for all the grain was eaten, so there was none to scatter in the furrows.

The three sons told their father how sweet was the spring weather; but, alas! They had no seed corn.

"Go, my sons," he bade, "to the cottage, and pull down the thatch from the roof, and perchance among the old straw you will find seeds still remaining. Take them and sow."

This, therefore, they did. They sowed and waited; and lo! crops of wheat came up, and barley, and buckwheat, and millet.

In the rest of the land the fields were brown and bare. On the farm of the three sons the harvest grew full and fair.

Word came to the king that in one spot alone in this country did the corn appear. Such was the plenty of the brothers' crops that they had enough for themselves and for all others who came to beg.

He commanded that the three young men should appear at his court. They first went to their father and wept: "We are found out! The king has sent for us. What shall we do?"

"Go and tell all, my children, and let him do as he lists."

Then the king said, "How is it, fellows, that you have corn when others lack?"

"Our dear father told us to get seed from the thatch."

"Is your father still alive?"

"He is."

"You have kept alive an aged person against my will?"

"We have."

"You knew you were running the risk of death?"

112

"We did." Then they threw themselves to the ground and asked the mercy of the king.

"Rise," said the king, "for now I see I was wrong. *You had respect for the aged, and you have lost nothing by your kindness.*" The king's messengers brought the old man from his hiding place in the barn, and he was called up to sit at the right hand of the throne, and to his words the young ruler gave ear as to the counsel of a wise man. Also the sons were raised high in the royal service; and the corn of their fields fed thousands of mouths.

✳   ✳   ✳

A MOON TO BARK AT

IF YOU are fortunate enough to summer on Cape Cod you know the Yankee toymakers who whittle while they work, and suddenly, miraculously, pull out of a spray of shavings a bird, or a rabbit, or a baby in a garden dress, as lovely and as alluring as Venus lifted by Jove from the foam of the sea.

As salty as that and just as nonchalant was Uncle Jeb, a Yankee miracle man immortalized by the play *Shavings*. According to the yarn which all Cape Codders know and which Joseph Lincoln tells exquisitely, Uncle Jeb was whiling away a summer evening by whittling a whirligig for a small boy friend. Suddenly, somewhere beyond the meadows and the cranberry bog, a beagle hound began to bay at the moon. The boy was pleased but puzzled.

"Uncle Jeb," he asked, "why does a dog bark at the moon?"

Uncle Jeb knew something about moons. He had seen several of them; also he had had a sweetheart once, moons and moons ago. She had loved him a little, but not so much as the man she had married. Nevertheless Uncle Jeb still loved her, especially when the moonlight was on the meadows. Be that as it was, he answered very conventionally, very prosaically, "Oh, he thinks it's a piece of green cheese."

113

"But, Uncle Jeb, the moon isn't a piece of green cheese, is it?"

"Nope, Sonny, but he's a lucky dog to have a moon to bark at."

And so he was and so are all of us—lucky to have a light outside of ourselves that lures us on to higher things and maybe makes us miracle men.

Michael Pupin, the great inventor, philosopher, and teacher, would be the first to credit his modern miracles to such a light. In fact, he tells us in his autobiography, *From Immigrant to Inventor*, that he first became interested in scientific research when he was a shepherd boy in the Hungarian hills. He used to watch the stars and wonder what gave them light enough to shine all night through the farthest dark. Also he used to marvel that the shepherds could signal to each other across the hills by thrusting a spear into the ground and throwing it into murmurous vibrations. Even as a boy he thought there was some connection between the stars and that vibration, between light and music. Both were communication, maybe, and certainly illumination. That became his moon to bark at, even after he emigrated to America and got the education which made possible his epoch-making inventions in the fields of light and radio sound. It also gave him a philosophy of life as comforting as Uncle Jeb's, out of which he could say with reverence, beyond nonchalance:

I found in the light of stars a heavenly language which proclaims the glory of God. Each burning star is a focus of energy, of life-giving activity which it pours out lavishly into every direction; it pours out the life of its own heart, in order to beget new life. What a vista that opens to our imagination! What new beauties are disclosed in the words of Genesis: 'God . . . breathed into his nostrils the breath of life; and man became a living soul.' The light of the stars is a part of the life-giving breath of God. I never look now upon the starlit vault of heaven without feeling this divine breath and its quickening action upon my soul.

✳   ✳   ✳

"THERE'S THE WIND ON THE HEATH, BROTHER"

WHEN old tales turn up again it gives us joy and laughter in our souls, doesn't it, my friends?

Somewhere, in the long ago, I used to hear the tale I am about to tell you and loved that haunting phrase, "There's the Wind on the Heath, Brother." It lingered in my mind like the scent of lilac on a spring day; or the perfume of a red, red rose after the sun had been shining on it for an hour some hot day; or the mists that used to hover over the Ohio in Moundsville in the early morning hours.

Then a few months ago one of my friends sent me this story which contains that phrase, and my heart rejoiced at finding an old friend again, for stories can also be old friends to us.

In *Lavengro,* George Borrow describes how he met one of those noble souls who believe that the compensations of life outweigh all its disadvantages. He found the gypsy sitting on the heath, and sitting down beside him, asked the following question: "What is your opinion of death, Mr. Petulengro?"

The gypsy replied that when a man dies he is cast into the earth, and there is an end of the matter.

"And do you think that is the end of man?"

"There's an end of him, brother, more's the pity."

"Why do you say so? . . . Do you think so?"

"Think so! There's night and day, brother, both sweet things; sun, moon, and stars, brother, all sweet things; there's likewise a wind on the heath. Life is very sweet, brother; who would wish to die?"

"I would wish to die——"

"You talk like a gorgio—which is the same as talking like a fool. Were you a Rommany Chal you would talk wiser. Wish to die, indeed! A Rommany Chal would wish to live forever!"

"In sickness, Jasper?"

"There's the sun and the stars, brother."

"In blindness, Jasper?"

"There's the wind on the heath, brother; if I could only feel that I would gladly live forever."

This is one of the wisest pieces of philosophy that can be found in the annals of open-air life. The yearning for immortality is there, although the belief is absent. This is not unusual; for this longing is implanted in the hearts of all men, even unbelievers. Huxley wrote in 1883, when nearly sixty years of age: "It is a curious thought that I find my dislike to the thought of extinction increasing as I get older. It flashes across me at all sorts of times with horror, that in 1900 I shall probably know no more than I did in 1800. I had rather be in hell."

Life is sweet. Her compensations are many. The vision of things beautiful—the purple moors reaching to the eternal hills, the broad stretches of sunlit water, the exquisite loveliness of flowers, the music of the wind, and the voices of every living creature—fills the mind with contentment and the heart with praise.

The mysterious voices of nature turn our thoughts Godward. No one can appreciate the beauties of nature without feeling

> A presence that disturbs me with the joy
> Of elevated thoughts.

The compensations of life outweigh all its disadvantages. That was Mr. Petulengro's belief, and it is a belief worth having.

"In sickness, Jasper?"

"There's the sun and the stars, brother."

"In blindness, Jasper?"

"There's the wind on the heath, brother; if I could only feel that I would gladly live forever."

This belief will always be challenged by skeptics, but it is backed by the teaching of the Christian revelation.

Many who are sick testify that

> The innocent brightness of a new-born day
> Is lovely yet.

Even blindness is tolerable when one can hear the song of the wind, and enjoy its cool fragrance; for does it not remind the

116

sightless that they have their part in a beautiful world, which though they have not seen, nevertheless exists?

For the wind on the heath, which awakens in the wanderer's heart the desire to live forever, is a mighty symbol of the all-pervading Spirit of God, who stirs our blind souls, reminding us of a larger and more beautiful world—the unseen world of God —in which we have a place; and the same Spirit breathes eternal life into the soul, thus satisfying the yearning for immortality.

✳   ✳   ✳

ON STEPPING STONES

BERNARD SHAW, the famous English writer and philosopher, once said a universal thing in this sentence: "The only man who behaves sensibly is my tailor; he takes my measure anew every time he sees me, whilst all the rest go on with their old measurements, and expect them to fit me."

I have read nothing in recent years so universally applicable to life as that thought, for, almost without exception, people form a certain opinion of us in our personal or professional lives; and even though we ourselves, in the natural order of events, grow, develop, constantly change, if they are asked to express an opinion of us they are very apt to judge us by what they knew of us in a very early stage of our development.

I had this curiously illustrated in a letter I recently received from a dear eighty-year-old woman, a Mrs. Supple of Pittsburgh, Pennsylvania. She wrote me a nice letter which started off, "My dear Willie"; and I knew at once that she must have known me in Moundsville, West Virginia, when I was a child. And, sure enough, that was a good guess, for as the letter continued she said: "I remember you as the little seven-year-old boy, sitting high up in an apple tree, who spit on me when I passed under that tree."

Now it would not be quite fair to judge me today, at the half-century mark, by what I did when I was seven years of age. I have long since ceased either climbing apple trees, or spitting on innocent people who pass under apple trees. I hope I have grown a little since those days and have changed my ways a lot. I rather liked the way that letter opened; and I have received at least a dozen of them starting off "Dear Willie." It gives me a little touch of homesickness, but nevertheless I like it; but I don't want my Moundsville friends to think that I still throw stones at people, or spit on them.

I think that all of us, as well as Shaw, like to be judged by contemporary standards; for we like to think that we are growing as the years go by. But our families and our hometown friends are apt to think of us just as we were in childhood days. That also is a universal trait. In our professional lives we do certain things at certain stages. I myself in my early ministry employed rather startling methods, which I would not use today. Not that it was wrong to use them, but just that I hope I have outgrown them now, that I have changed with the changing times.

One of the most delightful experiences I have is finding out that people, as a whole, grow with the years. I remember certain individuals whom I did not like in college. I thought that they were cocky, egotistical, blatant, and prejudiced. I have carried that college conception of their characters through a quarter of a century. Then I have had occasion to see them again after twenty-five years have passed, and I have found, to my delight, that those very persons have mellowed with the years. Life has knocked the egotism and cockiness out of them, just as it has out of most of us. I have found them agreeable, charming persons; and I have regretted the intervening years when I have not had the privilege of watching them develop and grow into these mellower, kindlier, lovelier persons. This is true of both men and women.

Most of us are like the butterfly and moth. We have our larva stages, our cocoon stages, and our butterfly and moth stages, and we all grow mellower, finer, more intelligent and kindly; even more beautiful in our spirits as the different stages come and go; as our measurements change.

It is the old, old philosoph fittingly expressed by a great observer of life in the long ago when he said: "When I was a child, I spake as a child, I understood as a child, I thought as a child: but when I became a man, I put away childish things."

And most of us want to be judged; and I verily believe that most of us have a right to be judged or measured year by year; and that there is a certain injustice on the part of our friends when they judge us by what we did in earlier years. I think that all of us ought to assume that men and women grow with the years and not only change physically every seven years, but that they change mentally and spiritually.

I have known a few cases where this was not true. I remember a grown man who never got beyond being the coxswain on a Syracuse crew back in the early part of this century. That was the high point in his life, evidently. Twenty-five years after he was still talking about the great race when he was coxswain of the crew.

I know of another case. Bishop McDowell told me about him. We'll call him Jones. Jones was the outstanding student, orator, athlete, personality in a certain college, and everybody expected him to turn the world upside down. He seemed to have the brightest future of any of the students. A quarter of a century later Bishop McDowell met a woman graduate of that college and they got to talking over old times and old friends. Finally Bishop McDowell said: "And what has happened to Jones? We thought he would be in the United States Senate by now. And yet he has dropped out of sight as completely as if the sea had swallowed him up. What has happened to him?"

"Why, don't you know, Bishop, what happened to Jones?"

"No, what happened to him?"

"Why, Jones caught up with his own horizons, Bishop."

Yes, that does happen now and then, but it is unusual; for most men and women develop with the years and decades. They grow in the natural order of events, and we have no more right to judge them by their earlier years than Shaw's tailor had a right to assume that his physical measurements would remain the same throughout the years.

119

"EVERY CLOD"

WHAT a glorious month June is, with its marching processions of June brides down the aisles of churches, and its other beautiful processions of marching boys and girls across the campuses of the nation to the sound of merry laughter and almost hysterical ecstasy.

I stood a few years ago on Smith College campus watching a parade of young girls, including my own daughter; and with my usual disciplined and brave control I stood there and wept. Trying to hide my tears I turned to make a casual remark, "It is the wind." Then I saw another silly old male about six feet tall who looked as if he might have played football on a Yale team, and he was weeping too. When we looked at each other he said to me: "Mine's in there too—that one with the blond hair, the big tall beautiful one marching beside that little one with the glasses—and I guess a guy has a right to weep a little today. I haven't shed a tear in ten years."

"Yes," I replied. "Us girls have a right to take our hair down now and then and have a good cry. It's good for us!"

That afternoon I met Mary Ellen Chase and told her of the experience that we two stalwart fathers had had that morning. "Well," she replied, "let me tell you a story. One commencement they were having the annual parade of the old classes from 1880 down to modern times. They were dressed in all sorts of outlandish costumes—pirates, sailors, oriental potentates, jockeys, bellboys, and what have you. Two men stood on the sidelines. They were utter strangers, one from Georgia and one from California. They had evidently come back with their Smith College wives to see their own daughters graduate just as you have. They had not as yet spoken to each other, but suddenly an unusually ridiculuous class came by of the vintage of around the late nineties. They were wearing pirate outfits. Most of them were fat, and one lady who weighed around two hundred looked particularly ridiculous.

"The two men started to grin. Up to that time they had not spoken a word to each other; but that group of fat ladies dressed

120

as pirates was too much for their male sense of humor, so the man from Georgia said to the man from California: 'Wow! And isn't that a circus? And that fat old lady there on the left with her pirate hat on the side of her head, isn't she a beaut?'

" 'Yes,' replied his new-found friend from California. 'That's my wife, and I told her this morning when she dressed up in that outfit that she looked like the devil!' "

Yes, June is a glorious month, as Lowell sang long ago:

> And what is so rare as a day in June?
> Then, if ever, come perfect days;
> And Heaven tries earth if it be in tune,
> And over it softly her warm ear lays;
> Whether we look, or whether we listen,
> We hear life murmur, or see it glisten;
> And every clod feels a stir of might,
> An instinct within it that reaches and towers,
> And, groping blindly above it for light,
> Climbs to a soul in grass and flowers.

That's it. Climbs to a soul! That is what June does, not only for every clod of earth but for every clod of humanity.

That's it. "Every clod feels a stir of might"—and that means all of us, even those of us who have reached mid-life.

While Angela Morgan was visiting us recently, I told her about this first of June story, and she pointed out to me a poem of her own, called "June Rapture," and told me I might use it.

> Green! What a world of green! My startled soul
> Panting for beauty long denied,
> Leaps in a passion of high gratitude
> To meet the wild embraces of the wood;
> Rushes and flings itself upon the whole
> Mad miracle of green, with senses wide;
> Clings to the glory, hugs and holds it fast,
> As one who finds a long-lost love at last.
> Billows of green that break upon the sight
> In bounteous crescendos of delight;
> Wind-hurried verdure hastening up the hills

To where the sun its highest rapture spills;
Cascades of color tumbling down the height
In golden gushes of delicious light—
God! Can I bear the beauty of this day,
Or shall I be swept utterly away? . . .

Praised be the gods that made my spirit mad,
Kept me aflame and raw to beauty's touch,
Lashed me and scourged me with the whip of fate,
Gave me so often agony for mate;
Tore from my heart the things that make men glad—
Praised be the gods! If I, at last, by such
Relentless means may know the sacred bliss,
The anguished rapture of an hour like this.
Smite me, O Life, and bruise me if thou must;
Mock me and starve me with thy bitter crust,
But, keep me thus aquiver and awake,
Enamored of my life, for living's sake!

This were the tragedy—that I should pass,
Dull and indifferent through the glowing grass.
And this the reason I was born, I say—
That I might know the passion of this day!

Angela Morgan, Lowell, Life, and June have said it all for us,
and every clod of us feels a stir of might during June days.

*   *   *

"THERE SHALL BE WINGS"

A LONG time ago, even before man came to the earth to live, the
birds had sweet voices with which to sing; they had beautiful
colors with which to make the world bright, but they had no
wings. They hopped from place to place, and thus often en-
dangered their lives, but they could not fly.

Now, there was some work to be done in the animal world,

and God chose one and another animal to help him. Some scattered seeds, some carried messages, some worked to make the world more beautiful. But none of the animals wished to bear burdens from one place to another.

The lion said, "I am too great to carry bundles."

The rabbit said, "I am too small to carry bundles."

The sheep said, "I give wool, so why should I carry bundles?"

The chipmunk said, "I must run fast and far, so how can I carry bundles?"

One and another of them asked to be excused—all but the birds. When they saw that the bundles had to be carried, they said to the great God who guarded them: "We are very small and cannot carry much. But we are glad to do what we can. Make the bundles small and we can help to do the work. There are many of us; perhaps we can do it all."

So the bundles were put on their backs. Sometimes they staggered under the weight of them, but still they carried; and they sang their sweet songs as they hopped along. They could still pick up bits of food as they went along. At first their songs could not be understood, but gradually the other animals found that they were singing: "Never mind about the burdens. We will do our very best."

And as the days went by, the burdens seemed lighter. Soon the burdens seemed to be lifting them instead of their lifting the burdens. Then, lo! when the winter was over and the spring-time came again, the burdens rolled away and in their place were wings—wings with which they could fly away from danger and spend their days in the beautiful sky and in the tree tops. They had learned how to carry the burden, and the burden had become wings to lift them nearer to God, for whom they had done the work.

Which reminds me of an interesting experience I had many years ago in the Pitti Palace, in Florence, Italy. I was talking with a guide and he showed me a most interesting design of an airship made by Leonardo da Vinci, the great painter, sculptor, and all-around genius—he who not only was a master in the field of art, but also made musical instruments and wrote his own

123

music; he who was a great military designer and drew plans for military defenses for his own city of Florence. But the most interesting thing he ever did back in the fifteenth century was to draw the blueprints of an airship. An even more interesting thing than that was a single line which he wrote as a caption beneath that drawing—a line which read with prophetic vigor: "There shall be wings!"

But let us go back to the simple legend with which I started this talk and to the eternal truth that we grow wings through having needs and burdens to carry—for, after all, "Necessity is is the mother of invention." Life had taught us all that. It seems in God's wise plans that the greater our burdens the greater strength we develop for the bearing of those burdens. It is always true in a mother's work.

Yes, strangely enough, a woman in her home always seems to get strength for her needs. And in the final analysis the very things she does for her children lift her on wings of joy, the joy of serving; and the people I have known who seem to get the most out of life are those mothers who bear the heaviest burdens for their children.

Angela Morgan expressed this in "The Housewife's Hymn:"

Somehow, Father—be it not shame to me!—
'Tis in such humble ways I compass thee.
I seem to see thee in the simplest things:
Foamy water that bubbles and sings,
Bursting in rainbows over the washtub's rim;
The clean, sweet clothes filling my basket to the brim—
How white they flutter at the wind's brisk will
That whips them whiter still! . . .

Yea, human love and human things: the touch
Of well-worn objects that I love so much—
Cushion and chair, dishes and pan and broom,
The comradeship of a familiar room;
My plants there in the window, and the glow
Of shining tin things hanging in a row. . . .

O God, I seem to find thee everywhere!
The steam that rises from the kettle there
Seems more a miracle, somehow, to me
Than all the heavenly marvels that I see.
The hum of homey things upon the range
Fills me with rapture; Father, is it strange
Since these thy products are of grain and food
And thou thyself hast called them very good?"

Yes, those who bear the everyday burdens of life are finally given wings to carry their burdens, and insight to see that they are most beautiful when they are done in the service of love, for Love lifts the soul on wings of joy to higher heights.

✳   ✳   ✳

THE LONG LOOK

DR. C. M. McCONNELL brings us this story.

A friend once asked Charles Darwin's gardener about his employer's health, and how he had been progressing lately. "Oh," he said, "my poor employer has been failing lately. I wish he had something to do. He mopes around in the garden, and I have seen him stand before a flower, doing nothing, for ten minutes at a time. Think of that! Just watching a flower for ten minutes at a time. If he only had something to occupy his mind I really think he would be better."

Perhaps no one ever saw more while watching a single flower for ten minutes than did Charles Darwin. He was one of the world's greatest naturalists; and in 1859 his book, *The Origin of Species,* created a sensation in the scientific world which still goes on.

In that ten-minute look at the flower in his garden Darwin saw not only the flower before him in its present state, but his eye saw the first flower. He was retracing zoölogical history, determining the stages through which plants have passed in their development. He saw the effects of soil climate and cultivation upon this flower. In his mind he was building up his theory of natural selection by which this flower had won in its fight for survival.

A ten-minute look to Charles Darwin meant that he was touching "the hem of eternity"—something which has been captured for us in an old Chinese manuscript of the story of Lao-Kung.

When Lao-Kung, Chinese artist, felt that his end was approaching, he asked that all his pupils might gather around him. And so they came and found the old painter in his workshop, sitting before his easel, brushes and paints around him. As his pupils sat sorrowfully, one spoke and his words were as follows: "Master, we are sad at heart when we contemplate your fate. We would like to ask you one question. Has life on your part been really worth while?"

The old man slowly raised his head and his face became like that of a mighty conqueror at the moment of his greatest triumph: "I have spent well nigh a hundred years on this earth. Oft I went hungry, and more than once, if it had not been for the kindness of my friends, I would have been without shelter or raiment. I surrendered all hope of personal gain that I might better devote myself to my art. I deliberately turned my back upon all that which could have been my own had I but cared to pit cunning against cunning and greed against greed. But in obeying the inner voice that bade me follow my solitary path, I have achieved the highest purpose to which any of us may hope to aspire."

"Will you not tell us what that highest purpose may be to which mortal man may aspire?" asked the oldest of the old man's pupils.

A strange light came into the eyes of Lao-Kung as he lifted himself from his seat. His trembling feet carried him across the room to the spot where stood the one picture that he loved best. It was a blade of grass, hastily painted with the strokes of his mighty brush. But that blade of grass lived and breathed. It was not merely a blade of grass, for within itself it contained the spirit of every blade of grass that had ever grown since the beginning of time.

"There," the old man said, "is my answer. I have made myself the equal of the gods, for I too through that single blade of grass have touched the hem of Eternity."

Thereupon he blessed his pupils and they laid him down upon his couch and he died.

Elizabeth Barrett Browning has caught the spirit of both Darwin and Lao-Kung in her lines from *Aurora Leigh*.

> Earth's crammed with heaven
> And every common bush afire with God;
> But only he who sees takes off his shoes;
> The rest sit round it and pluck blackberries.

Which always makes me think of something that Lorado Taft said to me years ago when we were out lecturing on the Chautauqua Circuit. We were talking about the needs of contemporary life, and Taft said: "What you preachers, what we sculptors, what every individual needs to remember is that we are a part of the eternal cycle and because of that we are tremendously important as personalities. We need to take the long look at life and to remember that we are immortal beings. We need to get the hint of eternity back into our work and our thoughts. When we do that we can have no small dealings with each other; no little thinking, no unkindness, no hate; and then every individual has a meaning in life's eternal plan and in God's eyes. When we remember that we are all made in God's image, just a little lower than the angels, then we stand up and quit us like men, and through each individual we get the long look and touch the hem of the Eternal. That makes life superbly worth living."

* * *

"SOME GLIMMER OF THE DAWN"

IN CERTAIN parts of China there are to be found guilds of artists who are called ancestor painters. Now, in America, when we desire a portrait of our ancestor, we dig out of the attic a faded daguerreotype, take it to a modern studio, and call for it a few weeks later to find it magically restored. There is Grandfather Brown with the determined chin, or Grandmother, perhaps, with her patrician grace—both of them unmistakably our ancestors. For have we not always been told that we got our strong will from Grandfather Brown? Or have not our easy-going ways been ascribed over and over again to our inheritance from Grandmother? We look at them and acknowledge, however reluctantly, that they are, indeed, our ancestors and there is nothing we can do about it.

But in China ancestor painting is a very different matter. We make a visit to the ancestor painter and say to him, "Oh, most honorable sir, I desire a portrait of my ancestor." He obligingly unrolls his charts: one filled with pictures of eyes of every shape and color; one bearing photographs of mouths; another chart covered with noses of every type. And we make our selection after the manner of our own desire. We say to him, perhaps, "Paint me such and such eyes, for I like their color and shape. As for noses, I prefer that one in the lower right-hand corner of the chart. The mouth that suits me best is that one with the cupid's bow." And presto! In a few days we return for the likeness of our ancestor and there he is, an ancestor of our own choosing.

Most of us have moments of wishing that we might have so chosen our own ancestors. But while we cannot choose or change our ancestors, we can at least determine the kind of ancestors we will be.

In other words, we are now about the big business of creating ancestors for the years to come. A critic said in Boston a few months ago, when Anton Chekhov's *The Sea Gull* was being played there: "You have grown up in the soil of modernity and in the soil of the historic past, but there is something in you which belongs to tomorrow and the days after."

A few weeks ago a friend of mine used a simple story to illustrate the obligation we have in this day to build a new world even while we carry on as best we can the business of the contemporary world.

Some years ago the New York Central Railroad discovered that it must have a new terminal station in New York City. The old Grand Central Station was inadequate, inconvenient, dirty, and dangerous. But, meanwhile, the business of the railroad must go on, for the life of the metropolis depended upon its uninterrupted operation. Through a period of many months the old station was taken down, and the great new station slowly and painfully erected in its place. And through all this stupendous labor of destruction and construction, going on together as though it were a single process, not a train stopped running, not a wheel ceased turning.

It is for engineering of this type that our civilization calls today—a new world that shall not destroy but fulfill the life of men!

This story is in the spirit of a voice I heard from England on the short-wave radio a while ago—a voice which quoted a good old English workman who cheerfully said, "The world ain't all you want, but it's all you 'ave, so stick a geranium in your 'at and be 'appy."

My friend William J. Cameron understands what I am talking about and so does Mr. Ford, for a few years ago I received a letter from Mr. Cameron which illustrates this principle better than I can do it:

DEAR DR. STIDGER:

We have just pulled off our thirtieth Ford Motor Company birthday today, without any band or fireworks. This morning when we were shoving his first little car out of the old Bagley Street woodshed, which was his first shop, I'll be hanged if, without any prearrangement or staging, the man who stepped up to help the Boss was not the very man (J. W. Bishop) who helped Henry Ford shove out that same car into the rain at 3 A.M. of a morning forty years ago. It was the morning the Boss put his last touches on the car, and couldn't wait till daylight to see if it ran. She did run, you remember—but she wouldn't back up. Well, it was all very interesting.

But already this episode is miles behind in the roster of today's events. For at this moment the Boss is keenest about a little operetta the kids are giving in the village tonight. He sat for hours at their rehearsals— their ages run from six to thirteen—and he thinks it's a more important occasion than the anniversary. It probably is. No use bothering about adults any more; the best investment now is in the children. You had better take a good look at them as they pass you on the street; they are the ones who are going to live under the new system. You know how we used to look at men who had been afar—Africa, out on the plains, even to Chicago; well, these little people are the ones who are *going* to go. Maybe we can catch some glimmer of the dawn on their faces.

✷   ✷   ✷

IN THE MUD AND SCUM OF THINGS

SOME of the most beautiful stories I get come in letters which I receive from friends who have read my books or who have heard me speak on the platform or on the radio. One such recent letter reads:

DEAR DR. STIDGER:

Your program comes at just the psychological moment. Tired from the many irritating concerns and duties of the morning and the preparation of the noonday meal, the fifteen minutes of spiritual uplift from your talk and the music and the rest give me the tranquillity to meet the children when they return for luncheon. My ruffled spirit has absorbed enough peace to be able to meet them and greet them as I had always dreamed a mother should greet her children.

You sometimes include in your broadcasts a human-interest story. I am writing this one just as it happened to me.

During convalescence from a very serious illness, I took one of my first walks accompanied by my two small children, Barbara, aged five, and William, aged two and a half, and also the child of a neighbor whom I shall give the name of Jane.

It was an exquisite late afternoon in June. Our home, in Hartford, Connecticut, was situated on a street high on a hill above the city. The three children and I walked slowly to the end of the street. As my strength was little, we paused to rest there. The sun was very bright, a breeze had whipped roses into the cheeks of the children.

Coming up the hill toward us was an elderly woman. She wore the clothes of a charwoman; in her hand were a few wild flowers which she had picked on the way. She approached us and stopped. A smile dis-

130

closed the fact that she was almost toothless. She looked at the children and back at me and then aked:

"Are they yours?"

I nodded my head "yes." They were all dressed in regulation navy-blue coats; there seemed no need to explain that one was a neighbor's child.

"What lovely children," she said, and handed a wild flower to Barbara, who accepted it very graciously, then to little Bill, and last of all to Jane. Now Jane's ancestry could be traced back to the "Mayflower," and Jane, although only seven years of age, had previously remarked that she never played with children who attended public school. Well, to go on with my story, Jane drew back with an almost repugnant look and would not accept the flower. The old woman smiled and went her way. We started down the hill and as we did so little Barbara looked up into my eyes and reverently and breathlessly said:

"Mother, wasn't she beautiful?"

Most sincerely,
Helen M. Burkhardt.

Some wise philosopher of old has said: "There is no particular virtue in loving the beautiful. It is an easy thing to respond to a beautiful rose, sunset, tree, or person. We human beings do not find it much of a problem to go out to a beautiful person—man, woman, or child. But the glorious thing is to have the ability to find something beautiful in the unlovely; to look beneath the exterior of an ugly body and find a beautiful soul. There is something divine in that."

One of the most unusual stories I ever heard was a story about two famous foreigners who later became American citizens of note.

Dr. George A. Gordon, the famous Boston preacher, on one of his early trips to America found that his cabin mate was a funny looking, hunchbacked, rather hideous man who looked like a deformed dwarf. So he went to the purser, gave him his money, and said to him: "I am sorry to have to do this, but my cabin mate is a hideous looking ruffian. He looks like a brigand, and I am afraid to leave my valuables in the cabin."

The purser, who knew Dr. Gordon well, said to him: "Now

that's a strange thing, Dr. Gordon, but your cabin mate was here a moment ago saying the same thing about you and asking if he might leave his valuables with me. His name is Steinmetz and he is an electrical engineer from the General Electric Company of Schenectady, New York."

Later Dr. Gordon and Dr. Steinmetz came to be the best of friends. It was understandable that Dr. Gordon should think that this little hunchback, with his deformed dwarflike body, should be a thug and a robber. So even among the great of the earth we discover a failure to see behind an ugly body a beautiful soul and spirit. For the world now knows that Dr. Steinmetz was the little giant who played with lightning and thunderbolts in laboratories and turned out to be one of the greatest scientists America ever welcomed to its shores.

And those who knew him say that he was one of the gentlest spirits who ever lived, with a soul as white and as kindly as a dawn in springtime. As we now look back on his achievements and his spirit we hear an inner voice hushed with awe and appreciation saying over and over, "Mother of Creation, wasn't he beautiful? Wasn't he beautiful!"

* * *

THE HAZARDS OF GOING ON

THE following incident in Amelia Earhart's first flight across the Atlantic was related by her in a public address made in Boston:

When I got out about five hundred miles over the Atlantic from Halifax, I suddenly began to have trouble with my engine. It sputtered and backfired, and sounded like it was going to give up. I lowered the plane and flew close to the sea so that I might make a desperate attempt to float it. I had to make a quick decision. I figured the distance I had already come and that which I had to go before I reached Ireland. I decided to go on as long as I could keep the ship in the air, for the hazards of going on were no greater than the hazards of going back.

Daring pioneers who have made new pathways on land and

sea and air have always had such moments of threatening danger. Columbus discovered America by sailing on. He overcame the fears of his crew, and stuck to his course when they threatened to throw him overboard and return to Spain. As Edwin Markham puts it:

The long day and the longer night,
And seas rushed by in eager flight.
Then frightened sailors raised a cry:
"We feel the terror of the sky.
Turn back, great Admiral," they moan:
"We cannot dare the dark unknown.
Soon we shall totter on the brink;
Soon into utter darkness sink!"
"No, no," the daring chief replied:
"The earth is round, the sea is wide;
Keep all the sails aloft, and steer
Into the west: the shores are near!"
They plowed and plunged for days and days;
Then horror struck, and wild amaze.
The Needle felt some secret jar
And seemed to shake the Polar Star.
The pilots paled with sudden awe:
Nature seemed crashing out of law.
Had they then swung to another realm?
Would the void open and overwhelm?
But no fear shook the captain, none,
From sunset to the rise of sun.
He stood there sleepless on the prow;
With wild hopes singing in his breast;
With gray eyes glued upon the west,
He stood there, beating against bars—
Stood all the night till drunk with stars.
At last, near twelve, he suddenly saw
A thing of mystery and awe;
It was a light afar—a light;
It moved, and there was no more night!
Now let this startling thing be said;
If land had not been on ahead,
So mighty had been his gallant dare,
God's glad hand would have put it there!

133

There is a story told about Daniel Boone and his wanderings in the forests of Kentucky. He was trying to find new lands for settlers and better roads through the wilderness to some promised land beyond.

"Were you ever lost in the woods?" an old settler once asked Daniel Boone.

"No, not exactly lost, but I have been *bewildered* for days on end, once for more than a week, but I kept going on."

Bewilderment is the best description of our state of mind today. Millions of people seem to be bewildered.

The people of the world are bewildered today about their security—about what we Americans call "the right to life, liberty, and the pursuit of happiness."

Our very being is grounded in this right. James Bryce, the English statesman, once said, "The remedy for democracy is more democracy."

And forward, for us, means more democracy.

But forward to more political freedom includes moving forward toward the good of the common man. We are trying to raise the people on the lowest rungs of our economic ladder to levels of economic decency. Were we to revert to a national policy of do-nothing about the unemployed, the poor and hungry, we should be turning back and facing the older hazards which are greater than the hazards of going on.

This principle works with you and me too. Life is a bewildering thing at best and we are forced to ask the question, "What is forward?"

It is continued self-improvement, the carrying on of our tasks, large or small, toward the goal of their completion. Forward means clinging to the old ideals which we have set for ourselves. Backward means giving up, letting loose our hold, and sinking down into discouragement and the acceptance of defeat as inevitable and permanent.

The words of Tennyson's "Ulysses" come to us to match those of Amelia Earhart and Edwin Markham:

'Tis not too late to seek a newer world.
Push off, and sitting well in order smite
The sounding furrows; for my purpose holds
To sail beyond the sunset, and the baths
Of all the western stars, until I die. . . .
To strive, to seek, to find, and not to yield.

✶   ✶   ✶

"EXCEPT, SOMETIMES, IN THE DARK"

ALFRED NOYES once said a great thing in two lines of poetry:

> And Bos'n Bill was an atheist still—
> Except, sometimes, in the dark.

Dr. C. M. McConnell illustrates that universal truth in an experience he had as a boy. He says:

I'll never forget the time Billy Compton's barn burned. Billy was our nearest neighbor and he had a barn stored full of hay and grain. One Sunday night about ten o'clock it caught on fire, and what a fire it was.

About bedtime I went out to pump some water. Just as I started to pump myself a drink, I looked up and saw the whole western sky ablaze. It looked like a wall of fire, and great chunks of burning hay and straw with blazing shingles from the barn roof were soaring out over the tree tops in the woods which came up almost to the well. I dropped the water bucket, let out a yell which brought the family to the door and windows—"Help, help, the world's on fire."

Mother and my two older brothers hurried off to the fire, leaving my sister, about fifteen years old, and myself, about eight, alone at home. We were paralyzed with fear. Afraid to look out the windows or door, we huddled together in an old rocking-chair. "What will we do? What will we do?" we moaned in our fright and anguish, for every minute we expected to be burned alive right there in the house, which seemed only temporarily safe.

I had seen many family crises before, and always in such moments my mother would read the Bible, and pray under both ordinary and un-

135

usual circumstances. I suggested to my older sister that we get the old worn Bible and read it. I took the first turn and read verse after verse. Then my sister read, and she said, "Let's try praying!" So we did as we had seen mother do—knelt down by the old armchair and prayed. It was for safety from the fire that we prayed, and the prayer was mostly, "Lord, don't let us burn up"—and we did not burn. After a while the brothers and Mother came home, and found us asleep in the rocking-chair. Rather sheepishly we admitted that we had read the Bible and had prayed while the world was burning right over our heads.

It was a childish fancy and fear my friend tells about, but it is what all of us eventually do in times of stress and peril; in famine, trouble, and pain; in the face of doubt and death.

> For Bos'n Bill was an atheist still—
> Except, sometimes, in the dark.

And when we pray in such moments we know the Father hears and heeds. I have an experience parallel to that of my friend, and I have no doubt that you could duplicate it in your lives.

One Christmas down in Moundsville, West Virginia, I got an air rifle for a present. Christmas Day was deep with snow and we could not play out of doors, so my brother and I stayed in our father's office in the courthouse. Since the air rifle was new it was our chief plaything. We put up little pieces of paper on the walls of Father's office and shot at them. Most of the shots missed the paper and went into the wall. It did not matter to us that Marshall County had just spent ten thousand dollars frescoing the walls of the courthouse. When we had filled one wall with shot we transferred our mark to another wall. Then, running out of walls to shoot into, I decided that it would be an exciting adventure to have my brother stand on a chair with a spool over the end of the air gun and shoot through the hole in the spool. Just as I was ready to shoot, my brother decided to look and see if the spool was on the air rifle properly, but he did not inform me of his intention and I pulled the trigger. The BB shot hit him a glancing blow in the eye. He let out a yell. I saw a tiny drop of blood on his eyeball. We were both paralyzed with fear. I was sure that younger brother would die. What should we do? The first thing that occurred to me was to open the window and throw the air rifle out into the deep snow. At least we would get rid of that nefarious instrument of sin.

Then I threw all the shot I had left out into the snow. Then I took my brother into the big stone vault where they kept the county records and made him kneel down on the cement floor. I knelt with him. I prayed. Then I made him pray. He said: "I can't pray! I don't know how!" I replied: "Dumbbell, you gotta pray if you save that eye and you may die if you don't!" So he prayed. Then we sang a hymn.

Finally it occurred to me that we had better go over to old Dr. Hall's office, which was just across from the courthouse, so I dragged my brother over. I rang the bell. The old doctor came to the door. I told him the trouble and what we had already done in the emergency. He looked at the eye and said: "That's a very serious matter. You had better go home and do some more praying!"

If we had had our wits about us, we might have known that it was not a very serious matter, or Dr. Hall would never have sent us scurrying home. But we were literalists, took him at his word, and tore home; I, as the older, dragging my younger brother. When we got home Father asked us what the trouble was. I didn't even stop to tell him. I simply said: "We gotta pray, don't bother us! We gotta pray! Read's been shot in the eye! Dr. Hall said we gotta pray!"

It was a very serious matter with us, but in a few days, when the eye was better, both my brother and I went down to the courthouse, dug into the snow and rescued the air rifle and all the shot we could find and started in filling walls and what have you with BB shot. But, after all, we *did* have our moments of devotion; and I learned through that childhood experience the universal truth of the fact that

Bos'n Bill was an atheist still,
Except, sometimes, in the dark.

SOMETHING TO TOUCH IN THE DARK

WHEN my daughter was a baby she used to like to take a favorite rag doll to bed with her, and when I asked her why she would say to us: "Because I want something to touch in the dark, Daddy!" How like that child most of us really are!

Kagawa, the great Japanese Christian leader, tells this amazing story. A man was brought into a hospital suffering from a terrible Oriental skin disease which was rapidly taking his life. It was one of those cases for which science had as yet found no cure. The doctors had only one remedy, a chemical solution to relieve the suffering. For the chemical to be effective the man's body had to be entirely submerged. So, condemned to a living death, he stepped into a bath tub filled with the prescription, where he was forced to live, day and night, for seven years. Even his arms were pinioned beneath the water.

As the days dragged by with throbbing monotony, a ray of light filtered into his pain-drugged brain—the Gospel Story! Perhaps he had heard it before, as so many have, but thrust it aside because he saw no immediate need of uplift. I do not know. But in his great affliction he opened the gates of his being, and a flood tide of comfort and power surged into that wasted body. He was no longer "the man in the bath tub." God took from him his prison number and put in its place—a name!

A New Testament, at his request, was fastened on a long string and tied to the ceiling. The book hung on a level with his eyes. Day after day, month after month, he drank in the life-giving words. His useless body was almost forgotten in the abiding peace which filled his crumbled world. As his strength failed his soul enlarged, until the bath tub became an altar.

World-weary people from everywhere came to hear this story and look with awe upon the yellow, eaten pages of his New Testament. He could lift his hands from the chemical water long enough to turn the pages.

There is no way of knowing how many people left that room of triumph feeling they had been on holy ground. As Kagawa put it in his Oriental stacatto, pausing before each word, "It is hard to have faith in a bath tub!"

There is a beautiful young woman whom I know, a former school teacher, who has been confined to her bed for ten years, a hopeless victim of arthritis. Her arms and legs are so cruelly crippled that she is unable to sit up. Yet her faith is unfettered. Her pastor, who goes to give her comfort, leaves that room having received more than he has given. She is the sun of inspiration, shining on many whose bodies have outgrown their souls.

Blind Fanny Crosby, the immortal hymn writer, beheld more "visions of rapture" through the cathedral windows of her darkness than we who have sight, but, seeing, do not see. The little poem, "Blind," seems to express this spirit of strength emerging from weakness.

> Give no pity because my feet
> Stumble along the dark, hard street,
> And stub against the hostile stones,
> Coldly deaf to the world's numb moans.
>
> The days move by on sullen wing
> Like migrant birds that cannot sing,
> Merging at last with a starless night,
> Forever denied the lift of light.
>
> Silent—I climb the anguished dark,
> Still I can hear a heaven-bound lark.
> Sightless—I see! And, seeing, find
> Soul-vision though my eyes are blind!

Which reminds me of the first time I ever met Helen Keller, the blind, deaf and dumb woman. It was in Cleveland and we were both going out for a season of Chautauqua lecturing. Helen made a speech to the talent assembled there. When she had finished there was a round of applause; and Helen, who is supposed to be unable to hear anything, fairly danced with joy over that applause and clapped her hands. The chairman asked her through Miss Sullivan how she heard the applause and she said, "Through the vibrations in my feet." Then she was asked what her favorite book was and she fairly shouted: "The Bible. It is the most wonderful book in the world. The Bible. It is beautiful!"

When she was asked why the Bible meant so much to her she replied, in the very spirit of Kagawa's story, "It is because, in my darkness, the Bible makes me see the Great Light!"

What a glow and glory there is in such stories for all of us! Sometimes we think that we are badly off and get into the habit of self-pity, but in the light of that Japanese boy's suffering, Fanny Crosby and Helen Keller's blindness, we learn how to get more out of life through the courage they show under handicaps.

*   *   *

"BLESSED ARE THE DEBONAIR"

ACCORDING to Dr. Earl Marlatt, one of the modern poets insists that he prays to a "God with a sense of humor." Another makes no special profession but exemplifies a deliciously divine sense of humor when he says that while hearing long prayers "that stretch like elastic bands" he always holds his breath in hopes that they will "snap back and hit the preacher in the nose." Dwight L. Moody had another way of dealing with long prayers, and that was what won Wilfred Grenfell to him. When Grenfell stepped into one of Moody's meetings, through sheer curiosity, a visitor was praying a long-winded prayer; just as Grenfell came in, Mr. Moody said, "While the brother is finishing his prayer the congregation will sing hymn number 86."

No, my friends, that is not irreverence. Beyond its piquancy is a profundity which redeems its seeming blasphemy. It is a layman's protest against the sour-faced, long-ranting piosity of professional religionists.

The late Clarence Day, who did so much to make the grim thirties more like the gay nineties, voiced the same plea for reality and gayety in religion in a magazine article about his grandfather's French Bible. Mostly it was a disappointment to him when, as a boy, he was allowed on rare occasions to read it. It made the regal "leviathan" of the King James version the plebeian *"le crocodile,"* and where he was accustomed to the spine-tingling "Behold now Behemoth!" he found, without a tremor, the commonplace *"Voici l'hippopotame!"* That was no more than small boys shouted at the zoo: "Oh, look! Here's the hippopotamus!" It wasn't Biblical, surely. There was the same sickening sense of let-down when Moses and the Lord were merely *"irrité,"* rather than magnificently, divinely "wroth" with the children of Israel. But all of this disgust was swallowed up in ecstasy the day he reached the Beatitudes and found, instead of "Blessed are the meek"—he had never liked that—"Blessed" or "Happy are the debonair!" That was what his father was, and St. Francis, and God. The Kingdom belonged to men like that. They would remake the world.

Waiving the textual problem here—the Greek word translated "debonair" really means "gentle, mild, meek"—the sainted Frenchman responsible for this rendering undoubtedly used the word in its original sense: "of a good disposition, characterized by grace and light-heartedness"—gayety, courtesy, gallantry. Thus construed debonairness is not the recklessness which leaps from Temple spires and expects "legions of angels" to prevent disaster; nor is it the jocund indifference which popular thought idealizes as "nonchalance." To be debonair is to be high-spirited but not narrow-minded, ardent but not dogmatic, sincere but not intolerant. It is to take one's cause seriously but oneself not so seriously. It is, then, a kind of meekness which allows differences without rancor, and so promotes individual development through common kindliness.

Mary Magdalene, "breaking a box of ointment of spikenard, precious, very costly," that its scented coolness might trickle over a Friend's dust-burned feet, was debonair. Simon, the ungracious host, sneered at her, and Judas, the betrayer, rebuked her bitterly. But the Master, who loved beauty, gayety, and extravagant sincerity, said: "Let her alone. She hath done a beautiful thing."

Francesco Bernadone, selling his evening clothes and his

blooded horses to rebuild a chapel and heal the wounds of lepers, was debonair. His playboy friends took his name out of the social register and his father disinherited him, but posterity called him "blessed." And today men, when they separate in gayety or grief, repeat the benediction which St. Francis taught them:

> The Lord bless thee and keep thee.
> The Lord make his face to shine upon thee
>   and be gracious unto thee.
> The Lord lift up his countenance upon thee
>   and give thee peace.

Albert Schweitzer, leaving the acclaim of Continental music-masters to be a medical missionary on the rim of the jungle, was debonair. Wilfred Grenfell, forsaking a fashionable practice in London to be a country doctor in Labrador, was debonair. Kagawa, praying for the Chinese suffering from Japanese ruthlessness, and T. Z. Koo, the Chinese Christian leader, saying of these same Japanese invaders, "My enemies are waiting to be loved on my very doorstep"—both are debonair, gallant, good-spirited.

✳   ✳   ✳

"THAT'S WHY I'M A VERY REMARKABLE FELLOW"

ONE of my friends, Dr. Charles M. Tibbetts, recently told me a good story about a childhood experience which has a universal touch in it. He said in that story:

When I was a small boy a chimney was built on the outside of a church which stood near my home. With a boy's curiosity I watched the men as they proceeded with the work. And how I did long to climb the ladder and stand on the staging as it rose above the very top of the lofty roof. But my mother had warned me that I was not to interfere with the workmen and, of all things, I was not to climb ladders. So I had to content myself with watching from my humble place on the ground.

Then, one day, one of the men leaned out over the edge of the staging and shouted down to me, "Boy, there's a trowel down there on the ground. Bring it up here." That was the most thrilling moment in my young life. I grasped the trowel firmly and climbed with it to the height where the men were working.

As I approached the staging I heard the other man say to the one who had told me to come up, "You ought not to have got him up here. When he looks down he will be so scared he may fall." For the moment my attention was fixed upon the importance of my errand—the delivery of the trowel. But when that was done, true to the perversity of our natures, I looked down to see for myself what it was that would frighten me so greatly as to make me liable to fall. Being a mere child the distance was appalling. I felt sick and dizzy. Overwhelmed, I would have fallen had I not, at that instant, heard the assuring voice of my friend saying, "Look up, lad; keep looking up." Strength and control returned to my muscles and nerves. As I descended I kept my eyes turned upward to the men on the staging, and all the while, as he laid his bricks, one of them kept saying, "Look up, lad; keep looking up."

When I reached the ground, still looking up, I could see, against the ineffable blue of the sky, two men calmly laying bricks, and hear, like a cadence from another world, "Look up, lad; keep looking up."

So it is that through all the years of my life, whenever difficulties and dangers have attacked with appalling frightfulness, I have looked upward for safety.

That story brought back to my memory that glorious motion picture most of us saw both in the silents and in the talkies, *Seventh Heaven*. None of us shall ever forget that scene down in the dirty sewers of Paris with Chico and the Rat working away, when suddenly a deluge of vile water poured down through the manhole above and swept the Rat into the sewer. Chico pulled him out and saved him from drowning. As the Rat sat on the edge of the sewer Chico turned loose on him some of his own philosophy of life when he said, "I work in the sewers, Rat, but I live near the stars!"

Then he added, with a gesture of confidence and appealing nonchalance: "Never look down! Always look up! I never look down! I always look up! That's why I'm a very remarkable fellow!"

The Rat was duly impressed with this important person, Chico, and listened to his wisdom with open mouth and spirit. For had not Chico just rescued him from death in those sewers? Such a fellow was worth listening to; and perhaps never more so than when he said those immortal words: "For those who will climb it, Rat, there is a ladder which leads from the depths to the heights; from the sewer to the stars! And as you climb, fellow, keep looking up! I always look up! I never look down! That's why I'm a very remarkable fellow!"

And, as we remember the play, Chico's philosophy worked, for he did climb from the sewer to the street level of life; and then from the street level of life to the "Seventh Heaven" of life which was love!

Buoyant, optimistic, self-reliant, self-confident Chico; what a tonic he is to all of us! That very human, universal phrase wins our hearts, for we all of us have a little of the Chico in us—thank God!

$$* \quad * \quad *$$

THE STONE REJECTED

Long after the American continent had yielded to the coming of the white man, an aged Indian, half-naked and famished, wandered into one of the Western trading posts begging for food. He was wearing a bright-colored ribbon around his neck, of which he was proud. A leather pouch, frayed at the edges and worn thin in places, hung from the ribbon. The poor old Indian was asked what the pouch contained. In his broken English he replied that it was a "charm" given him in his younger days when he had left the United States Army. Willingly the Indian opened the leather pouch and showed its contents to the curious settlers. Inside there was a faded paper which had been carried by the Indian in the leather pouch for a lifetime. It was a regular discharge from the army, entitling him to a good pension for life.

Many of us lack the knowledge to recognize the real value of the talents, capacity to love, the friends, health, and faith we already have.

The average person has some talent, skill, or ability which has value far beyond the knowledge of its possessor. Take just one type of ability, that of writing. Margaret Mitchell did not know she could write while she was writing her sensational first novel, *Gone With the Wind*. But when a skilled editor got hold of the rough draft of her manuscript he lost no time in publishing it in a book which millions have evaluated highly. We can rarely judge correctly our own ability. But we can find people who can properly evaluate our kind of ability.

One of the soldiers of Alexander the Great was searching for treasures in the palace of Darius. He found a leather bag containing the almost priceless crown jewels of Persia. They were worth millions, but the stupid soldier was ignorant of the value of jewels. In fact, he did not know a jewel when he saw one. So he shook out the little glittering stones into the rubbish heap and saved the leather bag. He went around boasting about the fine bag he had found for carrying his food.

But the man of expert skill, the artist, can tell true value in any surroundings or wherever found. Michelangelo was walking with some friends one day through an obscure street in Florence. He saw a block of marble, rough, shapeless, stained, lying amid a heap of rubbish. Others had passed it by carelessly, but his own keen eye saw that it was a treasure, and he began to clean away the filth that obscured it. "What are you doing with that worthless rock?" said one of his companions. "There is an angel in that stone," said Angelo, "and I must get it out."

Once I told some students the story of the Chinese tramp who had picked up a lot of brightly shining stones he found in the mountains. He carried them on his back to a city in the valley of the Yellow River. One morning he lay starving with his head pillowed on that bag. Some of the stones had fallen out of the bag and were lying in the sunlight. A stranger came up to the starving tramp and said, "What are you doing here?" The tramp replied, "I'm starving to death. I haven't had a bite to eat in days."

The stranger picked up one of the stones, examined it carefully and said, "Yes, you are like the average Chinaman; you are starving with a bag of gold in your possession."

Ernest Poole once wrote a great novel on that theme and called it *Beggars' Gold,* and in that novel he set forth the real truth that most of us are "Beggars Sitting on Bags of Gold." And he was right, for most of us do have the gold of friendship, loved ones, a civilized community in which to live; a nation which is at peace while so much of the world is at war; we are citizens of a government which is determined to bring to the people everlasting peace and security. We most of us have health or the possibilities of health within our grasp if we but reach out for it. We have schools, libraries, art galleries, public parks and playgrounds for the asking. We have sanitation, hospitals such as no other nation on earth has. We have the radio reaching out to us; and all we have to do is to turn a little knob and the truth, beauty, art, and news of the world are ours. But many of us pass it up as if it were not there. We are like that old Indian; we are "Beggars Sitting on Bags of Gold."

* * *

FORGET-ME-NOTS

FLOWERS cheer us! They tell us of God and remind us of our kind heavenly Father who made them and us. There is a pretty legend about the first flowers that ever bloomed upon the earth.

After God had made them all and given them their names there was one little flower who forgot her name. So she went back to God and said, "Please, dear Father, I forgot my name," and God replied, "I am glad you did not forget me. I shall call you 'Little Forget-Me-Not.'"

Flowers are messengers of love, cheer, and sympathy. They

146

can speak to others for us. That's why we have the slogan, "Say it with flowers!"

A story is told of a great German poet named Uhland. He was a very learned but modest man, and when the King of Prussia offered to give him the badge of an order that many famous people were glad to receive he declined to accept it.

While the poet was explaining to his wife the reason which moved him to refuse the honor there was a knock at the door. A little peasant girl from the neighborhood entered and, presenting to Mr. Uhland a bunch of "Little Forget-Me-Nots," said, "This is a gift from my mother."

"Your mother, child!" replied the poet. "I thought she died last autumn."

"That is true, Herr Uhland," said the little girl, "and I begged you at that time to make a little verse for her grave, and you kindly sent me a beautiful poem. These are the first 'forget-me-nots' which have bloomed on Mother's grave. I have plucked them, and I like to think she sends them to you with her greetings."

The poet's eyes moistened as he took the flowers, and, putting them into his buttonhole, he said to his wife, "There, dear woman, is not that something more valuable than any king can give?"

The precious thing about all this is that this grace of heart—this gentle, generous, loving interest in others, which is so fascinating, and this fragrance of a sympathetic and kindly nature, which is always so attractive—is in the reach of every one of us.

There are certain unforgettable people whom we meet in life. I have many of them in mind myself. One is Miss Mary I. Scott of Moundsville, West Virginia. There was a family of children in that town—five of them, to be exact—and their mother died when the oldest of those children was nine years old and the youngest nine months. Miss Mary was only a girl herself, but she felt a great sense of responsibility for that motherless family, and took them under her wings like a mother hen. She used to go into that home and talk with those children. She later invited them into her home and gave them of a culture and idealism that they would not have gotten otherwise. Finally, one by one she talked college to them and saw most of them off to a university; they hardly knowing what was happening to them, it was done so tactfully. Miss Mary is one of the unforgettable persons in my life. Then there was Mrs. Wendt, who taught an unruly boy to love the poets and books and the beautiful things in life. Then there was an old gray-haired teacher in a business college in Wheeling, West Virginia, whose name was Stevenson. I went to that school to catch up in my mathematics to get ready for my entrance examinations for college. The head of that business college turned me over to Mr. Stevenson. He took me into a little room to teach me mathematics. The first thing he did was to read to me from Young's *Night Thoughts*. That took all the morning of my first lesson in mathematics. So, day by day, it went on that summer. He taught me to know Tennyson, Shelley, Byron, Keats. I learned little mathematics that summer —just enough to get into college—but I did come to know and appreciate the great poets and masters of all time. And because he did introduce me to them that old gray-haired teacher is one of the Forget-Me-Nots in my life. The world is full of them. There are those who do some kindly deed for others each day; those who point out to us a beautiful poem, sunset, tree, river, mountain peak or flower; those who come to us in a moment of suffering, bewilderment, and sorrow; those who sacrifice for us without stint; those who battle for us and help us to keep faith in ourselves because they have faith in us—these are the unforgettable personalities of life; these are the forget-me-not flowers of the human ways.

* * *

BRIDGES TO THE MOON

HENRY DAVID THOREAU, the New England philosopher, once said of man that in youth he gets together the materials to build a bridge to the moon and in middle life he uses those materials to make a woodshed out of them.

That sounds like a pessimistic utterance, if one does not stop to examine it carefully and if one does not happen to be a realist in life.

The fact of the matter is that in youth one ought to be about the business of hitching his wagon to the stars, and of gathering the material to build a bridge to the moon. He ought to have what Dickens called "Great Expectations." I remember once in youth that I took charge of a certain secondary Methodist school in Rhode Island. It was a down-and-out, run-down-at-the-heels, dilapidated, ramshackle school. Its buildings were ready for the dump heap; its curriculum was antiquated; its teaching staff ready for the morgue. But a young group of us took hold of it, because we didn't have any better sense. We just didn't know enough to know that that school could never be resuscitated. We were too young to know that it couldn't be kept alive. So we planned to make it one of the great schools of America.

We used to go about New England speaking on that school and our plans for it; and it must have sounded like so much bombast to the oldtimers. I remember one evening speaking in a certain New England church on the subject of that school and what we were going to do with it. I know now that I was a whirlwind of fantasy in that speech. Then a kindly old gray-haired bishop got up. He was six feet tall and had lived in New England all his days. I remember what he said about my speech. It wasn't much but it meant a lot. He said, "I make it a point never to throw cold water on the enthusiasms of youth." What he meant was that even he didn't think it could be done, but he wouldn't be one who would discourage a young fellow who thought that it could be done. And he didn't. And it was done! That school still stands, and it got its chief impetus from those five years we spent in it because we didn't know that it could not be saved.

Yes, youth ought to spend its time gathering material to build a bridge to the moon; but as the years go by youth will discover that it is not going to use those materials to do that particular thing.

I remember a young chap with whom I used to work who had a phrase, "I've got the world by the tail and I'm swinging it around my head." In the exuberance of his youthful experience he actually felt that the world was his oyster to open at his will; and he fully expected every oyster to have a pearl in it. I have watched that particular man develop. He expected to be one of the great of the earth. He has never realized that dream. But I have also watched him, in a very matter-of-fact way, in a very practical fashion, take all the material he had gathered together to build a bridge to the moon—and he is now actually running a co-operative farm down in Louisiana, and he is doing a fine job of it. He did not do all that he dreamed he would. But he is doing something very useful and practical.

I know a mother who in her girlhood was a great musician. She went to New York City, stormed the gates of the Metropolitan Opera, won her way in an audition, and was acclaimed all over the United States as another Jenny Lind. The newspapers were full of her spectacular story. I doubt if there ever has been a more dramatic Cinderella story. Then in two years she was through as a Metropolitan singer. Her voice was not up to it. It was a great disappointment to her and to her friends. Then she retired for two years. Now she has come back in a different field—the field of radio—and she has a very happy and successful career in this field. She took the material which she originally intended to use in building a bridge to the moon and used it to make a happy life in a lesser field.

It is a universal trait that most of us in youth expect to turn the world upside down. That is characteristic of youth. But, also, most of us soon learn that that supreme achievement is not for us. We learn that ninety per cent of the people of the world are failures as far as their early ambitions and aims are concerned. That is why Dr. Parker, one of the greatest preachers in the world, at the end of his career said, "If I had my ministry to live over again I would preach more to broken hearts." He meant by that that the majority of human beings meet defeat, never realize their dreams, look upon themselves as failures. However, the practical man, the realist, the philosopher of life,

150

is the man who takes the material with which he originally intended to build a bridge to the moon, and builds out of it a woodshed, a home, a small business in a small town; he builds a reputation as a good common everyday citizen, a comrade, a brother to his fellow man in the spirit of this poem:

I have hoped, I have planned, I have striven,
  To the will I have added the deed;
The best that was in me I've given,
  I have prayed but the gods would not heed.

I have dared and reached only disaster,
  I have battled and broken my lance;
I am bruised by a listless master
  That the weak and the timid call Chance.

I am old, I am bent, I am cheated
  Of all that Youth urged me to win;
But name me not with the defeated.
  Tomorrow again I begin.

Tomorrow I build me a mansion
  Of simple and unadorned wood,
A hut on the hill for my family,
  A shelter for love and my brood.

I am through with the stars and the planets;
  I'm ready to settle for life
In a house or a hut in the commonplace way
  With children and friends and my wife.

*   *   *

"WE JES' LIVE"

Dr. C. M. McConnell, one of America's great naturalists and authorities on rural matters, recently told me this story:

One summer day a back-road farmer in one of Vermont's narrow valleys was sitting, half asleep, under an old maple tree in his front yard. A car load of "summer people" drove up to the farmhouse and stopped. The driver inquired the way to a nearby historic spot. They got the desired information in a few words, for the farmer was not one to waste language. Not content with the information about directions, the questioner added, "For mercy sake, what do you people do all the time, away off here so far from everything?"

The farmer looked around him at the lovely sloping lines of the mountains which rimmed the valley, at the river flowing through the fields, at the familiar sights around his homestead, and answered in astonishment at the ignorance of the questioner, "Do? Why, we jes' live."

Millions have found the abundant life in the remote and quiet countryside as well as in tiny villages and hamlets. Richard Henry Stoddard put in verse something of this fine flavor of country life:

> Happy the man who tills his field,
>   Content with rustic labor;
> Earth does to him her fullness yield,
>   Hap what may to his neighbor.
> Well days, sound nights—oh, can there be
> A life more rational and free?

The one man in American life who found time to "jes' live" close to nature and interpret the common things about him more than anyone else was Henry D. Thoreau.

In March, 1845, Ellery Channing wrote to Thoreau: "I see nothing for you in this earth but that field which I once christened 'Briars.' Go out upon that, build yourself a hut, and there begin the process of devouring yourself alive." Thoreau took his advice, borrowed an ax from his neighbor, Bronson Alcott, cut down some white-pine timber beside Walden Pond to build a hut, moved into it, and lived there alone for two years.

"Devouring yourself alive" meant—to this man who had set out to live—watching and listening, studying, thinking, dreaming, attending to the varying moods of the pond; writing in his journal; testing the virtues of the great world outside by the simple truths he learned from his secluded existence. But Thoreau can tell us in his own words why he lived close to nature:

I went to the woods because I wished to live deliberately, to front only the essential facts of life, to see if I could learn what it had to teach, and not, when I came to die, to discover that I had not lived. I wanted to live deep, to live so sturdily and Spartan-like as to put to rout all that was not life.

All health and success does me good, however far off and withdrawn it may appear; all disease and failure helps to make me sad and does me evil, however much sympathy it may have with me or I with it. If, then, we would indeed restore mankind by truly natural means, let us first be as simple and well as nature ourselves, and take up a little life into our pores.

When, near the close of his life, someone inquired if he had made his peace with God, he replied, "We have never quarreled."

The trouble with most of us is that we have never learned to live in any full, free sense. We run a routine. We allow ourselves to be regimented. We have certain beaten paths along certain village or city streets, and we take those same paths daily and ceaselessly and never get out of them. We allow ourselves to be routined and regimented by things. Things weigh us down. We never get a chance to live. And it is no fault of God's or life or fate. Men who have deserted the cities and gone to cast their lot with nature have learned to live. Henry David Thoreau, John Muir, John Burroughs—what a glorious lot they are! And when John Muir died, Charles L. Edson wrote of him in the New York *Evening Mail:*

> John o' the mountains, wonderful John,
> Is past the summit and traveling on;
> The turn of the trail on the mountain side,
> A smile and "Hail!" where the glaciers slide,
> A streak of red where the condors ride,
> And John is over the Great Divide.
>
> John o' the mountains camps today
> On a level spot by the Milky Way;

And God is telling him how He rolled
The smoking earth from the iron mold,
And hammered the mountains till they were cold,
And planted the redwood trees of old.

And John o' the mountains says: "I knew,
And I wanted to grapple the hand o' you;
And now we're sure to be friends and chums
And camp together till chaos comes."

$*$ $*$ $*$

"FACE YOUR FEARS, FRIEND!"

IN HIS first inaugural address and several times before, President
Roosevelt made a statement which I am sure all of us remember.
"The only thing we have to fear," he said, "is fear itself—name-
less, unreasoning, unjustified terror which paralyzes needed efforts to convert retreat into advance."

How perfectly that truth applies to the following story of the
people of a former day who were also harassed and driven by a
fear which proved to be groundless. Some four centuries ago, at
the time of the last Tartar invasion of Russia, there took place
one of the most unusual incidents in all history, an amazing example of the desperation to which people are sometimes driven
by *fear,* fear of evils which do not even exist.

It was during the war between the Tartars and the Russians in
the fall of 1462 that the two armies met on the opposite banks
of the Oka River, about two hundred miles east of Moscow, for
the final decisive battle of the war. For several days the two
opposing forces had been engaged in bitter fighting across the
waters of the Oka. Every attempt of the invaders to cross the
river was frustrated by the terrific onslaughts of the Russian
soldiers, who time and again drove the Tartar hordes back to the
opposite shore. The Russian defenders were far inferior in numbers, but the waters of the Oka were their protection, and it be-

gan to appear as if that natural line of defense would enable them to hold the barbarians at bay.

Then something happened which struck fear into the hearts of the Russians. A cold wave suddenly swept down the snow-clad peaks of the Ural Mountains, and the waters of the Oka began to freeze over. Once the ice was strong enough to support them, the Tartars could cross over, and, with their superior numbers, annihilate the forces of the Russian army.

Night had fallen, and the noise of the day's battle had ceased. Around the camp fires groups of Russian soldiers began to mutter in excited tones about the threat of the thickening ice and the advantage it would give to the enemy. As the force of the gale increased and the weather became steadily colder, their fears grew to a panic, and before midnight the entire army took to flight.

On the following morning, when dawn began to appear and the Tartar sentries were able to see across the river to the opposite shores, they found, to their amazement, that the enemy had vanished. Immediately they suspected a trick; perhaps the Russians had crossed the river several miles to the east and would suddenly attack from the rear. Some of the officers began to urge a retreat. Fear of what the Russians were up to, uncertainty as to their tactics, soon spread throughout the camp, and in less than two hours the entire Tartar host had abandoned its tents and was in full retreat. The two panic-stricken armies were running away from each other!

The Russians did not stop until they had reached the walls of Moscow, a distance of almost two hundred miles, and the Tartars continued their headlong flight until they arrived at the banks of the Volga River. Fear had driven the two armies in opposite directions as they fled from a danger which existed only in their imaginations. And history records this to be the last serious invasion of Russia by the Tartars.

Think of the millions of people who in their own personal lives are continually running away from something which doesn't really exist—driven by the haunting fear of an evil which lives only in their own imaginations. Our sanitariums are filled with thousands of such people.

We would all do well to recall, now and then, the words of Thomas Jefferson, "How much pain have cost us the evils which have never happened!"

One of the most practical phrases I ever heard is, "Face your fears!"

That is what happened in John Masefield's "The Hell Hounds," when all the countryside was terrorized by the shadowy Hounds of Hell which drove the people indoors at night. But when the priest actually faced the leader of these Hell Hounds he found a shriveled old woman, weak and cowardly, and cried out:

> Open the doors and let Him in,
>   That beauty with the sword;
> The hounds are silly shapes of sin,
>   They shrivel at a word.

✳   ✳   ✳

THE GOOD EARTH

MRS. MARIE POWELL knows how to tell a good story, and here is proof of it. She says:

Monica Shannon has written a delightful story for young people about Dobry, the Bulgarian peasant boy who longed to be an artist and fashion in tangible form the dreams of beauty which haunted him, but whose mother, Rhoda, felt that his place was tilling the soil as his fathers had done before him.

It was Grandfather, seventy years old and still lusty and full of the zest of life, who alone understood the boy's urge to create and who finally persuaded Rhoda to let the boy go to an art school in Sofia.

But that consent was given only after one Christmas Eve when Dobry, coming down the hill from the village church at the close of the quaint Byzantine service, lingered behind the rest of the villagers, all bobbing homeward with their lighted candles. Out in the icy cold Dobry worked the night through, fashioning of ice and snow a Nativity—a Nativity born of the peasant earth itself, for Mary, Joseph, and the Child were all peasants—his Joseph looking for all the world like Grandfather himself. For oxen he modeled his own two and, last of all, he added the little goat they all loved.

In the morning Grandfather and Rhoda, hurrying out to do the morning chores, were caught and held spellbound by the beauty of the scene, and knelt without knowing that they did so. After a long silence Rhoda said: "You are right. God made Dobry an artist, and who am I to set my heart against it?"

But Grandfather's greatest gift to Dobry was in making Dobry conscious of his heritage of the good earth; in making their days in the open close to the earth a sacrament. It was Grandfather who glorified those long days of plowing and sowing by saying: "You carry there under your arm a whole field of tall blowing wheat. A whole wheat field! Every little seed is alive, all of life in it. You are carrying all our next winter's bread!" And Dobry felt very strong and proud.

It was Grandfather who said, as he picked up a golden autumn leaf and placed it in his sash: "You see, the autumn leaf is the most prized leaf, most beautiful. That's the way old age should be always, the most beautiful time of life."

They were on the hillside with Asan, the shepherd boy, as Grandfather spoke; and the two boys, looking at Grandfather, so tall, so erect, so full of life, felt that his words were indeed true. Asan said, "And you are the greatest story-teller in the whole Balkans too!" Asan felt the questioning wonder everybody feels when he sees a really living person who warms other people with that spark of God he always keeps burning in himself.

Grandfather took their lunch out of his capacious sash and, breaking the bread across his knee, divided the food, and said as he did that: "When we eat the good bread we are eating months of sunlight, weeks of rain and snow from the sky, richness out of the earth. We eat everything now—clouds even. It all becomes part of us—sun, clouds, rain, snow, and the rich earth. We should be great, full of music and full of stories; able to run the

157

way the clouds do, able to dance like the snow and the rain."

So it was that Dobry, the peasant boy, when he became Dobry, the artist, could never throw off the spell of the good earth, but would see it through the years as a part of himself.

In the same spirit Lawrence of Arabia relates a curious incident which reveals man's hunger for something far more fundamental than represented by his own design and craftsmanship. With an Arab friend he rode far out in the desert to the ruins of an ancient palace which, according to tradition, had been erected by a Roman ruler for his queen. Legend has it that the mortar was kneaded, not with water, but with the essential oil of flowers. In each room the odor was different. The Arab led Lawrence about, explaining that this was the rose room, this the jasmine room, that the violet room, and they sniffed the atmosphere for the lingering scent of those lovely flowers. At length the Arab said, "But, come, smell the best odor of all," and, taking him to a broken casement, they smelled the clean air off the desert. It had come long and lazily over hundreds of miles from the far-away Euphrates, over vast expanse of desert where no human habitation is found. Lovingly it had whispered among the grasses and played with the sands until it possessed within itself the essence of the good earth, the mother of all mankind. Deeply the two men smelled, drinking it into their souls in that mystic affinity which man feels for the dust from whence he came and to which he shall at last return.

And Bishop Quayle once said, as we stood on his prairie farm in Kansas on a hot summer day: "William, the desert is brewing clean air for a continent to breath today." He knew the glory of the good earth.

*　　*　　*

"TRUSTING THE COMMONPLACE"

THE morning had been a particularly nerve-racking one in the office of the manager and so at noon he decided to take a brief

158

stroll about the mine. It was a famous diamond mine in the interior of southern Africa, intensely interesting to the few chance visitors, but indeed commonplace and ordinary to him. Only a few minutes had slipped by before his attention was abruptly snatched from his leisurely dreaming to a large sparkling object at his feet. At first he thought it to be nothing but a mere piece of broken bottle, but upon closer examination it turned out to be a large and beautiful diamond. It was about the size of a small lemon, perfect in every detail and outstanding in size, the mine's largest diamond.

Almost immediately the question arose, how was such a large and priceless gem to be transported safely all the way from southern interior Africa to busy London? Amid much difficulty and perplexity, anxiety and worry, a method of transportation was finally decided upon.

Four husky men heavily armed were given a little square package to carry in their careful custody on a long journey. They had to walk sixty miles through the jungle in order to reach the railroad. During that time two of the men stayed on guard constantly; never for one split second did they dare let the package out of their sight. When finally they reached the railroad a special car was chartered to carry them to the seacoast. On the ship which was to take them to England a new and extra-heavy safe was, at considerable expense, constructed in the hull. When finally the men reached England an entire special train was waiting to take them, under heavy police guard, to London, where they were to deliver the little box.

The great moment arrived, and with extensive police guard outside, and general excitement reigning within, the excited guests pressed eagerly forward, each one on his toes, stretching his neck just a bit that he might get the first glimpse of the glittering object. When the box was unwrapped they saw, to their utter surprise and complete astonishment, nothing but a little chunk of black coal. And where was that precious diamond? Let me tell you the rest of the scheme.

Back at the mine the wise manager had wrapped that priceless gem in ordinary cotton wool, put it in an ordinary pasteboard

159

box, wrapped it up in ordinary brown paper, tied it with ordinary string, and, what is even more surprising, had it sent through the ordinary, common parcel-post system without even the postal officials being aware of his plans. This valuable diamond had been sent all the way from the black and desolate interior of southern Africa to London, over land and sea, through sparsely and densely populated sections, by the mere common, ordinary everyday method of life. It had received no more attention than a postcard greeting which perhaps some mythical Mr. Jones had hurriedly dispatched to his little wife at home bearing the wholly original greeting, "wish you were here." Nor had this priceless gem received any more attention than the thousands of circulars blaring forth the miraculous results of a bottle of Madam Astolot's Peppy Pills for Pious People. The diamond, of course, arrived safely, and when questioned about the plan the manager remarked: "For years the postal system has been doing its task in a trustworthy manner. So dependable and careful has it been with the lesser and almost insignificant things that I knew the gem would be perfectly safe. When you find folks who handle the little tasks of life dependably and well, valuable things may safely be trusted with them."

What a parallel to life! Dependability and perfection in the smaller tasks lead to greater responsibility and opportunity. That is the law of success. When one is faithful over a little, new opportunities will present themselves continually. The task that may seem meager and mean today, when well done will lead to a greater tomorrow. To get the most out of life, one must master the insignificant daily tasks naturally and thus open the doors to the more valuable experiences of life.

It is a universal experience that most of us have to trust the most valuable and precious things of life to the ordinary, everyday vehicles and people, the trusted, tried, and true things we live by.

The food we eat comes to us through most ordinary hands from garden, field, store, and home. The average human being never travels in state, but he has to take the average, everyday public vehicles of life. After all, there is a place for all of us in this scheme of things: the ordinary, everyday, faithful, homely, uneducated, even uncultured human being, providing he has been faithful through the tests of life to the ordinary tasks which have been entrusted to him. That is the glow and the glory of the commonplace.

God often entrusts his most precious jewels of personality to ordinary, everyday parents and homes. I cannot forget Abraham Lincoln, nor the fact that Saint-Gaudens, America's most famous sculptor, was born over a livery stable in New York City to a livery-stable keeper and an Irish washerwoman. Nor can I forget that when God the Father sent his only begotten Son to this earth he made the first announcement of that arrival to shepherds watching in their fields by night; and when Jesus, in turn, planned to propagate his gospel he gave it over to twelve uncouth, uncultured men, horny-handed men of the sea and soil; farmers, fishermen, and men of the common walks of life.

✳   ✳   ✳

STRENGTH AND BEAUTY THROUGH STRUGGLE

Dr. Joseph Fort Newton once told a group of preachers a beautiful story which I want to use to launch the ship of this chapter.

It was the story of a certain amateur naturalist who watched an emperor moth slowly making its laborious way from the chrysalis stage. Day by day it struggled, strove, and squirmed its way, trying to emerge from its cocoon. As he watched this process he seemed to hear a cry like the cry of the unborn babe, "I want to be born! I want to be born!" in a drama of a few years ago entitled *The World We Live In.*

The opening of that cocoon was so narrow that the amateur naturalist decided to give that emperor moth some help from the outside, so he took his penknife and cut into the narrow end of the cocoon, slightly enlarging the opening so that it would be

161

easier for the moth to emerge. It seemed to him that so harsh a struggle ought to be ended as quickly as possible. He felt sorry for that moth just as many of us parents in this day feel sorry for our children when we see them battling through some hard problem; struggling through a dense wood, or a denser experience. We hate to see them puzzled, bewildered or hurt so we lift the load for them, make life easier for them by stepping in and helping them. We even go so far as to make it so easy for them that they never know the joy of getting up before daylight in the morning to go to the pasture for the cows, warming their cold bare feet in the spot where the cows laid all night. We make it so easy for them that they never know the joy and delight of overcoming hard things; having certain definite chores to do on Saturday morning—a cow to milk, wood to cut; newspapers to deliver in the early morning hours, dishes to wash, rooms to sweep. We want to save them from all the hard things of life, just as that amateur naturalist did for that emperor moth emerging from the cocoon into its new life. So we cut a hole in the cocoon, and the next day or the next month or year we discover what the naturalist discovered.

The struggler has, indeed, ended his conflict and the moth has arrived into a new world. But its wings are imperfect; it can flutter feebly on the ground but it cannot fly. It is feeble and frail, and before night it has sickened and died or its natural ground enemies have eaten it. It cannot battle its own way in its environment because its wings did not go through the long hard process of struggle which is necessary to develop large strong wings. By too much kindness that amateur naturalist had been an enemy to that moth. Too soft-hearted, he had unwittingly deprived the moth of the strength to be developed only by severe struggle and achievement of its way out of that old cocoon into its new level of life. Struggle is God and nature's way to development and strength—even to beauty, for strong wings are even more symmetrical and beautiful than weak wings. So are a strong body and a strong character more beautiful in a child than weak ones. Struggle puts iron in the blood, color in the cheeks, light in the eyes, confidence in the soul.

George Gray Barnard said it beautifully in his famous white statue, "The Struggle Between the Two Natures." I had the rare privilege of having that great sculptor take me to the Metropolitan Museum in New York City once and interpret that group to me. You will remember it as two glorious white marble male figures, exactly alike; one lying on the earth, the other standing on top of the lower figure with one foot on his thigh and one on his neck. As you look at those two vibrant figures they seem to be alive. They are like two wrestlers with every muscle bulging in struggle. They are exactly alike. No man can tell the difference between the two. I asked Mr. Barnard what he intended to say. He replied: "It is the everlasting struggle that goes on between our lower or physical natures and our higher or spiritual natures. Some people call it 'The Two Natures,' but I like to think of it as 'The Struggle.'" Then I said to him, "Mr. Barnard, which is winning?"

He replied, with a smile: "I do not tell that. Sometimes the physical wins, and sometimes the spiritual nature wins. It is different in different lives. It is not the sculptor's task to say which wins. It is his task to picture the struggle, for only through constant struggle do we grow or do we attain victory. The struggle is the important thing in life."

And what nature pictures for us in this story and what that marble and a great sculptor confirms, a great poet, Robert Browning, in "Rabbi Ben Ezra," puts into unforgettable lines:

> Then, welcome each rebuff
> That turns earth's smoothness rough,
> Each sting that bids nor sit nor stand but go!
> Be our joys three-parts pain!
> Strive, hold cheap the strain;
> Learn, nor account the pang; dare, never grudge the throe!

✶   ✶   ✶

THE RAPTURE OF REBEGINNINGS

A GLOWING story has come to me recently from a famous newspaper editor in Detroit, Michigan, the Hon. James Schermerhorn, who founded the Detroit *Times,* and originated the famous Brisbane column, "Today." He is a man who himself has known illness, defeat, and disappointment, but who has risen above them all to achieve what he calls "The Rapture of Rebeginning" —as brave a man as ever lived, and who at seventy-three is still achieving.

He sends me the tale of Thomas Carlyle, which has an uplifting challenge for all of us today. Living in abject poverty for years, Thomas Carlyle toiled on *The History of the French Revolution,* the work that was to lift him above want and to raise him to a towering pinnacle in the eyes of the literary world. The manuscript of the first volume, finished by dint of tremendous industry and self-denial, he entrusted to a friend, John Stuart Mill, and feverishly awaited this authority's opinion of the work. Instead of gladdening Carlyle with the expected high appraisal, Mill visited the plodding historian one morning with heart-rending news. A housemaid had taken the result of Carlyle's labors from a desk and started a fire with it. What it cost the friend to convey such tragic tidings was nothing compared with the desolating effect upon the author. In his stricken mental state Carlyle felt he would never be able to write again.

But one day, brooding over the emptiness of his days, he looked through the window of his study upon a group of masons lifting in completeness and beauty a new building, brick upon brick, row upon row. In that example of patient construction Carlyle came upon the rapture of rebeginning.

Thrilled with the spectacle of persistent, painstaking effort, he sobbingly assured himself that he could restore, letter and line, the lost book. Thus, by recalling and rewriting the manuscript, *The History of the French Revolution* was saved for an applauding world—all because the uncapitulating Carlyle had seized the glory of another chance. And those of us who have read Carlyle's *History of the French Revolution* know that his fame will rest longer on that monumental work than on any other thing he ever did.

Some wise man of old once said that the chief glory of man is not that he never fails in his enterprise of life, but that he rises from each failure every time he fails. The Salvation Army puts it: "A man may be down, but he is never out!" And a poet has put it: "A man may rise on stepping stones of his dead self to higher things." Robert Louis Stevenson sang it: "The day returns and brings us the petty rounds of irritating concerns and duties. Help us to play the man!"

And an everyday father once wrote to a struggling son who had met some tragic disappointment: "Forget the rotten yesterdays; they don't come back. You are bound to make mistakes and many of them; and so do all men, including your boss. If you make anything you will make mistakes. The point is that you must never make the same mistake twice."

Which reminds us of some famous writers who failed and lost all of their money in mid-life. Edwin Markham, of whom I have spoken before, lost the savings of a lifetime at sixty-five—all the money he had hoped would keep him in his old age. But he began again and lived the most productive period of his life, spending his last years in economic security which he attained by the sweat of his brow in the years when other men would be retired and resting. General U. S. Grant lost his entire fortune in a book-publishing venture after he was sixty, and yet turned in and worked the last years of his life and paid every cent of his debt. Samuel L. Clemens (Mark Twain) did exactly the same thing, as did Sir Walter Scott, the famous novelist. Those are glorious and inspiring illustrations of men who in their old age had the rapture of rebeginnings.

But there is an even more human and dramatic story of Eugene Field. He had come to a full stop with his column in the Chicago days and was floored.

Finally, in that cut-glass handwriting, he sent this note to the managing editor: "I give up. There'll be no column tomorrow."

As he was slipping into his coat for Jake's around the corner, a reply came: "There's a printer downstairs whose three children are dangerously ill with scarlet fever. He's not giving up."

Field removed his coat and knocked out one of the best columns of his career.

The most exquisite writings flower from the depths. Heywood Broun never wrote a more graceful essay than the one that followed within a few hours the passing of his former wife, Ruth Hale.

The finest editorial I recall was William Allen White's brokenhearted farewell to his beautiful daughter, tragically killed by a fall from a horse.

*   *   *

THE HOUSE BEAUTIFUL

OUT of the wreckage of the World War there has been saved at least the redeeming memory of a village priest in Flanders who tried to rebuild his little church out of scraps of stone, stained-glass windows, broken pews, a part of the altar place salvaged from shell holes into which the debris of his church had been blown. There was even a part of the gold cross from the church spire still intact. When it became painfully obvious, however, that this devoted priest could not succeed in rebuilding his church, his friends volunteered the doubtful comfort that, "After all, it was only a house of stone and wood."

"Yes," admitted the priest, "but it had a *soul* and its soul was fighting for France."

Carl Sandburg had exactly the same feeling about the national Capitol at Washington when he saw its gilded dome against a midnight sky, shining in almost ethereal splendor; and looking beyond that shining golden dome to the Washington Monument, rising in slender grace, he saw another symbol of a great personality, the first President of our nation; and beyond that he looked to the Lincoln Memorial and was reminded that the great leaders give a nation its soul. And Carl Sandburg, knowing that even beyond the Washington Monument and the Lincoln Memorial was the Arlington National Cemetery, once exclaimed, "There is something there that men die for!" And Sandburg is right. There is something in that Capitol building, the Washington Monument, the Lincoln Memorial, the Arlington Cemetery that men die for; and they remind us every day that, in spite of political bickerings and selfishness, America has a soul.

And just as it is true that a church has a soul and a great city or national building, so is it true that a house has a soul if it has been lived in for long years by those who love each other, suffer together, laugh together, play together, and build up a community of interests through the years; watch children born and grow into childhood, into youth, and finally into manhood and womanhood. Two of my own friends have seen this eternal truth and have written graphically about it: Channing Pollock in that unforgettably human drama *The House Beautiful,* and Edgar A. Guest in his well-known verse, "It Takes a Heap o' Livin' in a House to Make It Home."

I have long wanted to say a word about divorce in this book, but I have waited until I could say a heartening word about divorce news; for somehow, since divorce is news the few times that it happens compared with the innumerable homes in which it does not happen, it gets news space out of all proportion to its percentage. In fact, we see so many stories of divorce that we get to thinking that it is general. It seems to me that it is about time somebody called attention to the prominent homes in which divorce has *not* occurred. I have had the privilege, for instance, of being in the lovely home of Fred Stone, the comedian. I have never seen a more glorious spirit of love, affection, and fun than they have in that home. Culture and affection are also there; freedom and a chance for each individual to develop in his own way. One day when I was lunching with the Stones we all went into the living room and spent an hour reading poetry, the girls, Dorothea, Paula, and Carol, lying on the floor and Fred and Mrs. Stone sitting in a big chair together. That home has been going for forty years with never a whisper of anything but complete happiness. It was the same thing in

167

the Will Rogers' home, and I once heard Will say, "I have the unique distinction in Hollywood of having lived with the same wife for thirty years and I intend to keep on doing it to the end." Cecil DeMille was once telling me about the influence that family prayers had had on him in his boyhood home, and I said to him, "Then if it was that important to your boyhood home, may I ask you if you still maintain that habit in your own home?" He replied with great reverence, "Yes, we do, and if we neglected it my guess is that the children would be the first to protest." And who can forget the affection that Theodore Roosevelt had for his home, nor the day following his defeat on the Progressive ticket when he wired Mrs. Roosevelt: "We are defeated, but nothing matters as long as I have you and the children."

No, not all the homes of the great of this nation are broken up through divorce. In Detroit a story is told of how a wealthy business man came into the Detroit Athletic Club and said to Mr. Hughes, the secretary, "Is it true that Eddie Guest is getting a divorce?"

"Of course it isn't true. That just couldn't happen," replied Mr. Hughes.

"Well, I'm glad to hear that, for my wife heard it on the train the other day and she cried all night long."

And thank God there is, deep in the heart of America, a reverence and a respect for those who keep their homes intact and who remain true to their marriage vows through the years; who look upon a marriage vow as a partnership of love. And it is that spirit in a house which makes it beautiful and gives it a soul.

$*$ $*$ $*$

"THE COWARDS NEVER STARTED"

THERE's a powerful never-say-die story in Carl Sandburg's tremendously gripping volume, *Abraham Lincoln: The Prairie*

Years. If present troubles seem beyond one's power of endurance turn to the chapter in which the seven-year-old Lincoln is awakened in his father's hut in Indiana by smoke from the log fire getting into his nostrils, and he goes to the window to gaze wonderingly at the moon. This is a part of the author's painfully vivid picture of the pioneer hardships and deprivations of the Middle West in the year 1816.

Then the poet-historian proceeds to answer the boy's imagined question as he gazes up at the moon, which is looking down on the loneliness of the Indiana wilds. "What do you see?" the boy Lincoln asks. The moon saw, in that year of 1816, sixteen thousand wagons come along one turnpike in Pennsylvania with people hungry for new land, a new home, just like Tom Lincoln. It saw eight million people in the United States, white men who had pushed the Indians over the Eastern mountains. It saw these home-seekers take from six weeks to six months crossing the Atlantic, suffering terrible sickness from old and sharply salted food and meat and bad and foul water. In wagons these thousands were slipping through the passes of the Allegheny Mountains, heading west for two-dollar-an-acre government land. At first the stream of wagons and settlers moving west had kept close to the Ohio River. Then it began spreading in fan shape up north and west. Then Sandburg sketches the terrible cost of this migration in the light of the moon that young Lincoln gazed upon from the window of his father's pole shed on Little Pigeon Creek, while the hoot owl cried and the branches of the beeches and walnut trees shook outside. The moon saw, along the pikes, roads and trails heading west; broken wagon wheels with prairie grass growing up over the spokes and hubs; and near by, sometimes, a rusty skillet, empty moccasins, and the bones of horses and men. In the hot days, in the long rains, in the casual blizzards, they had stuck it out and lost. There came a saying, a pithy, perhaps a brutal folk proverb: *"The cowards never started and the weak ones died by the way."*

Surely it will banish the faint-heartedness of the descendants of the valorous and the venturesome in this present troubled day if they will look thoughtfully and teachably at what Carl

Sandburg's moon saw in the period and at the time of the beginning of the Great Emancipator's preparedness for his destiny —the Abraham Lincoln of the Prairie Years.

> Must I be carried to the skies
>   On flowery beds of ease,
> While others fought to win the prize,
>   And sailed through bloody seas?

We are the heirs of all the ages, and it is good for our easily dismayed spirits to hear the voices that come out of the storied past, inspiring us to be worthy of our inheritance.

William Allen White caught the meaning of this pioneering spirit of other days in his book on Calvin Coolidge when he said: "The worst thing you could say about the Coolidge family is that none of them ever went West."

Perhaps the classical example of pioneering courage and tragedy is the immortal American story of the Donner family, which started from Lincoln's home town, Springfield, Illinois, and got caught in the twenty-foot snows of California near what is now called Donner Lake, in the Sierra Mountains, and most of them died of freezing and starvation. Out of one hundred who started only four or five survived. I talked with one of them, a Mrs. Houghton, in San Jose, California, when I was a young preacher in that city. The story of the Donner party is one of the great epics of American pioneer life and is a perfect illustration of the theme of this talk, that "The cowards never started and the weak ones died on the way," for "There were giants in the land in those days." And what we need today in these times of trouble and anxiety is to get back into our spirit something which is worthy of this magnificent lineage. The pioneers of a new nation who became martyrs to the cause of developing an unknown West ought to be an inspiration to us today as we, too, are called upon to pioneer a new social civilization. None but the brave and venturesome, none but the energetic and courageous, dared to undertake such a journey as the Donner party made and as men and women of Lincoln's day and town battled through. A certain grandeur, a certain heroism, clings about the men and women of those rugged days. Our trials are trivial compared with the things they went through to seek a new land, a new social order.

We in this day of new ventures should catch the spirit of a legend I saw on a gravestone in Sleepy Hollow Cemetery in Concord, Massachusetts. I scraped away the moss and found this sentence: "The grave of Ezra Ripley. He came of a long line of Pilgrim ancestors and Concord ministers and he was worthy of his lineage!"

✳ ✳ ✳

"I WAS BORN TO BE A KING"

IT IS in the days of the bloody Commune in Paris. Hear the rumble and roar of the mob as it sweeps down the Rue de Madelaine and out into the Place de Guillotine. Now they are pounding down the gates of the Tuileries gardens; and now they are thundering at the doors of the palace. They drag out Louis XVI. They bind him hand and foot and place his head upon the cruel block. They touch the spring, and the knife severs the head from the body. Again to the palace. They bring out the queen, Marie Antoinette. They lead her to the same cruel block and the same awful fate. Now they bring out the little Dauphin, the heir to the French throne, he who is to be Louis XVII, but never becomes such. There he stands with his golden locks falling down upon his shoulders, clad in softest velvet, trembling and fearing for his life. The mob shouts: "To the guillotine with the Dauphin! An end of royalty!"

As they were about to lead him to the bloody block, one man in the crowd cried, "Hold! Don't do that! You will only send him to heaven; I'll tell you what to do"—but before he could speak the mob cried, "Vive la Republique! Vive la Republique! To the guillotine with the Dauphin!" When the mob had

171

shouted itself hoarse and had ceased for a moment, this man cried out again, "Don't do that. I'll tell you what to do; hand the little fellow over to Old Meg [she was the vilest woman in Paris]; let her clothe him in rags, feed him on filth, teach him to lie and to steal and to swear, and all the practices of the gamin of the town; let Old Meg damn his soul and send the little devil to hell!"

Somehow the diabolical suggestion caught the fancy of the cruel mob. And so, according to some historians—we know they differ—they handed the little Dauphin over to Old Meg. She clad him in rags. She fed him with the cast-out food gathered from the barrels on the boulevard early in the morning. She taught him to lie, and swear, and steal, and all the wicked ways of the gamin. But it is said that every now and then when Old Meg would have him speak a word a little viler than any he had yet spoken, he would clench his little royal fists, and stamp his little royal foot, and say, "I will not say it! I will not say it! I will not say it! I was born to be a king, and I will not say it!"

Which reminds me this day of a long-ago dialogue from the New Testament between Pilate and Jesus in the Trial before Pilate's Court:

Pilate: "Art thou indeed a king?"
Christ: "To this end was I born, for this cause came I into the world—
to bear witness to the truth."

The little Dauphin was right; Jesus was right. Aren't we all of us kings in a very real sense, made in the image of God, born to have dominion over seaways, skyways, earthways; a little lower than the angels; or, as in some translations, "a little lower than the Godhead"? When we get that feeling about ourselves there can be "no small dealings," no little thinking, no unholy or unkind talking or acting; no living by lower laws in the presence of higher laws; no playing the game unfairly; no blows below the belt; no petty gossiping or cruel social conduct. Indeed, we have a right to have a great conceit of ourselves when we remember that we are all born to be kings.

172

Even the weak Dauphin in the story of Saint Joan turned into a courageous son of a king when Joan of Arc reminded him that he was of kingly lineage. You will remember the scene where a trap is set for Joan, and Bluebeard pretends to be the young Dauphin to see if Joan's spiritual powers of discernment are as true as she claims. Then they parade Bluebeard before her and she detects that deceit and immediately points out the Dauphin, drags him to the center of the stage, and tells him that she has a message for him from God. Charles tells her that he does not want any message from God and Joan says to him: "I tell thee, Charles, it is God's business we are here to do, not our own. I have a message to thee from God, and thou must listen to it, though thy heart break with the terror of it."

"But I am afraid," the Dauphin replies to her. And Joan says, "I shall put courage into thee."

Then Charles says that he doesn't want to have courage put into him; that he wants to sleep in a comfortable bed, and not live in a continual terror of being killed or wounded; and adds, "Put courage into the others, and let them have their bellyful of fighting; but let me alone."

And Joan adds: "It's no use, Charlie, thou art the son of a king. Thou canst not escape that. Thou must face what God puts on thee."

And so must all of us, since we are all made in the image of the King of Kings!

$*$ $*$ $*$

"HERE THEY ARE ALL HEROES"

ON THE highway to the Argonne Forest in France sped an American car in the rear seat of which sat a woman dressed in deep black. Her eyes were red from weeping and her face showed marks of her grief. Far from America she had come, at the close of the World War, to find the grave of her only boy. Early in the war, long before America had entered the World War, he had volunteered to help and he had given many months of service to France before he fell. All along the way from Rheims she had been thinking of him. Perhaps he had been in these trenches, perhaps in some dugout that she had passed; she did not know. But she felt that he had died bravely.

As she saw the desolation of the little towns, the great barren tracts of country, the lack of men and boys everywhere, the women doing heavy work in the fields, there grew more and more bitterness in her heart against Germany, that nation which had robbed her of her boy, the idol of her home.

She finally arrived at the cemetery, where there were thousands of crosses. On the one side there were many white ones, marking the graves of those who fought for France. On the other side there were equally as many black crosses to mark the graves of those who had worn the German uniform. On some of the graves were flowers which friends had left there.

Down the long row she made her way, looking often at the slip of paper sent her by the government to tell her in what section of the cemetery her boy was buried. And then at the very end of the cemetery she saw his name in black letters on the white cross. "Franklin Meade. Jan. 15, 1918. Mort pour la France."

For a long time the mother knelt by the little cross. She prayed for her boy and then for herself, that she might be as true as he had been to what she saw was right and good.

Finally she rose, unwrapped the great bundles that the chauffeur had brought from the car, and began to place the beautiful flowers on the grave. That was all she could do—at least his grave should be beautiful when she left it. She would cover it completely with all these flowers which he had loved so much. Stepping aside to arrange them more carefully, she suddenly became aware of a black cross close beside the white cross of her son; another one was just behind it. Why had they laid him beside the Germans? Her whole nature rose in revolt. Why should he have been put here when he gave so much freely for France? She could not understand it. She wanted him to lie surrounded by comrades, or else she would have brought him to the home cemetery.

So she stood by the grave and looked down the long lines on both sides. And then she realized that every black cross meant a boy or a man. Every one had meant as much to some mother as her Franklin had meant to her. In her mind she seemed to see a German mother kneeling by the grave next to her, angry that her son should lie by the side of the soldiers who had made her home desolate. How many mothers there would be if one were kneeling by every white and black cross! Oh, how much the mothers of the world had suffered! Unconsciously there was creeping into her face a look of great tenderness. The little black crosses no longer spoke of enemies; they told the story of boys and men who had obeyed the call of their country to protect their homes from what they believed was evil.

Once more she looked at her white cross, "Mort pour la France." Then she took a beautiful rose from the grave of her own son and laid it on the grave at the right which was marked with a cross of black. And then she laid flowers on all the black crosses in the neighborhood, and the red poppies made the place look cheerful. "A mother's love is big enough to take all boys in," she said softly to herself. "I am glad now that my boy has been laid here with other boys who loved their homes and their country. The boys were not to blame. When they have been put here they are all 'dead for their country.' How beautiful this little corner looks and how much better than if all the flowers had been heaped on Franklin's grave. I am sure he would have had it so."

The sun was sinking in the west and the sky was alight with color as she rose to go. So with a long last look she went back through the cemetery, thinking deeply of what she had seen. Then as she softly closed the gate behind her she said: "God keep them all, as he loved them all, and help the mothers of the world to teach the love that makes war impossible. Here they are all heroes."

✳   ✳   ✳

WHEN TO CUT AN ASH STICK

IN THE country where wood is plentiful there is much discussion among woodchoppers as to what is the best time to cut trees for firewood. "The best time to cut wood," an old New Hampshire farmer said to his neighbor who went to him for advice, "is when you have the time."

This wise remark of a man who knew well the difficulty of finding a convenient season for woodcutting calls to mind a story by Joseph Bentley about John the Yorkshireman and his master, Squire Brookley, an old English country gentleman.

John had been employed at one of the English country fairs by the squire for his shrewd common sense and integrity, along with a gift of plain blunt speech. John came to be sort of a handy reference man to whom all matters calling for a common-sense opinion were referred. These occasions arose frequently when the Squire and his friends sat late around the fireplace and argued about questions ranging from politics to farm practices.

For example, on one occasion when the Squire had two good friends with him for dinner the conversation turned to what was the best time of year to cut an ash stick.

At that time it was the custom for almost every man, young or old, rich or poor, to carry an ash stick. It was needful in walking narrow country lanes, in which either straying cattle or droves were likely to be met, and after sunset in lonely districts. It was by no means to be despised as a weapon of defense against the assault of the numerous footpads who infested the countryside.

The stick must be straight, of good proportions, and the handle must be a natural crook, or a thick piece which had grown at right angles with the stick. Such sticks were uncommon and hard to find. In the argument about the right time to cut such a stick there was a division of opinion among the Squire's friends. Should it be cut in the spring when the sap was rising in the wood, in the summer when the wood was at the top of its form, or in the autumn when the sap had matured and perfected the wood? The stick cut would then be strong, reliable, and enduring. The argument was heated and there was

176

no chance of an agreement among the Squire and his friends. Finally the question was put up to John.

"Now, John," said the Squire, "my friends and I have a dispute as to which is the best time of the year to cut an ash stick—spring, summer, or autumn. Can you tell us which is best?"

"When you see it," promptly responded John.

The wisdom of John's reply was fully appreciated by these countrymen who knew how hard a good ash stick is to find in the woods and how easily it is lost sight of. To mark the spot and try to return is as difficult as finding a new ash stick elsewhere. "Cut it when you see it" applies to a stick and "Cut your wood when you have the time" is the best advice about the proper time to cut firewood.

And this homely advice is good in other lines of work. How many times have you seen a rare beauty spot along a highway or in the woods and have said: "What a picture that would make. If I only had my camera along with me now." That's why you see signs along the highway, "Kodak as you go." The time to catch a rare scene, an unusual event, or a striking bit of beauty, is when you see it.

> There is a tide in the affairs of men,
> Which, taken at the flood, leads on to fortune

is the poet's way of saying, "Cut an ash stick when you see it." Or, as James Russell Lowell wrote in his "Present Crisis":

Once to every man and nation comes the moment to decide,
In the strife of truth with falsehood, for the good or evil side; . . . .
And the choice goes by forever 'twixt that darkness and that light.

I have traveled all over the world and I early learned a great lesson from an experienced wayfarer. Most people say to themselves, "I'll see that beauty spot, cathedral or art gallery the next time I visit Paris." Then there may be no next time. So my friend said to me: "See as much of everything worth seeing while you can. Don't put it off."

I have also had that experience with beautiful poetry and fine things I read in a magazine or paper. I like something; say to myself, "I'll cut that out"; lay the paper aside and forget to do it—and lose it forever. I am having that very experience with a poem a friend once sent me. It told all about that friend's impulse to write "Jim," his friend, a letter. He kept putting it off from time to time; but, always, in his heart, he meant to write to Jim. Years passed and he received a telegram simply saying, "Jim died today!" I wish I had that poem to illustrate this talk. It is haunting my memory, but when I saw it last, years ago, I failed to keep it. I meant to keep it; I wish I had when the impulse came. Perhaps some of you know it and will send it to me. Yes, the time to say that kindly, loving word to wife, child, teacher, business associate, secretary, friend is *now!*

* * *

OUR LITTLE IRON BEDS

THERE is recounted in Grecian mythology the story of a famous bandit named Procrustes, who lived in Attica. He had the unpleasant habit of forcing his victims to lie down on an iron bed which was part of his robber's equipment. If the unfortunate traveler were too long to fit the bed he lopped off as much of his limbs as would suffice to make the fit perfect. If the traveler were shorter than the iron bed Procrustes would put him on a rack and stretch him until he had reached the right length. And this inhuman torture satisfied Procrustes. He felt that all the travelers were very much better off inasmuch as they were now all of an equal length. One day a Grecian youth named Theseus, who had just come into warrior's estate and who was known for his courage and swordsmanship, decided to visit the home of his parents, taking the road where Procrustes lay in wait for the unwary. His grandfather vainly besought Theseus to take the water route and avoid the robber, but the young man was confident that he could successfully conquer the monster.

178

Consequently he clothed himself in his best suit of armor, clasped his faithful sword, mounted his prancing white charger and set forth on the road which led past Procrustes' dwelling. As he had anticipated, he no sooner reached Procrustes' section of land than the bandit attempted to hold him up. After a terrific struggle Theseus slew the giant robber. But he did not finish the job. Theseus only destroyed the bandit; he left the iron bed intact. Today the world is covered with little iron beds into which each owner tries to fit everyone else, lopping off limbs here and stretching bodies there.

We still have our little iron beds. Parents have them when they try to make their children over into models of themselves; when they refuse to allow a child to have an independent opinion of his own. Wives and husbands do it with each other; each trying to dominate the other and make the other fit into his or her picture of what a husband or wife should be; frequently creating untold suffering throughout a lifetime in a partnership which should be happy and inspiring for each. Dictators are our modern Procrustes; and God grant that we shall never allow one to regiment us and lay us out on some Hitler, Stalin, or Mussolini political or governmental bed of spikes.

Critics try to do it. They are perhaps a more universal breed of Procrustes than any other type, for we have them everywhere —in our homes, our towns, our cities, and throughout the nation. They hounded Washington, Lincoln, Wilson; and our incumbent Chief Executive is no exception.

Faultfinders try to put us all into little iron beds, because when people find fault it is usually on account of a feeling of inferiority they themselves have, and the only way they know to build up their own ego is to tear others down to their own level. Always remember that about chronic critics and faultfinders and it will comfort you who are victims of their spleen.

The school system of the nation is very apt to be a process of preparing little iron beds for humanity, training children in a way that stretches them out and cuts them down to fit a certain system rather than helping to develop the talents, genius, and personalities they have in embryo.

My dear friend Dr. Charles W. Gordon, the Ralph Connor of
Sky Pilot and *Black Rock* fame, visited my home in Boston and
we talked about an autobiography he was writing. He died a
few months later and the autobiography has since been published, entitled *Postscript to Adventure*—and what a book it is.
He knew about this matter I am discussing today—the little iron
beds—and says of them: "Everything seems to be made for us
today by someone else and somewhere else, far away. We are
cribbed, cabined, and confined by civilization. At times we feel
like reverting to our primitive barbarism."

But the best statement ever made on this universal desire we
all have to make people over into some form to fit our own ideas
was said by Robert Louis Stevenson when he hurled this terrific
indictment: "Most of us seem to think that it is our bounden
duty to make people good, but it is not. It is our sublime privilege to make them happy. If they are happy they will be good,
and we shall be pleased with them then."

$$* \quad * \quad *$$

"LOOK FOR ME IN THE STREET
TOMORROW"

MARTIN lived in Russia in a poor little town. He had a little
shoe-repair shop and used to sit at his bench all day, fixing the
worn and ragged shoes of the peasants who lived near. He was
very poor himself, but he was the kind of man who would never
accept very much money from people, so that he had to get
along with the barest necessities of life. However, Martin's life
was not bare, nor was it dull. Every day he did something kind
for people who needed help. No matter how little he had he
was always eager to share it with someone in need.

He enjoyed nothing more at night than to sit by the light of
the candle and read his Bible. He had come to know his Master
and to walk very closely with him. His heart yearned someday

to hear the voice of Jesus and to look on his face. But he was very happy in reading the precious words of the Bible.

One night as Martin lay asleep on his cot, he seemed to dream that he was working at his bench, and then suddenly he heard a clear, deep voice speaking to him. "Martin! Martin! In your heart you desire to see your Master. Look for me in the street tomorrow." And the voice died away. It surprised Martin so much that he awoke with a start, jumped from his bed and looked around the room. He saw nothing, but he felt a deep thrill of happiness because he had dreamed that he heard the voice of Jesus, and he went to bed anxious for the dawn to come. All day long he would look in the street, to see if by any chance his dream would come true.

In the morning the dawn seemed even brighter than it had ever been before, and Martin went to his bench eager for whatever the day might bring. As he worked, he watched constantly out upon the street through the narrow little window, but nothing unusual happened. The dreary day made Martin feel a little disappointed. He wanted so much to know the meaning of his dream and he felt sure that something would happen.

Suddenly there was a loud call in the street; the angry voice of a woman scolding a little boy. Martin went to the door to see what was happening and found that a street urchin had stolen an apple from the cart of the old lady on the corner. The woman complained in loud tones to Martin, and the little boy, being caught for his misdeed, was already sorry. "Come in," said Martin, "and let us talk it over." The boy put the apple back on the cart; but Martin knew he must be very hungry so he gave the apple to the boy and some money to the applewoman. The boy apologized to the woman and helped her to wheel the cart away.

Martin went back to his work, but before he had gotten well started again he heard sounds of weeping, and looking up into his little street window he noticed that a mother, carrying a tiny baby, was leaning against the building trying to protect the baby from the chill of the cold air. In his heart Martin sorrowed for the woman and for the little child. He went to his door and asked the mother to come in and warm herself and the baby by his humble fire. With tears of gratitude she eagerly hovered over the fire to warm the tiny precious bundle. Martin poured some tea and the two of them sat down in the warmth and comfort of the little fire, and the woman told Martin of her struggle for existence since her husband had died. Martin went to his beloved Bible and read a few lines to her, until her face shone with radiance and peace. When she arose to go, Martin took off his coat and wrapped it around the baby, and the woman went away happy.

Back to work Martin went. Though the room was chilly, his heart was warm. But he still watched the windows in the street.

Soon a knock came to the door and Martin opened it. A wounded soldier stood there. His arm was bleeding and he was faint and weary. Martin helped him carefully into the room, placed him on his own cot to rest, and tenderly bandaged the wounded arm. After the soldier had rested a while he went away feeling strong again.

Now the day was nearly passed, and Martin went to his Bible to read. As he read, a voice like that of the street urchin called, "Martin, Martin." Martin looked up, but saw nothing. Again the voice called, in the tones of the mother, saying, "Martin, Martin." Martin stood up and looked around anxiously. Finally, in the deep voice came the words: "Well done, my good and faithful servant. I was hungry and ye gave me meat. I was cold and ye sheltered me. I was wounded and ye ministered unto me."

Martin's eyes fell upon his Bible, and with a rejoicing heart he read those words: "Inasmuch as ye have done it unto the least of these my brethren, ye have done it unto me."

*　　*　　*

"THE ERROR WAS MINE"

WHEN the St. Francis dam in Southern California broke and the water swept down the valley, causing terrible loss of life and property, there came the usual investigation and the customary effort to fix the blame. A coroner's jury called witnesses and experts from far and near and took reams of testimony. Among the many witnesses called was William Mulholland, chief engineer of the Los Angeles bureau of water and power.

This gray-haired official, whose age was seventy-two, met the questioners with this amazing utterance: "Don't blame anyone else. Whatever fault there was in this job, put it on me."

In an era like this when blame shifting is a common practice all along the line in public and in private life, we rub our eyes to see this veteran engineer standing up in his boots and saying in effect, "I am the man you are looking for. Shoulder the blame on me. My subordinates did not plan that structure. I am responsible for it. If there was any error of judgment—and it's human to make mistakes—the error was mine."

Strange words these, "The error was mine." But what a pleasant sound they have. And what an insight they give us into the character of William Mulholland.

"Did you ever find an automobile driver who said he was to blame for an accident?" I asked a traffic officer at the scene of an accident. "No, I should say not," came the quick reply. "If a driver who had hit another in plain sight of me should come to me and say, 'Officer, I am entirely to blame for this accident,' I would drop dead right there on the spot," added this veteran traffic officer. "And," said he, "it's a mystery to me how any accidents happen when no one is ever responsible for any of them."

Baseball players have a favorite expression which they use when a player tries to cover up an error on the field by picking up stones and throwing them off the field from the spot where he made an error. "He's a pebble finder," they say, and put the player down as one who tries to shift the blame.

> The fault, dear Brutus, is not in our stars,
> But in ourselves, that we are underlings.

In these two lines Shakespeare located the blame for most of human error.

And if this be true the virtue of fixing the blame is found in the avoidance of future errors. That coroner's jury in Los Angeles could not restore one human life nor a dollar of property lost by the breaking of the St. Francis dam. But by checking the blueprints, the materials used, the errors in calculations and the possible errors of judgment made in building the dam, William Mulholland might warn all future engineers of certain dangers and errors of construction.

When the blame is fixed on oneself or on anyone else it may mean the end of all future effort. But the effort has to be made, the work has to go on in spite of mistakes and failures. It's the errors we have to avoid instead of the efforts. It was the chief engineer who made the mistake while building the dam. And other dams must be built despite the possibility of error.

Old Honus Wagner is generally conceded to be one of the greatest baseball players of all time. For years he was the mainstay of the Pittsburgh Pirates of the National League. He was the idol of fans and players alike. One of his admirers gave this account of his own hero worship of Old Honus, who still travels around the circuit with the Pittsburgh Pirates as coach. "One year Honus was voted the most valuable player in the league. But to my amazement I found that Honus led the league in errors. I could not understand that at all and asked my father how it could be that the league's most valuable player could at the same time make the most errors. 'That one is easy, Son,' said my father. 'Old Honus goes after everything. There is nothing too hard for him to handle. He makes more errors than anyone else but he also makes more put-outs.'" With this explanation in mind I went to see him play. He was all over infield and outfield. Late in the game, with the score nine to two against his team, he made the greatest play I ever saw. The crowd cheered him for ten minutes, and had he missed the play after his desperate effort they would have cheered him just as loudly and as long. Had he missed, Honus Wagner would have thrown no pebbles from the playing field and would have gone right after the next hard one.

It may be that life itself has to be lived mostly by the trial-and-error method. Men who make no mistakes are very apt to be men who do little in life. The great of the earth have all made them, but the world soon forgets their mistakes because they do so many other things perfectly. The beloved "Teddy" Roosevelt made his share of them, but they are now forgotten. Indeed, he himself used to say: "I don't cry over spilt milk. I make a lot of mistakes, but I spend no time in regret. I go on to something else. When I find that a certain plan doesn't work I try another one—and make them forget the one that didn't work." And just as the great of the earth have made many errors, so we of a more humble walk of life have a right and may expect to make mistakes—mistakes which we should readily admit, and then go on to redeem them and to redeem ourselves. The bigger the man or woman, the quicker to admit mistakes.

*　　*　　*

A FRAGMENT OF THE ROCK OF AGES

ONE afternoon in the year 1662 the people on the streets of London and the shopkeepers from their doorways paused to watch a curious procession of about thirty men, with bundles on their shoulders, walking two by two through the main thoroughfares. Evidently they were men who had suffered, for some of them staggered from weakness and all of them looked pale and underfed.

The onlookers did not know at first that these men were Quakers who had been thrown into Newgate Prison for refusing to swear by an oath. "The law requires you to swear that your statements are true," had thundered the officers of the court.

To which the Quakers had replied, "Nay, a man's word is as binding as any oath can be, and we do not believe it is right to swear."

So, for months they had been herded in Newgate Prison in conditions so vile that one of their number had finally died. The day before this strange procession made its way through the busy streets of the city, a coroner's jury had appeared to hold an inquest over the death of this member of the group. The jury were so horrified at the conditions they discovered in the prison that they said, "It is a wonder that more of them have not died."

The prisoners had been utterly surprised when the key had grated in the lock the next day and they had seen in the blinding light of a torch, which illumined the dark corners of their prison, the turnkey and a sheriff. The sheriff had announced that he wished he could set them all free, but, as he could not do that, he would do the next best thing for them; he would send some of the number to the old Bridewell Prison and so relieve their crowded condition.

It was then that a very strange thing happened. The porter, who should have escorted them to their prison, announced: "You who are to go to the Bridewell know your way there. Your word is trustworthy; there is no need of my going with you. You may as well go there alone providing you promise to arrive at the prison before bedtime."

Imagine the surprise of those Quakers as Thomas Elwood and thirty more of them prepared to set out on this unescorted journey from one prison cell to another. And imagine the surprise of the curious passersby who stopped the little procession to ask the men where they were going and why, when they replied that they were prisoners, going from one prison to another. "What!" exclaimed the townsmen. "Without a keeper? Why don't you escape? This is your chance."

Thomas Elwood raised his head proudly as he replied for all of them, "No, for our word, which we have given, is our keeper."

We are often inclined to bewail the departure of the old-fashioned virtues and to feel that our present generation lacks those qualities of discipline, stanchness, and loyalty that have always been the characteristics of a pioneer people. Yet, a friend of mine tells of an interesting experience which she had last summer when she was traveling in England. She happened to be in London, and one noon was passing one of the larger concert halls when she noted from the bulletin in front of the building that a benefit program was being held for poor relief. The people were crowding into the building; and my friend also noted that the announcement advertised that Paul Robeson, the American Negro singer, would broadcast for this program at twelve o'clock from Russia, where he was living at the time.

Having no imperative engagement my friend decided to buy a ticket and hear an American Negro singer broadcasting from Russia to an English audience. She managed to obtain standing room. It was exactly the time when Mr. Robeson's broadcast was expected. Just on the dot of twelve o'clock the door at the left of the platform opened and the announcer of the program walked out to the center of the platform. The audience could detect a look of chagrin on his face, but they were not prepared for the shocking news he brought to them.

"My friends," he said, "I have a very disappointing announcement to make to you. You have gathered here to listen to the beautiful music of Mr. Paul Robeson. But at the last moment word has come that the Russian authorities have decided not to permit Mr. Robeson to make this broadcast." The announcer paused and a long murmur of disappointment rose from that crowded house of expectant listeners. They were stunned by that disappointing word. Even the man who had made the announcement stood stock still as if he himself ought to do something further about it; explain more fully what had happened. A sudden quiet fell upon that crowd and then a wave of disappointed exclamations. Then what was perhaps one of the most dramatic things that ever happened on a public platform took place, for the door of the stage opened and Paul Robeson himself walked in—not in dress clothes, to be sure, for he had not had time for that. Both audience and announcer looked puzzled—not to say bewildered. Then a burst of delighted applause broke forth. While that applause was rumbling through the great building the man who made the disappointing announcement bent over Robeson to find out himself what had happened. Robeson whispered to him: "The Russian authorities refused to allow me to broadcast, and, rather than disappoint this audience, I hired a plane at my own expense and flew to London. I just landed at Croyden Field, got a taxi, and here I am. I never break a promise or disappoint an audience if it is humanly possible to keep an engagement."

Then Paul Robeson stepped to the front of that platform and opened his program by singing an old Negro spiritual, smiling as he made his own announcement: "Flying through the clouds from Moscow I found myself humming 'Swing Low, Sweet Chariot, Comin' fo' to Carry Me Home,' so I'll open my program today with that number to limber my voice up."

*   *   *

"AND I NEVER SAW HER HALO"

THE wife of a preacher on Cape Cod, Mrs. Charles Hutchinson, recently sent me the story of an interesting everyday experience she had. As she tells it:

One Sunday, in a class of ten-year-old girls, we had been talking about Jesus, when one little girl interrupted to ask, "Mrs. Hutchinson, do you think that Jesus really had a halo like you see in all the pictures of him?" I said, "Girls, what do you think about it? Have you ever seen anyone whose face was all radiant with sunshine?" Before I could add more, to my amazement and embarrassment as well, they chorused, "Yes, you, Mrs. Hutchinson." I was so taken unawares that I could say nothing for a moment. Then before I added anything another little girl spoke up. "Perhaps I ought not to say this," she said, "but I lived with Mrs. Hutchinson for a week while my mother was away and I never saw her halo." It was said so earnestly and seriously.

Let me add, it was funny at the time. It was also convicting and challenging.

That story has both its humorous and its startling side, for it is just as certain as fate that those who live noble, beautiful lives *do* have a sort of halo about them, a radiance of personality, a beauty of countenance which illuminates their faces.

You and I have known many of them in life.

One whom I knew as a boy was Father Staley, an old six-foot giant of a blacksmith in Moundsville, West Virginia. I used to love to watch him shoe horses as I delivered the *Echo* to his shop every afternoon. I loved to watch him standing with the horse's leg resting on his knee, which was covered with a worn, burned leather apron. As he reached over and blew the bellows the sparks would fly upward, the fire would glow. It was then that Father Staley's face shone with a strange radiance as he smiled down on me from his great height.

But Father Staley's face would never have taken on that halo if he had not been so kindly and loving in his everyday life. He was the one man in our little town to whom all people went in their troubles. If a man wanted to run for office he would never think of running if he had not first consulted Father Staley. The story used to be told that the old town drunk once decided to run for constable and went to Father Staley's home to ask for his support. Father Staley listened kindly to his request and then said to the town drunk: "I'll think it over a while and, of course, I'll take it to God in prayer." The town drunk thanked him and started off. Then he had an afterthought, went back to Father Staley and said to him: "It's all right, Father Staley, for you to take that matter to God, but if you'll just as soon, please don't mention my name."

I used to love to hear Father Staley pray in church. The preacher always called on him. He would get squarely on both knees. Then he would start in slowly and softly, for all the world like his warm fire used to glow in the blacksmith shop before Father Staley started to work the bellows. Then he would warm up to his task of prayer, get louder and louder in his voice. Then he would start to slap his legs as he prayed. His voice would get a pleading tone in it. Then he would make demands. One night I remember hearing him pray for the preacher, and

189

he began to make demands on God, and these words thundered forth from his burning lips: "Now, see here, God! You've just got to stick to Brother King! You've just got to give him a revival! He's stuck to you and he's been doing your work faithfully—and God, you can't go back on him. No such nonsense as that, God, would become you! You've gotta stick to Brother King!"

Then he would lift up his face and the tears would stream down his cheeks as he prayed; and he looked for all the world like the fires in his shop when he got the bellows to going full blast. Then he would pound his own legs in a certain rhythm; and when that dear old man got into his full stride of prayer the very walls of the church thundered with his voice. There was lightning in his requests, and it all finally climaxed in a mighty roll of thunder as if something had been struck by lightning—perhaps an old tree on the Indian mound which stood next door to the church. Then it literally seemed as if the very heavens opened and we children could hear the voices of angelic hosts singing "alleluiahs." I used to look up at that point, for I never liked to miss Father Staley's face; and I swear to you, my friends of this indifferent age, that there was a halo of lovely light around that old man's gray hair and his face shone as with a divine glory.

You say it was just a child's imagination. Perhaps so, but I like to think of that old man just the same.

Mrs. Hutchinson talks about halos; I think I know what she means, for certainly the test of any good, brightly shining halo is whether it shines on the head of an everyday saint in the home, the grocery store, the accounting office, the kitchen, the blacksmith shop—in everyday living. Those are the halos which never tarnish.

✳   ✳   ✳

190

"TO BE BETTER OFF IS NOT
TO BE BETTER"

A FRIEND of mine recently sent me this story of one of the most interesting experiences of his life of travel and adventure. He says in his letter:

Through a friend I made the acquaintance of Dan Crawford, that eccentric and lovable man who spent twenty-seven unbroken years in the long-grass area of Central Africa as a missionary. We had brought together a company of ministers and laymen to meet Crawford at luncheon at the Strand Palace Hotel in London. Everyone present had read Dan Crawford's strange book, *Thinking Black,* and all were so eager to ply him with questions that the luncheon hour extended until teatime. When I was leaving I mentioned that I had Mr. Ernest Seton Thompson, the "Wild Animals at Home" naturalist, dining with me that night at my club. Stevenson suggested that it would be great fun to bring Dan Crawford and Seton Thompson together, and we agreed to make a dinner party of four. It was one of the oddest séances in my experience. Mr. Seton Thompson could not make head nor tail of Mr. Dan Crawford, and Mr. Dan Crawford did not know what to make of Mr. Seton Thompson. Suddenly both began slamming civilization, and instantly they were as bosom friends, knit together, it seemed, by a common hate. Both men loved the wild and had heard its call in their souls, and, figuratively speaking, they fell on each other's necks when they discovered that they both loathed the ways of cities and the dismal unsatisfying materialism of modern civilization.

Mr. Seton Thompson told a story of an old Indian whom he had brought down from one of the reservations to show him New York. He took the old red man down Broadway—"the Great White Way"—at night, took him over Brooklyn Bridge, took him on the elevated railroad and in the subway, showed him, in fact, all the feverish ways of the great American city. At last he took the bewildered old Indian to the Grand Central Station to see him back to his reservation. Not till then had he asked the old man what he thought of New York. Then he put the question. The old Indian thought in silence for a minute or two, and then replied: "Mr. Seton Thompson, in the land from which I come we have no bridges to span our great rivers, no great white way to spoil the darkness of the night sky, no trains under the land and over the land; but we, Mr. Seton Thompson, we have peace of mind."

Mr. Dan Crawford, delighted with the story, capped it with an even better one: "I have lived," he said, "so long in the long grass that I think like the blacks, and I never talk of Western European civilization. But just when I was coming home and was thinking perhaps tenderly of old scenes and faces, I did one night boast a bit about civilization to an old Bantu native who was sitting with me in my hut. I told him that I was going to my own country, where they had ships that went under the water, and still more ships that flew over the water. I told him that in English houses you turn a tap and the water flows, touch a button and the room is flooded with light. In fact, I gave him a glowing description of all the alleged triumphs of civilization. When I had catalogued as much as I could remember I stopped and waited for the old Negro to show his surprise. But the old Negro just said: 'Is that all, Mr. Crawford?'

" 'Yes, I think it is,' I replied.

"Then very slowly and very gravely the old Bantu said: 'Well, Mr. Crawford, you know, to be better off is not to be better.' "

Yes, the wise old African Negro was right. "To be better off is not to be better." We have all learned that in our experiences with machinery and things. I was talking about that very situation recently with the director of my broadcast. We were walking from Radio City to my hotel and were talking about the fact that New York City last year had seven successful shows on Broadway which dealt with religious matter, and that this year there are also several religious shows which prove that America has a nostalgia, an almost inexpressible homesickness, for "the ancient and beautiful things": the simple things; the simple things of the so-called "Gay Nineties"; the old hymns; the sincere, simple memories of childhood; in the days when life was not so complex as to bewilder us all. We are lonely for the great out of doors: the rivers, hills, meadows, twilights and still nights of country and small-town days and ways. No wonder Thornton Wilder's *Our Town* had such a long run and won the Pulitzer Prize a few years ago. It was the drama of a New England village; of simple, sincere, loving home folk who knew how to live the "Simple Life"; who respected their neighbors, helped them when they were in trouble, wept with them when they lost loved ones;

who went to bed at nine o'clock and were up with the first rooster crow and the first faint streaks of dawn. No, we do not make life better by getting more things; but we make life better by growing character, by building tried and true friendships, by living unostentatiously and kindly. No wonder the great naturalists and those who have lived close to nature are not enamored by our big, flagrant, blatant, turbulent, tumultuous, storm-tossed cities, "Where Cross the Crowded Ways of Life."

*　　*　　*

YOU NEVER CAN TELL

ONE of the stories my friend Dr. Miles H. Krumbine tells with fine effect is that of an elderly lady, humbly dressed, who once went to make a casual visit to a certain Canadian hospital, merely to be shown about the institution.

The superintendent was in the office when she arrived. He was one of those capable individuals who are never too busy to be gracious, and therefore offered to escort the unimpressive old lady himself, showed all there was to be seen, and answered such questions as she asked. At the end of the trip of inspection she said very gently, "Is there any particular thing you need in this hospital?" The superintendent suggested that they were badly in need of additional facilities for their orthopedic work. Crippled children would surely appeal to a dear old lady. His suggestion was really modest, for the total cost of the facilities he spoke of did not run beyond $150. The old lady assured him that that could be taken care of, but wasn't there something else? The courage of the superintendent grew. It was X-ray apparatus he now specified as their most insistent need, costing around five hundred dollars. Again the old lady assured him that that would be looked after. She now grew very impatient and a bit sternly said, "But isn't there something else that you need?" This time his courage was turned into daring. He grew really rash and told her the hospital needed desperately a whole new wing. The plans were already drawn up for it, the blueprints were made, and the total cost would be $250,000. Certainly he was not prepared for the answer he got. Very quietly the old lady said to him, "Let us go into your office and examine the plans. Since you seem to know exactly what you want and understand intelligently what you really need, I will write you out a check to do it."

Cyrus Dallin, the sculptor who created "The Appeal to the Great Spirit" in Boston, had an experience similar to that one. He was working away in his Arlington Heights Studio, near Boston, one day when a simply dressed woman came in. Mr. Dallin paid little attention to her and went on with his work. Presently she saw one of his major statues, called "The Last Arrow," and asked him how much it would cost. Mr. Dallin, thinking she was ignorant of the cost of major sculptor pieces, smiled condescendingly and said: "Lady, that is a museum piece. You couldn't afford to own that one." Then, thinking to suggest something within her means, he showed her several small items which he often sold to casual visitors in his studio. But she said again, "Nevertheless, I'd like to know what that statue would cost."

Once again Mr. Dallin courteously but firmly said, "But Madam, that is a museum piece or a statue that only a city could buy for some public park," and tried to turn her mind in more humble directions. However, that woman determined to know what that statue could be purchased for. Finally Mr. Dallin, to humor the whim of a childish woman, said, "Oh, that statue would cost around fifteen thousand dollars." "All right, I'll take it," she replied, without batting an eyelash, and sat down at his studio desk and wrote him a check for it, adding, "Send it to my estate in Madison, New Jersey." That particular lady happened to be one of the Rockefellers and that particular statue now adorns her driveway; and Mr. Cyrus Dallin has not even yet recovered from the shock he got that day when, as he says, "I was entertaining a financial angel unawares."

No, you never can tell these days. Some European crown prince may be waiting on you in your hotel; some princess may be cooking in your kitchen, or writing a novel, as actually happened recently in New England. You never can tell when you look at a child what destinies are wrapped up in that life, so it is best to do as Mr. William J. Cameron suggested to me in a recent letter: "The best investment is in the children. You had better take a good look at them as they pass you on the street, for they are the ones who are going to make a new world for you, and you can catch some glimmer of the dawn in their faces."

Nor shall we ever forget that the greatest Man ever born in this earth was born in a stable because there was no room in the inn. And I often wonder how that innkeeper would feel today if he knew whom he had turned out of his inn that night so long ago.

✳   ✳   ✳

"THE PATH-BORER"

IN 1889 Dan Crawford went into the far interior of Africa to carry on the work of David Livingstone, who had explored and opened up more of what was then called "The Dark Continent" than any other white man. Livingstone's last message to the outside world was: "Eight days south of Katanga the natives declare the fountains of the Nile to be. When I have found them I shall return." But it remained for Dan Crawford to make this journey and by the flare of African campfires to record his fulfillment of Livingstone's last desire in a thrilling book, *Thinking Black*. In 1912 Crawford came out of the far interior of Africa and announced, "I have found the uttermost man in the uttermost parts of the earth." Emerging from a long shut-in life in the Far Interior, Crawford told the story of his twenty-two years without a break in the long grass of Central Africa.

And it was in this long grass that Crawford found the meaning of the word "pioneer" in the African language to be "dew-drier" or "path-borer." He wrote it down in *Thinking Black* in words that drip with African dew and flood.

Often overgrown with thick grass, the trail is lost below it, and the terror of morning treks is to squeeze your way through this thick matted tangle. The drier the season, of course, the greater the deluge of the dew, and all to be negotiated in the cold, callous dawn. Often, too, you get out of your blankets to find another thick blanket of mist along your path.

The big black carriers have a way all of their own in clearing the drenching dew from the tall, thirteen-foot grass. They push shivering small boys ahead of them as 'dew-wipers' or 'human brooms,' to dry off the clammy dew on their naked bodies. Pushed on ahead in the dark dawn, of course, these little bits of black humanity run the chance of a hungry hyena or leopard lurking in the path to nab firstcomers.

The African has coined a phrase which is a fitting parable of David Livingstone and Dan Crawford staggering through the tall grass and jungles of the "Dark Continent." "The first along the dew-damp path in the morning [i. e., the pioneer] dries off on his own body the wet grass, for the benefit of those who follow him." Hence the African song which Dan Crawford translates thus:

> Lead thou the way in the wet grass drear,
> Then, only then, art thou pioneer:
> For Mr. First must get all the woes,
> That Mr. Second may find repose.

A few great names adorn the pages of history as pioneers. They went out to the ends of the trails of geography, science, business, art, religion, and bored new paths through the wet tangled grass. Usually they were scorned and hated by their own generation, only later to be acclaimed great by those who reaped the benefits of their hardships and daring disregard for things as they were. Progress has come largely through the efforts of these leaders.

But not all "dew-wipers" and "path-borers" have been found among the great men and women of the earth. There are millions who have done and are doing pioneer work along the well-worn paths of life. They go forward a little in thought by refusing to accept some well-established but outworn belief or doctrine and keep on standing by their own convictions at the risk of being called queer or stubborn by the crowd. Or it may be that it is some artisan rather than artist who insists on doing his work a little better or a bit different from others, giving it quality and personality. They are willing to go anywhere provided it is forward.

Coming back to Dan Crawford's *Thinking Black* we find this verse on the title page:

> There's a legion that never was listed,
> That carries no colors nor crest,
> But, split in a thousand detachments,
> Is breaking the road for the rest.

Among these are the thousands of mothers who get up early in the morning to prepare breakfast for their children; the other thousands of fathers who, to make the family living, awake to the clang of an alarm clock and rise in the cold and darkness of suburban towns to take up the daily grind of train, taxi, and office, then home again by dusk; those untold millions of workers on farms and in factories, mines and mills who go to work before daylight and get back home by dark, who never see the sun but who labor a lifetime to make it easier for those whom they love; that untold army of scientists, laboratory workers, nurses, doctors, milkmen, the clatter of whose horses' hoofs we hear dimly in the early morning hours—who all carry in their hearts the spirit of rugged old pioneers and serve their day in these humble but gracious ways, like the dew-wipers in the African jungles.

✳　　✳　　✳

DESTINY IN DISCARDED JUNK

ON WEEK days Jim MacDonald was an inventor's mechanic, but on Sundays he played the organ in the Methodist church in a town in Canada. Jim's burning ambition was to create. In his music he worked prodigiously and composed in every form, but his compositions proved to be just another anthem or piece; the form was perfect but the soul to make it live more than a week was just not there. He studied composition and used to say to his teacher: "How do these fellows do it? Handel writes a simple tune, the Largo, and centuries after he is dead the Largo is still the world's most popular melody. Whence came this melody and why?"

On week days Jim worked in an organ factory. The head of this factory was a real inventor, a really great genius. To hide his real identity today, for he is still famous, we will call him Hope-Jones. Mr. Hope-Jones invented, and Jim's job was to make the first model of the invention. Here, again, it irked Jim that he couldn't invent—and the more so since Hope-Jones inventions, once the first model appeared, seemed to be so very simple and obvious—but Jim's mind persisted in remaining a blank as far as original ideas were concerned.

Hope-Jones had invented a great many organ "stops"—or, to be a little clearer, pipes—which produced beautiful tones in the organ which had never before been heard. His "diaphone" was an unusually happy thought, for not alone was the tone very valuable in an organ, but it was found that a larger model could be heard fourteen miles at sea; so the United States government adopted the device as a fog signal on the Great Lakes. Encouraged by the success of the diaphone, Hope-Jones tried to eliminate the pipe altogether and produce organ tones with a ratchet and diaphragm. Jim MacDonald, his mechanic, finished the model and several friends were invited in to hear the new device. Jim wore such an unusually serious expression that they were sure the thing was going to be good; but when he pressed the key the most amazing thing happened. Such a racket no one had ever heard before. It was like an electric shock, and everyone jumped. Then everyone laughed, for a more unmusical sound was beyond the imagination. Hope-Jones promptly waved the crowd to the door. "At least I've got that out of my system," he said. "One has to try everything that comes into the old head or the gods might be offended. That thing is just a piece of junk. Better luck next time."

Just then Jim MacDonald, the mechanic, grabbed Hope-Jones by the arm and said, with deep emotion and earnestness in his voice: "The model! The model! Mr. Jones, you don't want it? May I have this? Will you give it to me?"

Hope-Jones, the great inventor, laughed and assured the excited mechanic that it was perfectly all right. He never wanted to see the thing again, so Jim was more than welcome to it.

With just a word of thanks Jim MacDonald put on his hat and coat, picked up the model and left the factory, while the group of more or less brilliant creators of new ideas followed his retreating form with no little amusement.

Jim went directly to a blacksmith's shop. As he entered, the smithie's back was to him. Jim gave a toot on the device he carried. The blacksmith jumped—and, incidentally, dropped a hammer on his toe. "What the Devil!" he exclaimed. "What you got there?"

"That," said Jim, *"is one million dollars.* Can't you see?—one toot and you jump; you can't help it. Here we have the ideal auto horn, and with cars becoming popular we can make a million."

Jim had become conservative. Inside of five years that patent had transformed the little Canadian blacksmith shop into one of America's greatest factories. In fact, Jim bought the organ factory to add another block to the plant; and auto drivers in every country of the world found no bend in the road that wasn't protected by a sign, "Sound your Claxon," urging them to toot Jim's exclusive auto horn which for years had no competition on account of the patent. That was the way the Claxon auto horn was invented.

Jim is no longer envious of George Friedrich Handel. As the head of one of America's sixty families—so to put it—he finds so many opportunities to help poor creative artists who have "the spark" that he is quite content to be Jim MacDonald, and he often wonders what good "the spark" would be to these composers if Jim MacDonald were not in a position to take care of them.

"AS COLUMBUS, FROM THE SHORES OF SPAIN"

WE USED to see a strange man walking up and down Mt. Vernon Street in Boston, back in 1910. He always seemed lost in meditation. He walked up and down our street, past the Boston University School of Theology, unaware of our august presence, seemingly unaware of the presence of anybody or anything.

Most of us came as callow young men from the Middle West, and our world was rather limited. What we did not know was that that man's name was an honored name in those parts, and in all parts where thinking men lived. He was Percival Lowell, brother of Amy Lowell, the poet, and Dr. A. Lawrence Lowell, once president of Harvard. Not knowing all of this, we students looked upon that strange, unseeing, meditative man as somewhat of a curiosity.

I left the school, went to California, traveled around the world, went to war in France, and served churches in San Francisco, Detroit, and Kansas City. Finally I was called back to Boston, in 1929, to teach in the same school where I was a student in 1910, and where I used to see this unusual man walking up and down Mt. Vernon Street.

Shortly after I took up my new teaching work in 1930 I picked up the newspapers on March 13, Percival Lowell's birthday. There, across the front page, were great black headlines—something a little short of the size they might use in announcing the millennium!—and under them a story about the discovery of a new planet which was later named Pluto. The first two letters in the name of that planet were the initials of Percival Lowell! Why? Because he had discovered the presence of that new planet by noting an unseen force tugging at Uranus. Yes, the man who made that discovery was the man we students used to watch as he walked up and down Beacon Hill.

But that is not all of the wonder of it.

Percival Lowell, through sheer mathematical calculations and intellectual imagination, discovered Pluto ten years before there was a telescope large enough to sight it if it was there—fifteen years before it was actually discovered by astronomers. He had so much faith in his calculations that he founded Lowell Observatory in Flagstaff, Arizona, to find Pluto if his calculations turned out to be correct. The planet itself was not actually located until fourteen years after he had died.

Some poet said, in recent years, speaking of the discovery of an unseen planet:

> We have not found it,
> But we feel it trembling along the line of our analysis
> As Columbus, from the shores of Spain,
> Once felt the new continent.

So these astronomers work, through sheer faith in their calculations—faith in the unseen, the invisible, the unknown.

I remember an editorial that appeared in the New York *Times* telling about the importance of the discovery of Pluto. I do not remember a thing the editorial said, but I do remember that it was headed, "Faith in the Unseen." And I liked that heading, for it was talking my language. It seemed good to hear the language of the parson creeping into the pages of a newspaper. "Faith in the Unseen." I liked that kind of newspaper talk, too, because it buttressed all that religious people have been gambling their lives on from the beginning of time.

We have been trained to believe in the reality of the invisible. Here was a great scientist who believed so much in it that he prophesied the position of Pluto long before it was discovered, before there was even a telescope large enough to find it. And he had so much faith in the accuracy of his calculations that he actually built an observatory to discover it, though he died before it was found.

Now, after all of these years, I take this way of apologizing to the whole Lowell family for our failure to see a prophet in our midst. I have a feeling that the Lowells, with a slightly ironical smile, will forgive us. For, after all, it is we who ought to be pioneers in the reality of the unseen and the invisible, for we are the followers of a man who said long, long ago: "We look not at the things which are seen, but at the things which are not seen; for the things which are seen are temporal; but the things which are not seen are eternal."

And I count this experience as one of the great spiritual adventures of my life—namely, to have seen that astronomer walking up and down Mt. Vernon Street in my student days, even though I did not realize his greatness; and to have arrived, later, on the same scene in Boston, in time to see that new planet, Pluto, heave its huge form across the horizons of our time to prove to me, and to all the world, the reality of the unseen.

> We have not found it,
> But we feel it trembling along the line of our analysis
> As Columbus, from the shores of Spain,
> Once felt the new continent.

✳   ✳   ✳

ETERNAL FIRES

IN THE rotogravure section of the Boston *Herald* recently there was a picture of an old man sitting by an open fireplace in a mountain cabin, playing a fiddle. The picture was interesting but not at all unusual, until your eye caught the single word "Eternal" printed in the upper corner of the picture. I read the rest of the story when I saw that word "Eternal."

And here it is. The fire on that hearth was lighted one hundred and forty-seven years ago and has never been allowed to go out. The old man fiddling before the fire is William Morris of Saluda, North Carolina, and he is seventy-seven years of age. The fire on this mountain hearth was lighted by his great-great-grandfather, John Morris, when he came with his young wife, Sarah, to that little mountain community as a pioneer from Philadelphia in 1790.

Lighting a fire was a tough assignment in the days before matches, so the fire was always kept burning. But the grandson has tended this wood fire through his lifetime for reasons other than the inconvenience of relighting it. So significant has this fire become to William Morris' neighbors that they have petitioned the National Park service to take over the fire and preserve it in the projected museum of the Great Smoky National Park. They are afraid that some morning they'll wake up and find that there's no smoke coming from Bill's chimney—that Bill and the fire have "gone out" together.

Now if anyone thinks this eternal fire down there in the Smoky Mountains has no symbolic meaning, may I mention some things which you and I may see in its curling smoke or glowing embers?

There is the earth beneath the hearthstone and chimney and around the old cabin. This was there when the great-great-grandfather of William Morris claimed it as a pioneer. His ancestors who tilled the tough acres on the mountainside have handed this bit of earth on from one generation to another as a means of livelihood.

William Morris himself is a continuation of that fire we call human life which began countless ages ago. The great-grandfather handed on to his son his life along with the fire upon the hearth.

In the old man's hands there is a fiddle. He is playing one of the old tunes which came down from the past—from his people: Anglo-Saxon ancestors down there in the Smokies, the oldest and purest strains of old English in this nation. Those mountain ballads and tunes are signs of that heritage of culture which is handed on from one generation to another as a burning fire upon the hearth.

Art, music, literature, religion—these are all rooted in that past, kept alive by faithful souls who hand them on by fiddle and string, by brush and pen, by word of mouth or by tending the ancient fires of faith upon the altars of the nation.

When I saw the picture and read the simple story of the eternal fire on the cabin's hearth, tended by William Morris, I thought of that ancient Hestia, goddess of the hearth and home. Her cult was widespread in all Greek lands. Every community had its common hearth where the sacred fire burned, and from which every colony took the sacred flame. The keeping of the fire was a sacred task entrusted only to the most faithful. The sacred hearth with the ever-burning fire was a place of worship. William Morris and every one of us are tenders of some sacred, ever-burning fire. The word that gives us and our fire meaning is "Eternal."

When I read that word "Eternal" my mind went back to an experience I had a few years ago in Paris.

The Advertising Clubs of America were visiting the famous Arc de Triomphe, which is a memorial to the French soldiers who died in the World War. It was Sunday morning and we had gathered to pay tribute to them, to lay a wreath on that sacred tomb, and to watch the daily ritual of replenishing the Eternal Flame which burns beneath the arch.

A crippled French captain walked up to the flickering blue flame, took out his sword, touched a button at its base which replenished the oil, and suddenly that flame spurted up a yard high. That was what they called the Ritual of Renewal. But that was not all of it. Suddenly one of those impetuous Americans who are not afraid to follow an inner impulse cried out: "It's Sunday morning, boys, and this is a sacred thing to these French people, so let's kneel down and have a word of prayer. What do you say?"

Moved by a common impulse, we all knelt down on those French cobblestones under the Arc de Triomphe. Then an American preacher offered prayer.

It was a strange and impressive sight to the French, and they liked it. The photographers took pictures of it, and the Paris papers gave it front-page headlines that evening. None of us shall ever forget that simple gesture of international friendship. But to me it was a symbol of something that ought always to be kept alive in human life: friendship, love, worship, and—the flame of faith.

*　　*　　*

THE GAME AND THE FLAME OF IT

For years the owner of a small drugstore looked around for an opportunity to do big things. He hated his drugstore, and spent his mornings looking for a "better opening" and his afternoons at the ball parks, leaving his business to shift for itself—with results as could be expected.

This is what a lot of us do. We look with envy at the other fellow, think he has an enjoyable job, and decide that ours is hopeless. We think he has all the luck and vainly wish that some would come our way. We can learn from this druggist how to overcome such an attitude. The way he did it was very simple. It involved nothing beyond the reach of any person, no matter what his position in life may be. One day he asked himself: "Why try to get into some other business about which I know nothing? Why try to get into another game? Why not play the drug game?"

He decided to do it. He began to develop the business as if it were the greatest sport in the nation; and he tells with great glee what fun he had building up his drug chain by giving his customers the very best of service.

"When someone who lived very near would call on the phone and I answered, I would hold up my hand to attract the clerk's attention and repeat loudly: 'Yes, Mrs. Hasbrook. Two bars of So-and-so's soap. All right. A three-ounce bottle of spirits of camphor. One-half pound of chocolate chips. That's all? Nice day, isn't it, Mrs. Hasbrook? By the way . . . .' And I'd go on talking with her about anything I could think of.

"But the minute I held up my hand and began to repeat the customer's order, my clerk would be scurrying around the store putting up the order. And the delivery boy, with a grin all the way across his friendly face, would be scrambling into his coat. Within a few seconds after the customer had repeated her order, the delivery boy would be on the run up the street with the goods. And I, for my part, would keep her at the telephone until she would say: 'Oh, wait a minute, Mr. Walgreen. There's the doorbell.'

"Then I'd chuckle and hold the line. In a minute she would come back. 'Why, Mr. Walgreen, that was the order I just gave you. I don't know how you manage to do it, but I think that's just wonderful service. It can't have been over half a minute since I called you up. I'll have to tell Mr. Hasbrook about that tonight!'

"Folks began trading with us from right under the noses of other druggists several blocks away. And pretty soon druggists from other parts of town were coming in to find out how I was building up my business so well."

That is the way in which Charles R. Walgreen branched out from his one store to become the most remarkable promoter of the chain drug business that this country has ever seen. Today he controls the second largest chain of drugstores in the country, a chain which is continuing to grow most remarkably.

He learned a little secret, namely: Opportunity lies right at your door if you will simply look at your own occupation as an interesting game and play it with enthusiasm.

Walgreen's opportunity depended more upon his attitude toward his work than upon the work itself. As soon as he looked upon his work as a challenge to a game, the tide turned in his favor. He accepted the challenge, studied the rules of the game, and then played it with all his might. It was easy. It was a game. It was fun. Why not try making a game of your home life, of your work, of your school, of your day?

Angela Morgan has caught the spirit of what I mean and calls it "Work—a Song of Triumph"; a poem she has graciously allowed me to use here:

> Work!
> Thank God for the might of it,
> The ardor, the urge, the delight of it—
> Work that springs from the heart's desire,
> Setting the brain and the soul on fire—
> Oh, what is so good as the heat of it,
> And what is so glad as the beat of it,
> And what is so kind as the stern command,
> Challenging brain and heart and hand?

206

Work!
Thank God for the pride of it,
For the beautiful, conquering tide of it,
Sweeping the life in its furious flood,
Thrilling the arteries, cleansing the blood,
Mastering stupor and dull despair,
Moving the dreamer to do and dare.
Oh, what is so good as the urge of it,
And what is so glad as the surge of it,
And what is so strong as the summons deep,
Rousing the torpid soul from sleep?

*　　*　　*

"BERRIES FOR THE KING'S PLATE"

THERE is an ancient story which has come down to us from the days of kings of how the servants used to go out into the garden at daylight, when the dew was still on the leaves and fruit, to pick a bushel basket of blackberries for the king's breakfast.

That servant would take the bushel basket of nice ripe berries to the kitchen, where a relay of servants would pick out the best of that bushel basket until it was down to a peck of the most luscious ones—culling out the unripe, blotched, and inferior ones.

Then another servant would cull that peck basket and further eliminate the ones which were too hard, selecting only the juiciest, softest, and sweetest berries, until what remained was put into a large blue bowl for the king's breakfast, and set before him with a huge pitcher of rich cream.

They called that "Berries for the King's Plate." And no matter what we think of the social implications of that selective process, it is an interesting law of life just the same.

Those of us who serve the public have to learn to do that very thing if we hope to survive in this competitive age of serving humanity. Only in this day the king happens to be the public, and they have been trained to expect that they, too, have a right to get "Berries for the King's Plate."

207

Especially is this true of preachers and public speakers, for the American public has been trained to expect the best, hearing over the radio the finest lectures in the nation. When they want to hear music these days all they have to do is to turn to a Toscanini or a Boston Symphony Orchestra, or the great Metropolitan Opera soloists. For now the American public expects to have prepared for it "Berries for the King's Plate"—and, what is more, they get it.

One of the most interesting lessons I learned from my experience in national broadcasting was how much extra material may actually be culled out. Every night before I went to the studio I ran through my talks, culling out the words and phrases with a blue pencil—trying always to make them better. I have learned that it doesn't hurt them, but helps them, to go through this process. I did it because I wanted to come as close as possible to offering "Berries for the King's Plate."

It is exactly the same process which Luther Burbank used in his creation of new plant forms and flowers. I remember driving once with Mr. Burbank from Santa Rosa to his experimental gardens at Sebastopol, California, a distance of only a few miles. When we had come within two miles of those gardens a sudden and beautiful wave of perfume swept upon us. The wind was blowing the scent of more than a half-million varied types of lilies on the morning breezes directly into our faces. I said to Mr. Burbank: "Why, it's like a hurricane of perfume. I never smelled anything so beautiful."

He smiled at my enthusiasm, for it was an old story to him. Then he said to me, as we drove along in his old car, "I have more than a half-million lilies growing in that garden, and most of them are now in full bloom."

"But how will you ever market that many lilies?"

Then he laughed out loud at my ignorance and replied with a chuckle: "Why, Son, we don't market them! We're culling them. My workmen will go through that half-million lilies, cull the half-dozen best specimens, selecting for length and strength of stem, beauty of perfume, contour of leaf and petal, vigor of body. When they have selected the half-dozen best lilies out of the half-million they will all be destroyed and turned back into the soil again. That is the simple mathematical process of selecting to get the best.

"They call me a wizard and I hate that word. I am not a genius. I am simply a plant craftsman. It is merely a mathematical process, a process of elimination and selection. It is like the old days when they used to select 'Berries for the King's Plate.'"

Then Luther Burbank proceeded to tell me the story which I have just passed on; and when he was through he said: "That's the way we work in our laboratories. We throw away a million flowers to get a single bud and plant. Indeed, the whole process of evolution has taken that trend. In other words, that is God's way of working and we learned it from him."

And I was glad to hear Luther Burbank use that very expression. I was overjoyed to know that he worked hand in hand and heart to heart with God and his supreme laws in the glorious process of discovering God's best for humanity—in gleaning "Berries for the King's Plate."

✳ ✳ ✳

A SURE CURE FOR SATIETY

Now and then I like the adventure of reading the dictionary. I once assigned to a young college student the task of writing me a review of the dictionary, in a competitive race for the editorship of the college newspaper. He handed in such a good review that we made him the editor.

Not long ago I myself got to thinking of the word satiety and turned to the dictionary to find out what it meant. I discovered that it had a real connection with our general theme, "Lifting the Levels of Life." The definition read: "State of being satiated; a fullness of gratification, either of the appetite or of any sensual desire; fullness beyond desire; an excess of gratification which excites wearisomeness or loathing; which finally creates boredom with life itself, and may end in thoughts of suicide; to surfeit; glut."

"Man alive!" I said to myself. "That's a terrible condition to be in. That's worse than having nothing!"

I knew what it meant, for once when I was a boy I entered a contest in an apple orchard. One Saturday morning, having nothing more important to do, five or six of us decided that a good game would be for each of us to take a tree, start at the outside circumference of the apples which had fallen, and see who could eat the furtherest in toward the trunk of the tree.

I won, and I think I had what might be called a satiety of apples for that day. The doctor called it colic.

I can reliably report that it is not a pleasant feeling. There used to be an old saying, "An apple a day keeps the doctor away." But too many apples in one day brings the doctor on the run, as I can testify.

Paralleling that story of satiety is one a friend, Mrs. Lucille LeSourd, told me not long ago.

Bob went to visit his favorite aunt. She said to him: "Bob, I want to give you, while you are here, the food you like best. What is it that you wish most of all?"

Bob hesitated only a moment and answered: "I never had enough pancakes in my life. Mother always says, 'Three are enough for any boy.' "

"Well," said his aunt, "you shall have pancakes and all you want."

So at his first breakfast the pancakes rolled in from the kitchen, one stack after another, until Bob began to slow down, and then suddenly stopped eating.

"Why, Bob," exclaimed his aunt, "don't you want any more pancakes?"

Slowly Bob answered, "No, I don't want any more—I don't even want those I've already had."

Contentment in life is not determined by what we have or do not have, where we live or do not live, but is based on a condition of mind and heart.

210

Dr. Fosdick once told me of a cruise he took along the coast of Maine. One day he stopped at a desolate little island where a tall lighthouse sent out its bright rays over the sea. He sat with the lighthouse keeper, and in their conversation the lighthouse keeper told how he lived alone there, but that once in two weeks a coast guard vessel brought him his necessary supplies. Amazed at the isolation within sight of land, Dr. Fosdick said: "Don't you get lonesome and bored out here all by yourself day after day? You seem to have very little in your life?"

Then the old weather-beaten man turned to Dr. Fosdick—and I shall always thrill to his simple reply: "Not since I saved my first life!"

Bored! Why should anyone be bored with life if he is rendering an effective service to his fellows? Was Livingstone bored in Africa as he opened up a continent? Was Walter Reed bored as he fought a plague that claimed tens of thousands of victims every year? Was Admiral Byrd pining away with pity for himself as he kept his lonely vigil at the outpost on the South Pole?

No! I interviewed Admiral Byrd and in that interview he said to me: "Those were, in many ways, the most completely contented hours and days of my whole life. I thought things through down in Little America, and in the silence there I came as near to a spiritual victory as I have ever come in all my adventuring days. I was never bored and never in danger until my illness came from the fumes of the stove. You can never get enough of silence."

Now let us turn from Admiral Byrd to a peculiar old genius, of a more humble walk in life. He too was a New Englander.

He opened an office in a certain New England town and painted a crude shingle to go up in front which read:

"A-CURE-FOR-THE-BLUES SPECIALIST!"

People flocked to his office and poured out their troubles, and when they had finished he invariably presented them with a little box bearing this line: "Do not open until overcome with a severe attack of the blues and boredom. Sure cure inside."

When the patient opened the little box he found a prescription inside folded up to imitate a powder capsule, and read these words:

When you find yourself getting blue,
Something for somebody else *go do!*

It was crude poetry but it was fine philosophy. For there is never a satiety in service.

✶   ✶   ✶

SAINTS IN SHINING ARMOR

WHEN Earl Marlatt published his book "Protestant Saints" he was asked by a small friend, Philip Fox, six years old, "Uncle Earl, what's your book about?"

Uncle Earl hesitated a moment before he answered: "I'm afraid, Phil, it's about something you never heard of—saints. Do you know what saints are?"

Phil's eyes lit up, as if he were remembering a room full of rainbows at Sunday school.

"Sure," he said. "I know what saints are. They're the men the light shines through."

And so they are, and so they have been from the time when the early Christians saw martyrs die in winding sheets of flame, and spoke of it as "shining armor." One of the greatest of them, St. Paul, knowing the glow which sacrificial service can give to any life, advised his friends to "put on the whole armor of God, that ye may be able to stand against the wiles of the devil."

Times have changed since then, but saints are still "the men the light shines through." They live among us in modern dress. We meet them and talk to them as casually as Channing Pollock met a friend of his, Jim, and talked to him on the way to work.

I want you to hear this story of St. Jim the way Mr. Pollock

first told it to me himself. Eventually it became his very successful play, *The House Beautiful*.

One morning I was hurrying from a suburban home to catch the eight
forty-five train to New York. As I walked toward the train I saw a
friend of many years walking ahead of me. I knew him as Jim. I
caught up with him, put my arm around his shoulders, and got to talking
about the thirty years we had spent together in that suburban town
near New York City. Remembering that he had never been away from
that town on a vacation as far back as I knew, I finally said to him:
"Now, Jim, why don't you take a long vacation in Europe? You and
Mary have the children all raised and in college. Why don't you take
a rest?"

I shall never forget the light that shone in his eyes when he turned to
me and replied: "Why, Channing, I never thought of that. In fact, I
don't dare think of it. Mary and I would love to go some place. We
have always wanted to. In fact, every summer we get all the steamship
catalogues and plan a trip we know we can never take. You see, we
have struggled for years to raise the children, then to get them through
college, then to see them settled in their own homes. I have never
earned more than a hundred and fifty dollars a month, but we are
somehow managing to make payments on our home. We want that
house secure so that the children can bring their babies home to it and
have it for a refuge if anything happens to them or us. I've also tried to
keep up a modest insurance for Mary. So we have never had any margin
to travel, as much as we should like to. But, Channing, we do have our
home, and that's enough. It's The House Beautiful to us, and I'm satisfied."

Then Jim's train came in and he hurried away to catch it as he had for
thirty years. As he ran the sun shone on his blue-serge suit. It was
shiny where blue-serge suits always get shiny. Suddenly he was not just
my friend Jim. He was a knight in shining armor. And out of that
episode came *The House Beautiful*.

And out of lives like that will come The World Beautiful, as
Earl Marlatt realized when he wrote something else about saints
in ancient or modern dress. It doesn't matter so long as those
who know them think of it as "Armor of Light." This time he
wrote it in poetry and set it to the glowing music of "Aurelia,"
familiar as the tune for another hymn, "The Church's One Foun-

213

dation." He did this deliberately, he says, because he honestly believes that the Church, or any agency benefiting all mankind, is built on the kind of "men the light shines through." He called his hymn "Shining Armor."

✳   ✳   ✳

A BOY WHISTLED

MARY LEE REED sat in the waiting room of the Union Station in Chicago. The long wooden bench was hard and the stone floor was cold. She felt a draft from the continual swing of the door, and a shiver shot up to the back of her neck. She got up and moved toward the other end of the heavy stone room, brushed peanut shells from the bench with an old newspaper and sat facing the door. She was alone in Chicago.

The constant rustle of newspapers reminded her of the impatient people on the benches. They were tired, worried, anxious, unsmiling and sullen. Mary Lee Reed became interested in all these people. They seemed so unhappy—so unsocial.

She sat silently watching the crowd milling and hurrying in thoughtless confusion. They all seemed to lack something. There was a certain emptiness in their faces. She wanted to help them! She sat up straight at the thought and smiled.

At that moment a young man came striding through the door whistling loudly.

Heads turned slowly as if searching for something. The young man felt the gaze and became embarrassed. He stopped whistling and in a few seconds disappeared.

But something had happened to that crowd. They had been transformed by that whistling. A woman across from Mary Lee Reed smiled at her. An old man laughed out loud. A child began to sing. It was as if some magic wand had been waved over that station. Suddenly Mary Reed had an idea—it was music that was needed in big, cold, unfeeling, impersonal rail-

214

road stations. All the way from Chicago to Denver that idea haunted her. It sang to her in the click of the wheels. It was so simple a thing she wondered that somebody else had not thought of it before.

When she arrived at her destination in Denver she began at once to put her plan into effect.

She had her piano moved from her home to the railroad station and filled the station with the waltz, opera, and hymn. As someone said later, "She filled that station with music that washes away from the soul the dust of everyday life."

That was in 1923. Now she plays a silver-toned organ loaned to her by a large organ company. Her peaceful, hope-inspiring music has filled the majority of the stations in the country. Before she left one station she always made arrangements for someone in that town to take her place and carry on her work. She and her friends now play in nearly one half of the large stations in the United States. They play for two-week periods at Thanksgiving, Christmas, and Easter, and she has further plans to organize playing units all over the nation in railroad stations.

She devotes her entire life to helping others by her splendid and inspiring music. For the past nine years she has been playing in Grand Central Station, New York City. Besides her station work she travels around the country organizing community sings, giving organ lessons, and training quartets and vocal groups. She is one of the happiest women I know. She has surely learned how to get the most out of life by helping others.

Many of you may have heard Mary Reed playing in Grand Central Station in New York City. But a friend of mine who told me this story also says of his friendship with her:

I drop in to see her at least once a year. I like to see her smiling face as her tiny hands run over the deep, powerful organ that brings joy to thousands. I shall never forget the first time I heard Mary Lee Reed. It was in 1929, her first year in Grand Central. I was hurrying from the lower level with a package under my arm, very intent on keeping an appointment. A beautiful sound caught my attention. Soon, without knowing it, I was moving slowly and mechanically. I drifted up the stairs to the peaceful strains of "Silent Night" played on an organ.

The music filled a part of me I had lost in the hurry of the day. Without realizing it I was standing perfectly still. I had forgotten my urgent appointment, to watch the people before me. They were standing in groups deep in thought. It was noon and the sun was streaming from the high arched windows and bathing the faces of that silent, entranced crowd. Before they moved on, their faces became alert and their eyes were shining. The station had been transformed by the magic of music into a beautiful cathedral.

✳   ✳   ✳

TOMORROW'S BRIDGES

IN MY church in Detroit I had a bridge engineer, Mr. L. A. Paddock, now president of the American Bridge Company. We used to sit by the hour in my home and talk about bridges. He had taken over the reconstruction of the world-famous Quebec bridge across the St. Lawrence River after the middle span had fallen and carried eighty men to death with it.

But what fascinated me in those days was what he told me about great bridges that were yet to be built. For instance, he used to tell me about a colossal bridge which would one day be built across Sidney Harbor in Australia. A year following this prediction he actually went to Sidney to study plans and make a bid on that gigantic bridge, stayed several months, but lost the contract.

Then he used to tell me about a great bridge that someday they surely would build across the bay in San Francisco. I had lived in San Francisco for three years before that, and his talk seemed to be the improbable dreamings of a poet and not the possible perdictions of a prophet. But in his own mind he had that bridge already built and talked about it as if it were a reality, just as he did about what he called an International Bridge which would be built from Detroit to Windsor, Canada. It was reality to him.

216

The strange thing about it all is that that bridge across San Francisco Bay was actually built. Even a stranger thing is that my friend, Mr. L. A. Paddock, was the man who built it. And, of course, the International Bridge from Detroit to Windsor is an accomplished feat of engineering too.

Then I remembered that "Tomorrow's Bridges" are always built in the minds of dreamers forty, fifty or even a hundred years before they are actually arches and spans across great bodies of water.

Inspired by some such dream and its coming into reality Edwin Markham once sent me a poem entitled "Tomorrow's Bridges":

Tomorrow's bridge, as I look ahead,
   Is a rickety thing to view;
Its piers are crumbled, its rails are down,
   Its floor would let me through.

The chasm it spans is dark and deep,
   And the waters foam and fret—
I have crossed that bridge a thousand times
   Though I never have reached it yet.

It has crashed beneath me to let me through,
   Although it is miles away;
But strange, the bridges that I have crossed
   Have all been safe today.

Perhaps I shall find when I reach the one
   That lies in the distant blue,
Some hand may have mended its rickety floor,
   And its piers may be strong and new.

And I can pass over, lighthearted, and free,
   As a bird on the buoyant air.
Forgive me, God, for my fearful heart,
   My anxious and foolish care.

Strangely enough, the very day that Mr. Markham sent me that poem I picked up the newspapers and read the dramatic story of the destruction of the bridge at Niagara Falls, which included these words:

A new and greater 'Honeymoon Bridge' was planned at Niagara Falls today, even as the gaunt skeleton of the old bridge which crashed yesterday continued to groan and settle into the ice-covered river.

The International Railway Company announced that architects will be asked at once to design a new and finer arch. It will rise from the site of the fallen bridge. The old structure succumbed after a thirty-hour battering by the worst Niagara River ice jam in thirty years.

✷   ✷   ✷

"I'M KEEPING MYSELF CLEAN FOR HER"

THE scene is Rome, Italy.

A group of American artists were living together in a little colony, finishing their studies.

A wealthy old man was a sort of godfather to all of them. He loved them, for they were all that he once hoped to be, but could not be, in the art world. Instead of that career he had gone into business and had made a fortune, which he was spending in helping young American artists in Rome.

He noticed that a certain young fellow kept himself aloof from the revelries and debaunches in which the others indulged from time to time in what they called "celebrations." Every time there was even half an excuse—Fourth of July, Memorial Day, Christmas—they made that day an excuse for some sort of hilarious celebration. Drinking was a part of this type of "party," and many an American boy and girl joined in on that celebration who would never have thought of so doing back home. But this chap did not enter into these "parties." The old man noticed this.

The boy was a good fellow just the same. They all respected and loved him because he would do anything for them. When the others were "broke" it was he to whom they went for a loan.

When they were blue and discouraged it was to his room that they went for good cheer. He was always doing some little thing for each of the colony. Therefore he did not lose their friendship because of his refusal to enter into their celebrations. Better than that, he gained in their estimation.

But the old man, who had watched this young chap for two years, was curious to know just why this boy kept himself apart; held to his ideals in Rome when it might have been so easy to do otherwise.

So he decided to find out for himself. One Sunday evening, while the others were gone, the old man and the young man took a walk up one of the "Seven Hills of Rome," just at sunset when a beautiful crimson, golden mountain range of clouds massed itself above the western horizon.

They stood on that great hill looking down upon the Eternal City, hushed by the beauty of that sunset. After ten minutes of silence the old man said: "John, I have been watching you for two years now and I cannot help noticing that you hold yourself aloof from these 'parties' the boys and girls have so frequently. I cannot help but feel that there is something in your life that helps you do that. What is it?"

The boy looked up into the old man's face, and then up into the glowing sunset, and, pointing his finger westward, said: "Do you see that sunset? Over westward beyond that sunset lies America, and in a little New England village there is a home, and in that home lives the girl I love. I'm keeping myself clean for her!"

It is a simple story and a true one.

Sometimes, when we are young, in a careless moment we trade off the glories of the future for the pleasures of a moment. We trade a "party" for a permanency; we barter off an inheritance of golden years of happiness for a mess of pottage; we give up a lifetime of happiness and love for an hour of nothing. My old philosophy teacher in Brown, Dean Michaeljohn, used to say: "We trade so much for so little at times. Sin is a bad bargain!"

One summer up in Colorado mountains I happened to be playing in a golf tournament. One afternoon I talked in the locker room with a young Yale student who was leading the tournament. I said to him, "Will you win it?"

He responded: "Not if Jim keeps sober. He can burn this course up and whip any man on it if he keeps sober. But it is his usual habit, on the night before the finals, to celebrate his victory beforehand by having a 'party' for his friends. Then he slumps and loses. He has done that several times. If he gets drunk I win. If he stays sober all of us lose. Drunk we can beat him. Sober he is invincible."

Naturally I watched Jim with a good deal of interest the rest of the tournament. The day before the final round he was playing 68. That broke the course record. That night, sure enough, he had a "party" to celebrate his breaking the course record. The next day he shot in the eighties and lost the tournament ignominiously. He was a charming, likable fellow. He traded that victory off for a "party."

"I'm keeping myself clean for her."

I'm keeping myself clean for the woman I love, for the children I expect to have or already have, for the home that shall some-day be mine, with all of its permanent values and happiness, for the career that I expect to work out, for the influence that I expect to assert in my community and in my nation. I am keep-ing myself clean for the emergencies of life that may come upon me. I am doing it for the sake of my father and mother, my brothers and sisters; for those who love me, trust me, idealize me, and believe in me; for those who are sacrificing for me and boasting about me; for those who may look to me—my children; those who are younger than I am, who look to me for leadership. "I am keeping myself clean for them."

✳   ✳   ✳

THAT NOBLE BIRD, THE CHANTICLEER

IN THE conclusion of the play *Chanticleer,* by Rostand, there is a beautiful thought on praise. That noble bird, the Chan-ticleer, thought for many a day that it was because of his crow-ing in the morning that the sun arose! Morning by morning, therefore, he crowed, and indeed the sun did rise! But there came a time when he was so worried with other things that he forgot to summon the dawn with his call. One day the sun arose and he had not crowed! Whereupon he suddenly realized that he, with his little ineffective part, had no bearing whatever upon the actions of the sky. To this conclusion he speaks profoundly and echoes the conviction of the believing soul of man: "It may be that it is not my poor voice which brings on the day, but this at least I can do, and nothing can deprive me of the joy of it: If I may not cause the sun to rise, I may lift up my voice to celebrate its rising."

Aye, there is the wise old bird! The Chanticleer knew how to turn his disappointments into assets; he even knew how to turn his humiliations into satisfactions. He suddenly realized something that it often takes a lifetime to discover: that he who honors a great man, or even recognizes and praises a great thought; even he who tells a fine story, passes on a great poem, has as great a part in the actual link of service as he who originally wrote that great poem.

> If I can lead a man who has been blind
>   To see the beauty in a blade of grass;
> If I can aid my fellow men to find
>   The friendliness of trees they daily pass;
>
> If I can stir a soul to view the dawn
>   With seeing eyes and hold the vision clear,
> So he may drink the rapture when 'tis gone,
>   To purify some sordid atmosphere;
>
> If I can help the human ear to hear
>   The gladness in the waterfall's refrain;
> The tenderness of robins piping clear;
>   The healing in the sound of falling rain;
>
> If I can rouse but one to that rebirth
>   Which sees God mirrored in each flower and tree,
> To feel his oneness with the whole of earth—
>   Why, that will be a priceless joy to me!

All of my own life I have been at the big business and delight of passing on the thoughts of others. I may not have done much creative work; I may never have written any lasting poetry, prose, or oratory; but I have had the fun of finding great thoughts which others have written and passing them on. My first book, written back in 1918, was entitled *Giant Hours with Poet Preachers,* and it was a series of chapters on the then contemporary poets of newly rising fame, including Edna St. Vincent Millay, Alfred Noyes, John Masefield, Rupert Brooke, Alan Seeger. I merely quoted those poets and interpreted them. That was my first book, and there have been forty since that one; but that one is still selling—not because of any merit I put into it, but because of the great quotations from those poets. That has carried that particular book, and one which followed it, entitled *Flames of Faith.* In fact, Dr. Hal Luccock once said to me: "Why don't you write a book someday expressing some of your own thoughts, if you have any—and there was a mean dig in that—and quit celebrating others and quoting the thoughts of others?"

My reply to that distinguished teacher and writer was, and still is, a part of the philosophy of my life: "I do not have any great awe, respect or confidence in my own writings; but I do have great respect for my ability to recognize greatness and beauty in the writing of others; and feel that perhaps my mission in life may be to pass on the great thoughts of others. I recognize my own limitations—which is better than I can say for many of my friends who are writing books, expecting them to make some original contribution to the sum total of learning; and fooling themselves." I was basing that simple statement of my philosophy and appraisal of my own talents on a saying of the immortal Bovee: "A great thought is a great boon for which God is to be first thanked; then he who is the first to utter it, and then, in a lesser, but still in a considerable degree, the man who is first to quote it to us."

It is the same thing which John Drinkwater expresses in his great play on Abraham Lincoln, in which he has the Chronicler open the curtains before that drama, step to the front of the stage, and say by way of introduction:

> When the high heart we magnify
> And the sure visions celebrate;
> And worship greatness passing by,
> Ourselves are great!

It is a universal plan of life and service, for it takes us all in. Most of us will not be able to do great things, write great books, paint great pictures; but the world of literature, art, music, also requires that we have one hundred persons who appreciate great things to one who can write them. No man or woman can be truly great without a great audience—men who can recognize, respond, and praise. So, after all, that old Chanticleer didn't choose a bad part.

$*$ $*$ $*$

"I ONLY DID WHAT ANYONE WOULD DO FOR HIS KID BROTHER"

THE bitterly cold waves were beating against his face; he had terrific cramps in his legs; his head was fuzzy, his eyes so blinded that he could not even see the shore line; his heart pounded against his chest until he felt it would burst. He no longer had any feelings. He just swam on and on with something driving him. Courage, will power, hope, love—call it what you will; it is something which beats in the heart of a brave boy—or man; for John Cole Le Suer fought on—for his kid brother—and a friend.

After that long swim was all over they tried to make a hero out of this eighteen-year-old Ohio boy, but he said, "I only did what anyone would do for his kid brother—and a friend!"

It happened on Chautauqua Lake last Easter Sunday. The expedition began when a neighbor, Mr. Erickson, invited these two brothers to go with him to see if they could find his boat, which had drifted away from its moorings. They borrowed a steel boat, attached an outboard motor and started about three o'clock; had gotten out three or four miles when one of those sudden early spring storms blew up—the worst in ten years, with rain pouring and the wind at hurricane force. The steel boat filled with water. The boys tried to bail it out, but the wind blew the bailing can out of their hands, and then they tried to bail with their hats. Finally the boat foundered, but the airtight compartment kept it afloat upside down. It was completely submerged with only the heads of the boys above water. They shouted for help, but the noise of the wind and rain made it impossible for those on the shore to hear them. It looked hopeless. They were there for an hour, with no help in sight, so finally John Le Suer, who had passed his Red Cross and Scout lifesaver's tests, decided to swim for shore. That seemed the only hope.

When he had gotten part way he became frightened and felt that he could not make it, so started back to the sinking boat. But he saw his two companions in the boat shouting for help, and turned again and started back for the shore, in spite of the fact that both Mr. Erickson and his younger brother begged him not to try it; to take a chance with them clinging to the submerged steel boat. But bravely that lad started again. Try to visualize the whole picture: John, starting a second time for shore against the pleading of both Bob, his younger brother, and their friend Mr. Erickson; fighting long cramps, using various strokes, floating now and then to catch a brief rest; two and one-half hours in the icy water; finally feeling sand beneath his feeble feet. Then his mind went blank as he reached shore. He fell unconscious, and firemen who had heard the cries of the men in the boat could find no slightest trace of a pulse, but used artificial respiration for over an hour.

Imagine the feelings of the younger brother in the sinking boat, who lost sight of John a minute after he left the boat the second time to risk his life for help; feeling certain he would never see his brother alive again. Imagine that young Robert, as they clung to the submerged boat, urging his friend Mr. Erickson to "keep his chin up," when he seemed to lose his courage and cried out: "It's no use! I can't hold out a minute longer!"

224

Perhaps Robert, the younger brother, was as much of a hero as the older one who swam to shore. At least, that's the picture.

No, that isn't all of the picture. Firemen heard their cries of distress, launched a boat, rowed out to the men in the water, brought them ashore, where they found John lying unconscious, and started in with the artificial respiration, working for an hour before they even saw a sign of life. Robert, his nerves still calm, watched while the firemen worked over his older brother who had risked his life—perhaps lost it, for all he knew at the time—watched closely for his older brother's return to consciousness.

Nelson and Sundberg, the firemen who rowed out and rescued the man and boy clinging to the sunken steel boat, had their troubles also. The two rescued ones were suffering so with cramps that they could not sit up in the boat, but fell on their faces. That made four, and the rescue boat sunk to the gunwales, with the waves washing over it. Many people who watched the rescue spoke of the danger to Nelson and Sundberg. One of them told reporters that he did not realize the danger to themselves until it was all over. "But now that I think of the risk, it gives me the jitters! But at that time the only thing we thought of was getting out to those fellows and bringing them back to shore!"

It's a glorious story of five heroes in everyday life; just such heroes and episodes as you will find a thousand times every summer on our lakes, seas, and rivers in this nation; for everyday people, born and bred in this nation, have a glorious habit of rising magnificently to emergencies; and I tell this story here as a tribute to all such heroic lives. Yes, John Le Suer, whom the firemen finally brought to life again, was right when he said, "I only did what anyone would do for his kid brother—and a friend!" Yes, John, that's the universal glory of it!

*　　*　　*

AUNT HANNAH

Dr. Merton Rice of Detroit once told me a glorious story which I pass on to my readers.

About twenty-five years ago a class in sociology at Johns Hopkins University made a study of one of the worst slum sections of Baltimore. The students went into the homes, noted also the good and bad influences in the community and tabulated the results on cards. Two hundred cards were marked "Headed for Jail." On each of the two hundred cards was the name of a boy or girl whose background, attitude toward life, and prospects indicated a life of crime ending in jail or worse. The cards were filed for future reference and study.

After a lapse of a twenty-five-year period another class in the same sociology course in Johns Hopkins, in looking about for a project for the year, found this bundle of two hundred cards marked "Headed for Jail." The task of checking up on every person listed on the two hundred cards was chosen by this class as a project. One by one the persons were investigated, but the students were due for a surprise. Only two of the persons whose cards were marked "Headed for Jail" actually got there. A mistake had apparently been made by the first class twenty-five years ago or the more recent one making the checkup.

Another study was made by the professor who had delegated the task to the students. He was not long in finding the reason why two hundred boys and girls "Headed for Jail" twenty-five years earlier had not arrived on schedule time.

"Aunt Hannah" was the reason. She was a schoolteacher in that slum section who had for forty years been teaching boys and girls in the grade school. She never even taught in high school, but taught over and over, year after year, the routine lessons of her grades.

The story of the two hundred, with two exceptions, ran true to the same pattern. "I was headed for jail, surely enough, until Aunt Hannah got hold of me and started me in the right direction," was the testimony of the majority. Here are just two cases chosen from the many that might be cited to illustrate the influence of "Aunt Hannah" in that Baltimore slum section.

"I sure was a bad egg," was the answer a doctor in that section gave to the professor. "I was the worst kid in the whole neighborhood, and how the cops did like to pin everything on me! And they were usually right. One day 'Aunt Hannah' kept me after school and I thought I was in for it again. But instead of scolding me and threatening me with expulsion from school, she just talked to me like a mother. I never knew what it was to have a mother, and that was new to me. She told me I was too smart a kid to be getting into trouble, and before I left she asked me to come to her home for Sunday dinner. I just never had the heart to let 'Aunt Hannah' down after that."

A corner grocer had a story to tell about his career of crime which came to a sudden end outside of jail. "I am one of 'Aunt Hannah's' alumni. Oh, yes, there are enough of us to form an 'Aunt Hannah Alumni Association' if all the people influenced by her were gotten together. While I was attending school in 'Aunt Hannah's' classes I was clerking evenings and Saturdays in a grocery store. I would steal money from the store and also candy and groceries for a gang of boys who had organized. Of course I got caught and the owner threatened to turn me over to the police. Things looked bad for me, but I just had sense enough to go and talk it over with Aunt Hannah. In a couple of days she kept me after school and told me she had fixed things up so I would not have to go to jail. But I was to pay her back all I had stolen. I kept on working in the grocery store and finally bought this store. That's why I ended in the grocery store instead of in jail, as my card was marked."

Aunt Hannah herself has a story to tell, but she will only say, "Oh, I just loved them like they were my own boys and girls. You see, I never had any of my own and they were all mine in a way." That's about all you can get from her when you visit her in a home for aged teachers down there in Baltimore. But that's all you need to know to explain why only two out of two hundred of her boys and girls "Headed for Jail" ever got there.

That's a great story and it comes out of everyday human life. You who read this tall tale could name an Aunt Hannah in every village and town. I know two or three of them in my home town, Moundsville, West Virginia. I have never had a church in all my ministry where I didn't have two or three Aunt Hannahs—God bless them all—who devoted themselves to the high and heroic business of befriending young people and leading them down the path that leads to useful citizenship and everlasting happiness. They are the uncrowned queens of our American life.

✳   ✳   ✳

"AND LINCOLN WAS THE LORD OF HIS EVENT!"

IT IS an interesting thing that Raymond Massey, a Canadian actor, played the part of Abraham Lincoln in the Broadway play, *Abe Lincoln in Illinois,* and that the great drama of Lincoln which came to the American stage a few years ago was written by John Drinkwater, an English poet; all of which means, of course, that Canada, England, and these United States are bound together by ties of kinship which make us one family, rooted in the same soil, the same language, the same culture, the same traditions. So Canadian people have a right to feel a certain pride that Mr. Massey on the legitimate stage and in the motion picture so beautifully interpreted our great Lincoln.

But it is back to the John Drinkwater drama of Lincoln that I want to go in this story to take my theme. Drinkwater has two Chroniclers step in front of the curtain to introduce the play. The first Chronicler says that Cromwell, who came to the front in one of the great crises of English history,

> Watched in lonely Huntington,
> A summons, and he went,
> And Tyranny was bound,
> And Cromwell was the lord of his event!

Then a second Chronicler steps to the front of the curtain and speaks of another great crisis in American history, and he uses the same phrase for Lincoln:

And then, from fifty fameless years
In quiet Illinois was sent
A word that still the Atlantic hears,
And Lincoln was the lord of his event!

Ah, yes, that is the great interpretative phrase of all time: "And Lincoln was the lord of his event!" Timid, shy, fearful, defeated, anxious; a failure in business, in love, in his home, in the law, as a lecturer; defeated even in ninety-nine per cent of the times he tried the political venture; looked upon by friends, family, Springfield, and even by himself as a failure in life, yet in the final analysis, and in the major crisis of his life, "Lincoln was the lord of his event!"

The major crisis of Lincoln's administration came after the election of 1862 when, in September, Maine chose a Republican governor by a majority of only 4,000 when it usually gave a Republican majority of from 10,000 to 20,000. And for the first time in history Maine sent a Democrat to Congress, which was looked upon as a direct repudiation of Lincoln. Ohio sent to the House of Representatives 14 Democrats and only 5 Republicans. In Pennsylvania, where in his first election Lincoln had a majority of 60,000, the Democrats exceeded the Republican votes by 4,000. New York State went Democratic by 10,000. Even Illinois, Lincoln's home state, went Democratic by 17,000 majority and sent 11 Democrats in her congressional delegation to 3 Republicans. This was a direct repudiation of Lincoln.

The President's support in Congress was almost nothing. A visitor came to Washington to be introduced to some of Lincoln's adherents. He was led over to the desk of Isaac Arnold because Arnold was the only man in the House who belonged to that group.

A caucus of Republicans was called against Lincoln. That caucus demanded that he dismiss his entire cabinet. Lincoln said: "They wish to get rid of me, and I am sometimes half disposed to gratify them. We are now on the brink of destruction. It appears to me the Almighty is against us, and I can hardly see a ray of hope. The committee from the caucus is to be up to see me at seven o'clock. Since I heard last night of the proceedings of the caucus I have been more distressed than by any event of my life."

Dr. Barton said to me one day in Boston about this matter: "Lincoln had promised God that if Lee were driven out of Maryland, he would issue the Proclamation of Emancipation. He issued it against the judgment of several members of his cabinet, believing it would commend itself to the favor of the people, and to the blessing of God. Apparently it did neither. Lincoln never felt more completely Godforsaken than in the weeks after that proclamation bore its fruit. It seemed to him that God was against him, and it seemed also that the people, whom he trusted next to God, had also cast him adrift. Repudiated at the polls, he was deserted by Congress and betrayed by members of his cabinet. The ballot failed him; the army failed him; the heavens above him were brass. Never was he nearer despair than on the night when that committee from the Republican caucus was on its way to the White House.

He met the committee courteously and received their report, which requested Lincoln to dismiss his whole cabinet and change his entire policy. He dismissed them with the request that they leave their report with him for consideration.

But when that committee came back the next day they found a new Lincoln; no longer forsaken and defeated. They found a Lincoln no longer despairing of his God, no longer hesitant; but a Lincoln who calmly, yet with adamantine certainty, said, "I'm master now!" And in that spirit he stood calmly with new faith in God and the cause for which he was fighting. "And Lincoln was the lord of his event!"

That faith was justified. The Proclamation of Emancipation raised up new friends in Great Britain, and dissuaded England from recognizing the Confederate Government. And again the armies prepared for battle, singing as they marched:

> We'll rally round the flag, boys,
> We'll rally once again,
> Shouting the battle cry of Freedom.

230

THE CHANT OF THE VOYAGER

A LITTLE Canadian boy years ago sat in an attic thumbing a dusty old book entitled *Lives of the Great Composers*. He came across the story of Paderewski and that inspired him to want to be a musician. Years passed and he became an accomplished pianist; but his old grandfather, with whom he lived, felt that it would be a disgrace to the family to turn out a mere musician; and this grandfather went so far as to have the old upright piano moved to the attic so the boy would not be always pounding it.

However, this boy would not be discouraged and used to sneak up to the attic to do his daily practicing.

After many years the startling news seeped through to the little Canadian town that Paderewski was to make his first visit to the United States and Canada and was to play in Montreal. The boy was chilly inside with excitement. He determined that he would hear the great Polish master. All of Canada was waiting with hushed hearts for the great event; but no heart was more hushed than this Canadian boy's.

He asked his grandfather if he might go to hear the master, but the grandfather was firm in his refusal. Besides, the boy had no way of traveling the 120 miles to Montreal in midwinter. The week of the recital finally came and this boy's heart was heavy. Yet he was just as determined to go as ever, even though his grandfather had forbidden it. But how?

Two nights before the concert a great blizzard came which broke down a big tree. The boy got up when he heard the crash of that snow-burdened tree. He noticed that it pointed directly toward Montreal and took that as a sign that he should go to hear Paderewski. So he dressed in warm clothes, took his snow-shoes and his bicycle and started off across the fields for the rail-road tracks. Being a boy, he knew that the wind and the snow-plows would have a space cleared in the middle of the tracks, where there would be a hard cinder path over which he could ride. Sure enough, the snow had been cleared away, and he started peddling the 120 miles to Montreal with the wind behind him. Most of the way was downhill, and through the zero air that boy peddled and coasted toward Montreal. However, he got to going so fast with the downhill grade and the wind at his back that he could hardly get his wheel stopped for the cow culverts, and about twenty-five miles from Montreal he ran into one, turned turtle and cut his knee; but, fortunately, he was near a small railroad town. He went into a drugstore, told the manager what had happened and said: "I have no money, but won't you please fix up my knee so I can get to Montreal, for I've just got to hear Paderewski. I've ridden a hundred miles on my bicycle today to get there."

Just at that minute a gentleman dressed in a big fur coat pricked up his ears and came over to the boy.

"Boy, you're a godsend to me. I'm Mr. Paderewski's press agent. If what you say is true you're going to hear him and you're going to sit on a front seat. When you get to Montreal come to the Windsor Hotel and hunt me up."

The boy continued his trip with a little song singing in his heart; but about twenty miles out of Montreal two mounted police stopped him and arrested him for riding on railroad property, took him in their buggy to Montreal and turned him over to the press agent in the hotel, who had wired ahead to have this done. There he was fêted, dined, and given a front seat in Mr. Paderewski's concert; afterward taken to a banquet in a hotel and seated next to the master. Then he was invited to play for the great Polish pianist, but when he was taken to the platform he said: "When I rode down on my bicycle the one thing I thought I wanted most of all was to have Mr. Paderewski hear me play. But not after hearing him play tonight. I now know that I am not ready to play for him." And he refused to play. But there in the audience sat Dominique Ducharme, the father of music in Canada and the greatest teacher of piano in all the Dominion. He ran up to that boy, hugged him, and said: "Come with me! My home shall be your home and you will study with me. Paderewski is to spend the night at my home. You shall play for both of us."

Out of that experience this ambitious lad was invited to live in the home of the master for four years and got his first real start as a pianist. This is almost a "Believe it or not" story, but the name of that young boy was and is Frank White, and he was the regular organist on a broadcast over a national hook-up which I carried on for three years from Radio City in New York.

✶ ✶ ✶

"LIKE THE FLUTTERING FEATHER FROM A SEA GULL'S WING"

ONE of the most beautiful, heartening, and inspiring things I know in American life is the hold that the great hymns of the Church have on our hearts. We all grew up with these great hymns ringing in our ears; and as we grow older they still haunt us and make our hearts happy when we hear them. No nation or human being can lose its character while it still sings and responds to the old and beautiful hymns.

I had a curious and dramatic illustration of the influence of the great hymns when I was coming home from France in 1918 after a year in the war.

The great transport "Matsonia" was cutting its way through three dangers: the submarine zone, a terrific storm beating from the west, and a night as dark as Erebus, with no lights showing.

I had the midnight to 4:00 A.M. watch on the "Aft Fire Control." Below me, on the aft gun deck, as the rain pounded, the wind howled, and the ship lurched, I could see the bulky forms of the boy gunners, two to each gun; two standing by with phone pieces to their ears, and six sleeping on the deck, ready for an emergency. That ship was carrying back to America a precious cargo of wounded officers from France.

For an hour I heard no sound from the boys below me. I watched their silent forms with a great feeling of respect and affection. The ship lurched through the storm on its zigzag course. Then suddenly I heard a familiar sound coming from one of the boys below me. It was from big, rawboned "Mon-

233

tana," as they called him. The sound was low at first, and because of the storm and the vibration of the ship I could not make
it out, although the melody was strangely familiar. Then the
boy on the port gun took the melody up, followed by the gunners
on the starboard, and I caught the old familiar words of:

> Jesus, Saviour, pilot me
> Over life's tempestuous sea;
> Unknown waves before me roll,
> Hiding rock and treacherous shoal;
> Chart and compass came from thee;
> Jesus, Saviour, pilot me.

Above the creaking and the vibrations of the great ship, above
the thunder of the storm, those American boy gunners all unconsciously, in that storm-tossed, tumultuous, turbulent sea, were
singing the old hymn which came back to them from their boyhood memories in little churches across this continent. I think
I never heard that wonderful hymn when it sounded sweeter or
more appropriately sung than it did that night, as the second
verse wafted up to me where I stood my watch on the aft gun
deck of the old transport "Matsonia":

> As a mother stills her child
> Thou canst hush the ocean wild;
> Boist'rous waves obey thy will
> When thou sayest to them, "Be still."
> Wondrous Sovereign of the sea,
> Jesus, Saviour, pilot me.

We heard a good deal in the days of the war of how our boys
sang "Hail! Hail! The Gang's All Here," "Where Do We Go
From Here, Boys?" "There's a Long, Long Trail A-Winding,"
"Keep the Home Fires Burning"—and they did. But when you
got those boys in a serious, thoughtful mood you found them
singing the great hymns of the Church. I remember that my
friend Bishop Francis J. McConnell was speaking to a crowd of
boys up on the Somme Line before a great drive. Half of the

boys to whom he was then speaking would never come back. He asked them what they wanted to sing, and unanimously they asked for "O God, Our Help in Ages Past, Our Hope for Years to Come."

The mothers and fathers of America knew, of course, that in their lighter moods the average American boy was singing the lighter songs in the war, but buried down deep in their hearts there was then, just as there is now, a reverence and love for the old hymns. Indeed, most of us, under circumstances of storm and stress, doubt and night, find ourselves with the old hymns ringing in our hearts. And that, my friends, is God. That is one of the most heartening and inspiring things in our American life.

That is why I think the singing of the old hymns will help us lift the levels of life. My guess is that after hearing a great hymn or humming it we find ourselves going about our work humming "Jesus, Saviour, pilot me over life's tempestuous sea," just as we hum or whistle a catchy tune coming out of a theater. It will give us a sense of peace and security in this too turbulent, storm-tossed world. How much we all need a place of peace and quiet in these tumultuous days!

I remember once, in Oakland, California, hearing the great Bishop William A. Quayle step into a pulpit and speak this benediction: "May the Peace of God fall on your souls like the fluttering feather from a sea gull's wing as it touches the white-tipped waves of the sea." He had evidently, that very morning, crossed the bay from San Francisco, and as he stood on the deck of the ferry, watching the sea gulls wheel around the wake of the boat, had seen something which inspired that simple and appealing prayer.

*   *   *

"OF WHOM SHALL I BE AFRAID?"

Dr. Burris Jenkins of Kansas City, Missouri, tells of how Otto Floto, one of the partners in the Sells-Floto Circus and sports editor of two Middle-Western papers, one time told him an amusing little story:

The circus had just landed in Cincinnati one day, got the tents up under great difficulties and in a great hurry, and some sort of order was just emerging from chaos, the manager all but tearing his hair with nervous anxiety and haste, when some rube, a saphead from the country, sidled up to him and asked him for a job, any kind of job, to make just enough to buy him something to eat. The manager, to get rid of him, said, "Well, clean out that tiger cage!" and pointed to a cage of Royal Bengal tigers—four of them—and hurried away from the menagerie tent into the other one. He had not been gone more than a quarter of an hour when a string of terrified employees came rushing to him, crying out, "That saphead has got all those tigers out of the cage; come in here quick!" The manager, with his heart in his throat, ran into the menagerie tent. He stood aghast at what he saw. That greenhorn had opened the cage, gone in and tied ropes around the necks of those beasts, led and dragged them outside and tied them to the wheels of their cage, had swept out their floor, put in fresh straw, and now, having untied one of the tigers, was trying to shove him back into the cage, slapping him and growling, "Get in there, you big cat!" Nobody dared to go near, but the whole circus company stood off breathlessly and watched until all four of the angry beasts were securely back in the cage and the door shut upon them. Then the observers collapsed; and the manager gasped, "I meant for him to take that rake, and work through the bars. The fool!"

Dr. Jenkins adds: "I do not know whether that story is fact or mere fiction. Otto, good reporter, so far as I could ascertain never told things as fact which were not fact; but whether fact or not, that story, it would appear to me, possesses solid truth. That poor 'sap,' to use the slang of Mr. Floto, did not know enough to be afraid of those Royal Bengal tigers; perhaps lacked imagination enough to recall to his mind their previous condition of freedom in the jungles of the Orient, their thousands of generations of man-eating heredity, and the possible recrudescence of their former savage proclivities. He therefore was able literally to get away with his ignorant and plebeian impudence to their four royal highnesses and to come off without a scratch."

Burris Jenkins is right in telling that story, whether it is fact or fiction, for the philosophy behind it is as old as the Bible, which says: "That which I feared hath come upon me."

We all remember when we were young and first learned to ride a bicycle. There in front of us was a water plug, a telephone pole, or a tree. We were afraid that we would run plunk into that tree; we wavered and waddled from side to side of the walk, our fears increasing with each foot; and, sure enough, did run into the object we feared. "That which I feared hath come upon me."

Then there is the immortal story of the woman who was entertaining a famous celebrity in her home. Mary Roberts Rinehart told it in her autobiography. This famous man had a deformed nose—what we called a strawberry nose—and he was sensitive about it. So the mother carefully coached her children before he came to dinner, admonishing them that they must not look at that man's large nose, and that they were not even to mention the word nose during the evening meal. She trained them for weeks, and the night of the dinner arrived. The dinner proceeded with perfect behavior on the part of the children. Then they all went into the living room for the after-dinner coffee and the mother helped to serve it. When she came to the celebrity with the deformed nose, she poured his coffee and then said, "Mr. Jones, will you have sugar and cream in your nose?" "That which I feared hath come upon me."

Most of us have pet fears. I have always been afraid of pain or illness, and from time to time have been certain that I had heart trouble, tuberculosis, mastoiditis, appendicitis, ulcer of the stomach, infantile paralysis, cancer—every possible disease, in fact, from chilblains to fallen arches; and yet the clinics have all given me a clean bill of health and say that I ought to go and forget myself—a thing which I have agreed to do. So I have quit being afraid of sickness. I have almost gotten to the place where that wild-eyed country boy arrived; until I would walk into a cage of diseases, take each one by the mane, put a rope around its neck, lead it out and clean out the Aegean stables of disease, for I have somehow caught the spirit of the psalmist who sang: "The Lord is my light and my salvation; whom shall I fear? the Lord is the strength of my life; of whom [and what] shall I be afraid?"

* * *

"AND OUR WORLD BE SWEETER"

A NEWS story recently told of a Milwaukee business man who sold a new house. Looking over the property before giving possession he found robins nesting on a window ledge and expecting newcomers. So he went back to his office and revised the sales agreement to provide that the purchaser must not disturb that nest until the mating season was over.

That story reminded me of one which Mr. Wm. J. Cameron once told me about Mr. Henry Ford. I had just come in from a walk with Mr. Ford through his Dearborn estate, during which time Mr. Ford showed me his Baltimore oriole nests which he had swung on fine piano wire because the oriole likes to nest in a habitation which will sway in the winds. After telling Mr. Cameron about the morning's talk he told me of an incident the summer before, when they were cutting wheat in a certain field and came upon a quail's nest in the wheat, and Mr. Ford ordered the men to cut around that corner of the field so as not to disturb the mother quail and her nestlings.

I wondered how many business men whom we would not suspect of having that much sentiment were actually interested to that extent in birds. I knew that I myself had been greatly enriched in my life because in college days I had a teacher who knew birds. He used to take us on bird walks. That was thirty years ago, but I can still tell you the exact spot where I saw, and learned to know by song, nest, and coloration, my first scarlet tanager, Baltimore oriole, with its orange wings flashing in the morning sunlight; a phoebe, a crimson cardinal, a red-winged blackbird, swaying on a swamp reed; a grosbeak on the tip of a pine tendril. All my life each spring and summer I have gotten more out of life because I know the birds and watch them come back one by one. Here is a simple and universal experience available to all; a way of getting more out of life if we take it. And many wise men have done that very thing.

Not many years ago Viscount Gray of England came to Harvard and made an informal talk to a group of students there. Most of them went expecting him to talk on politics or international affairs and were both surprised and refreshed when he said:

When I was at the Foreign Office in London I got a letter from Mr. Bryce, who was then British ambassador at Washington, saying that President Theodore Roosevelt intended to travel as soon as he was out of office; that he planned to travel in Africa, then to visit Europe, and come to England. He was planning his holiday so minutely as to time his visit to England for the spring, when the birds would be in full song.

It seemed to me very interesting that the executive of the most powerful country in the world should have this simple, healthy desire.

Time passed, and when Mr. Roosevelt retired from office he went to Africa and had much big-game shooting there. Then he came to England, and I received a letter from the English friend who was to be Colonel Roosevelt's host in London, telling me that Colonel Roosevelt had written reminding him of the promise of a bird trip. I saw Colonel Roosevelt soon after he came to London. The day was arranged, and at the appointed time we met at Waterloo Station.

So we went alone, and for some twenty hours were lost to the world in the little village of Titchborne. In the village of Titchborne there lives also the family of Titchborne. Evidence shows a continuous record of one family in one place for about eight hundred years. I forget whether we had time to go into the church and look at the tomb, but the songs of the birds which we had come to hear are far more ancient. They were the same songs that were heard by the inhabitants of England before the Romans came, for the songs of birds come down unchanged through great antiquity.

I found that Colonel Roosevelt had a remarkable interest in birds and a wonderful knowledge of birds. We began our walk, and when we heard a song I told him the name of the bird. As soon as I mentioned the name it was unnecessary to tell him more. He knew what the bird was like. It was not even necessary for him to see it. He knew the kind of bird it was, its habits and appearance. He had, too, a well-trained ear for bird songs, which cannot be acquired without spending much time in listening to them. If three or four birds were singing together he would pick out their songs, distinguish each, and ask to be told each separate name. Then farther on, when he heard any bird for a second time, he would remember the song from the first telling, and be able to name the bird himself.

Once we were passing under a fir tree when we heard a small song in the tree above us. As we stopped I said that was the song of a golden-crested wren. He listened very attentively while the bird repeated its little song, as is its habit. Then he said, "I think that is exactly the same as the song of a bird we have in America"; and that was the only English song that he recognized as being the same as any bird song in America. Some time afterward I related this incident to a bird expert in the Natural History Museum in London. He confirmed what Colonel Roosevelt had said, that the song of this bird is about the only song that the two countries have in common.

Edwin Markham knew the contribution that birds make to human life. One day when his son Virgil was about five years of age he was telling Virgil that there is poetry in everything—a tree, a board, a stone, a cliff; in food and drink and night and dark; in everything. While Virgil stood looking out of the window a bird's nest fell into his line of vision, and with a challenge in his young eyes he ran to his father, dragged him to that window and said, defiantly: "There's a bird's nest, Father! Let's see you write a poem about it!"

Whereupon his famous poet-father sat down in that boy's room and wrote one of the most beautiful poems of his career and called it "At Little Virgil's Window." I use it by special permission of Virgil Markham.

> There are three green eggs in a small brown pocket,
> And the breeze will swing and the gale will rock it,
> Till three little birds on the thin edge teeter,
> And our God be glad and the world be sweeter!

INDEX OF TITLES

243

INDEX OF PERSONS

245

Tibbetts, Charles, 142
Tolstoy, 53-55
Toscanini, 208
Twain, Mark, 106-7

Uhland, Johann Ludwig, 147

Vinci, Leonardo da, 18, 123

Wagner, Honus, 184-85
Wald, Lillian, 94-95
Walgreen, Charles R., 205-6
Walters, Zelia M., 13
Washington, George, 179
Weiderhold, Albert, 10

Wendt, Mrs., 148
Westphall, Clarence, 33
Weston, 34-35
White, Frank, 233
White, William Allen, 41, 166, 170
Whitman, Walt, 84
Wilder, Thornton, 192
Wilson, Herman, 37
Wilson, Jab, 37
Wilson, Woodrow, 179
Worsley, 44

Young, Edward, 148
Yudisthera, 38-39

INDEX OF TOPICS

250